The Occasional Man

*Travel, Life, and
an Uncommon Love*

Shirley White Pearl

ISBN: 978-0615791241

Book and Cover Design: Patti Frazee
Back Cover Copy: Gordon Thomas

Published by Ideal Living Press

I_LP

To Fred
An Extraordinary Ordinary Man

Table of Contents

Preface i

Introduction iii

Chapter One: *The Occasional Man* 1

Chapter Two: *The Principal and the Professor* 9

Chapter Three: *Endings, New Beginnings, & Rules of Engagement* 31

Chapter Four: *Smooth (and Not-so-Smooth) Sailing* 41

Chapter Five: *Penelope and Ulysses* 49

Chapter Six: *Whee eee!!!* 55

Chapter Seven: *Nobody's Perfect* 65

Chapter Eight: *Creative Ways to Get Around* 73

Chapter Nine: *Transitions* 85

Chapter Ten: *The Frugal Man's Moveable Feast* 91

Chapter Eleven: *Trouble on the Home Front* 121

Chapter Twelve: *Murder and Mayhem at Pearl Mansion* 133

Chapter Thirteen: *Busy Years* 141

Chapter Fourteen: *The Beat Goes On* 147

Chapter Fifteen: *Into Africa* 159

Chapter Sixteen: *England Mourns* 175

Chapter Seventeen: *The Ice Road* 191

Chapter Eighteen: *Far from Home* 205

Chapter Nineteen: *Last Trip Across the Pond* 219

Chapter Twenty: *Separate Ways* 231

Chapter Twenty-one: *Transitions* 247

Chapter Twenty-two: *Final Trip* 259

Chapter Twenty-three: *And Thus the Moveable Feast Ends* 269

Chapter Twenty-four: *Fred's Two Worlds Meet* 273

Chapter Twenty-Five: *What Next?* 281

Epilogue: *Havana, Cuba* 291

Acknowledgements 295

Preface

Some might say that crazy, wild romantic love is for the very young. For me, it has been for the young at heart. This is my love story, which began when I was forty-six-years-old and Fred was forty-eight. Our improbable romance lasted more than thirty-one years.

It was filled with love, joy, travels, and adventure. For me, it eclipsed all that had happened before I met him. It was almost as though my life began at the age of forty-six. Yet, in retrospect, all that happened before prepared me for that encounter.

It didn't occur to me to write about it. I was too busy living the happy adventurous life of a woman in love. I was of an age that I could invest my energies into this romantic endeavor without the usual encumbrances of youth: getting an education, a marriage, a career, a family, a mortgage. By the time one reaches those middle years, such challenges have been met and resolved one way or another. One is no longer "needed" in the same way by family, friends, or work. If one is lucky, even the mortgage may almost be paid.

I was open and ready for new adventures when Fred came into my life.

It was many years later — indeed thirty years later — that I decided my adventures with him might be a story worth writing.

This, then, is my love story.

If you are lucky enough to have lived in Paris as a young man, then wherever you go for the rest of your life, it stays with you, for Paris is a moveable feast.

—Ernest Hemingway to a Friend, 1950

Introduction

My dreams were heavily influenced by the Methodist Church and MGM movies in the '30s and '40s. Brought up in Marshalltown, Iowa by parents who took their responsibilities seriously, two constants in my young life were Sunday School and Saturday movie matinees. Like John Wesley, founder of Methodism, I wished to do all the good I could, by all the means I could, in all the ways I could. The teachings of Jesus inspired me to live by the Golden Rule, take the high road when indecisive in matters of conscience, discover and use the talents given me, and show appreciation for those gifts.

Like Doris Day, I yearned to meet the man of my dreams, who would whisk me off on exotic journeys, finding me up to the challenges, just like Maureen O'Hara was to John Wayne or Lauren Bacall was to Humphrey Bogart. I felt I was meant to live a life of adventure.

How were Fred's dreams formed? Like many boys of his generation, Fred grew up reading the short stories and novels of Ernest Hemingway, whose life included a home in Idaho's mountains where he hunted in winter; apartments in New York, Paris, and Venice; and a home in Cuba, where he housed a yacht that gave him easy access for fishing the Gulf Stream. Hemingway was said to walk the jungles of Africa as serenely as he walked the streets of New York.

I came into Fred's life able to immediately understand Fred's dreams. Though we couldn't rival Hemingway's appetite for adventure, or his genius for the way he saw life and lived it, we nonetheless created for ourselves a more frugal moveable feast.

Over the years we hiked the mountains of Colorado or British Columbia in the summer, sought out adventures across the pond in the fall, skied in the snow country of northern Minnesota, Yellowstone, or Whistler, British Columbia, then headed for the warmth of Mexico, Puerto Rico, or the British Virgins to sail and snorkel. We used spring to explore our own backyard in the Midwest or to go abroad with family or friends.

We had many journeys together, but the greatest adventure of all was the relationship we had with one another.

This is our love story.

Chapter One
The Occasional Man
1979

I HATED BEING LATE. One last look in my hallway mirror and I would be on my way. It was easy then to ignore how the house was falling apart. Paint peeling, wood floors creaky and scuffed. It was a beautiful old Victorian badly in need of repair.

Turning my head from one side to the other, I decided my hair passed the test. Being blond didn't hurt. And the new gray and white pinstriped suit with the jaunty pink bow tie, so popular that year, gave the right "dressed for success" look. It matched perfectly my gray purse and high heels. *Yes*, I thought, *it will do*.

Grabbing my car keys, I dashed out the front door of the old draughty house I owned with my soon-to-be ex-husband and jumped in my car. Thank goodness the state psychology convention was being held in downtown St. Paul, only about a ten-minute drive away.

I was going to cancel out, but my colleague Jimmy assured me, "Shirley, you can take my place, I can't make it. My seat is next to a college professor and I'm sure he'll share his notes with you."

The session was already going on when I arrived. I cautiously opened the door, hoping to go unnoticed. I slipped through the partially opened door and eased it into closing quietly behind me. I did not want to disrupt anyone.

Suddenly my name boomed over the loudspeaker. "Folks, this

is Dr. Shirley Pearl who runs the day school program for behavior-problem kids in St. Paul. I am very pleased to introduce her." The speaker was well-known to me and my work. As the crowd turned their attention my way, I smiled in what I hoped was a confident manner, gave a slight wave to — well…everyone — and began to look for the vacant seat Jimmy had mentioned. As soon as I found it, I slunked down into the chair, hoping to disappear. The man next to me, the college professor, whispered that his name was Fred and quietly offered his notes.

Fortunately, as the session went on I was able to remain just another person in the audience. When the session ended, Fred asked, "Would you like to join me and some others in my room for a drink?" Fred looked a bit nerdish in his light blue blazer and gray slacks, but his voice was warm and kind. There were several colleagues at the convention who looked quite interesting; I thought it would be nice to get to know some new people, so I accepted. Besides, what did I have to get home for? Fred pushed his horn-rimmed glasses back up on his nose and gave me his room number.

As I stood before his door, staring at the three-digit number embossed on a little plaque, I raised my hand to knock. Before my fist made contact with the door, it opened. "Go on in and make yourself at home; I'm just going to get some ice," Fred said as he raised the empty ice bucket. I was the first to arrive, so I sat on one of the chairs as I waited for Fred to come back. Upon returning, he put the ice bucket down next to the wet bar. "Drink?" he asked.

"Yes…sure."

He turned around and began making a drink. Ice rattled in the glass. He moved confidently, pouring liquid from one bottle and then the other. He mentioned that he had run into the others in the hallway and that they couldn't make it after all. The metal stirrer tinkled on the side of the glass. Fred licked his fingertip as he handed me a gin and tonic. "Cheers!" he said and we clinked our glasses together.

Maybe I should have been concerned, being in a room alone with a complete stranger. But there was something about Fred — I thought, *Maybe he is not the nerd I imagined him to be. This could be interesting.* Since part of his responsibilities was to train teachers to work with behavior-problem children, he seemed very interested in the work I was doing for the St. Paul Public Schools. In fact, Fred was hunting for programs like mine where he could place some of his students. "I'll have to visit you sometime and check out the work you're doing" he said, raising his glass as if saying "cheers."

We soon discovered we had both taken classes at the University of Iowa the same year from some of the same professors. For some reason, our paths never crossed.

"What a coincidence. Both of us doctoral candidates there at the same time. When did you get your degree?" I asked.

"I returned to Ohio State to finish my degree," he said.

"Oh..." my voice lilted into a tease. "Iowa was too difficult for you?"

He smiled at me, swirling the gin and tonic in his glass. "Too much of a cow college for me." He laughed. "Actually, I was from Ohio and did most my work there. I went to Iowa to get distance from a relationship that needed to end." He took a drink of his gin and tonic, looking over the glass at me.

"Sounds like both of us were single at the same time. I'm not now."

"I'm not either," Fred said. "My wife and I are both psychologists on the faculty at St. Cloud University."

"I'm about to become single again" I tentatively offered.

Fred hesitated, then dug an ice cube from his glass. He popped it in his mouth and slowly let it melt before saying, "I spend as much time as I can traveling."

I rattled ice around my nearly empty glass, "Like what kind?"

"Well, did you ever read Hemingway's book, *A Moveable Feast*? He had an insatiable desire to test himself in different worlds—like running the bulls in Spain, or going on safaris in Africa, and making wherever he went a celebration of life. Of course, my travels are more modest."

I leaned forward in my chair. "Like what?"

"Well, let me see. I've done a lot of sailing—once from Florida to Venezuela. And I got in a vodka-drinking contest with a bunch of Russians in Moscow. Oh, and some scuba diving in the Mediterranean. I love exploring the streets of London, my favorite town. And lots of downhill skiing in the mountains of Ontario." Again, his ice rattled around his glass. I loved the spark in his eyes as he talked about his travels; it was like he could see the world unfold before him as he talked. "There's more I'd like to do, like hiking Hadrian's Wall that separates England from Scotland. And I've always wanted to take the Transiberian Train from Vladivostak to Moscow."

I suddenly wanted to jump up and say *Let's go! Now!* but instead I just kept looking into those soulful brown eyes. "How's that for openers?" he asked.

I loved how determined this guy was to live his dreams. I began to think back to all of the library books and Saturday matinee movies I used to devour, dreaming of far-away places. "I used to say when I was a kid that I wanted to live as many lives in one life as I could. In a way, isn't that kind of what you're saying?" I asked.

"Exactly," Fred stood up and took the glass from my hand. Without asking, he began making us both another drink. "It's living now — while you can — all over the world."

"I used to wish I could backpack across Europe, but it seemed beyond me." I kicked off my high heels and pulled one of my legs up under me. "When I read Fitzgerald and Hemingway and how they lived in Paris in the '20s, well, I guess many of us would have liked to sample that. But the thing is, *you* have. You've figured out a way to have such adventures."

I wanted to shout, *take me with you*!!

He handed me another gin and tonic. "So what do you do when you aren't stamping out ignorance and such," he asked.

"Well, as a matter of fact I've done a wee bit of traveling myself. I grew up in the '40s watching movies of pretty damsels in distress playing the helpless card, needing to be saved, rescued, or taken care of. But by the '50s Maureen O'Hara could take very good care of herself whenever John Wayne was off herding cattle, fighting bad guys, or keeping the peace. It was as though she were saying to herself, 'if a guy has to do what a guy has to do, then a woman must do what a woman has to do.'" I took a drink, wondering if I sounded silly with all this movie talk.

Fred sat down on the edge of the bed and leaned forward. His eyes were focused intently on mine. I just wanted to sink into those eyes.

I took another drink and continued, "So my friend Sue and I decided to take off for Europe without our husbands to seek adventures on our own. We enrolled in an education class at River Falls that required a three-week home stay with an English family. That was fun and we managed to get to where we needed to be on our own.

"Once we figured out that we could make our way without a husband helping us, we wanted even more adventure." Fred smiled and didn't move his eyes away from me. I suddenly had the urge to reach out and touch him, but instead, I continued talking, craving to hold his attention. "We rented a car and drove to Scotland to visit the father of a friend of mine, and from there we flew to Cork, Ireland, to meet Sue's Mom and sister for another week of vacation. But the day of our flight, no tickets were available since it was the first day of holiday in the UK." I stopped to take a drink and wondered if I was rambling, going on too long, but I couldn't stop, and he didn't seem to want to stop me. "So we managed to get a seat in between two railroad cars to Stranhaur, Scotland, where we caught a ferry to Belfast. There we spent the night at the Europa Hotel before getting a train to Cork early the next morning. All this required the cock-eyed optimism of two fools going where angels feared to tread. We felt triumphant as we sipped our Bloody Mary drinks while waiting for Sue's mother and sister to arrive. By the way" I said, while standing up to stretch my legs, "how about another drink?"

Reaching out for my empty glass, he remarked, "That is impressive. When was that?"

"It was 1975, the last year a Brit, Virginia Wade, won a Wimbledon final. I knew that because watching tennis at Wimbledon was a national pastime. It couldn't be avoided."

Fred dropped ice cubes into my glass. "You mentioned earlier that your marriage was ending. This must be difficult for you."

Oh yes, my marriage. "It was probably a marriage doomed from the beginning, but that doesn't make it any easier. I hate having another marriage failure; this is my third. I've been talking with my friend Jimmy about maybe going for a legal separation instead. He thinks I need to rethink that."

Fred handed me a fresh drink. "Why?"

"Jimmy knows Harold pretty well. He thinks Harold would like me as an ace in the corner—in case his move to Arizona with his girlfriend doesn't work out. Jimmy feels Harold believes he has enough control over me that he could just move back in."

Fred shifted back from me, his psychologist wheels turning. "Wow. Is Jimmy right? Does Harold have that kind of control?"

"Well, he *thinks* he does," my tone started to rise and I tried to bring it back down, get it in control, but then my voice just quivered as I continued. "If I'm to be on my own, I will make all my decisions, thank you. To quote Harold, 'what I do is nobody's business but my own.' If I keep the house, the locks will all be changed!" I took a big inhale and sighed, as if releasing everything needed one last push. "I must admit, though, the idea of living alone both frightens and intrigues me. I've never lived alone."

Fred leaned forward and earnestly said, "Frankly, I would recommend you live alone ten years or so. You'd be surprised how much you learn." His relaxed tone somehow made me feel relaxed. "I was single ten years before I married Sonia. I don't plan to get a divorce, but if Sonia ever wanted one, I would not marry again." He drank his gin and tonic, keeping eye contact with me, then continued slowly while he twirled the ice in his glass. "I don't believe in sexual fidelity. It is idiotic to expect one could be sexually faithful to one person for a lifetime. But I am emotionally faithful to my wife. She is a strong, remarkable woman with whom I have much history. When we married, we agreed to an open marriage."

An open marriage? Curious. I said, "My first husband was intrigued by that idea but I wasn't. We were too young and inexperienced to handle such a complex lifestyle. How has it worked for you? Wouldn't you each wonder what the other was up to when not home?"

"Not really. We share what we want the other to know and are discreet in what we share. I would never do anything to embarrass her."

"Well, does she have lovers?" I asked.

"I don't know. I assume so."

"You're lucky you're not married to me," I finished off my third gin and tonic. I was starting to feel relaxed and brave. My voice got flirty, "I would want to know everything you did when not with me."

At that, Fred laughed and, standing up to stretch, said, "You wouldn't want to be married to me. I am not and never will be good husband material. Our marriage suits us, but it isn't for everyone."

Reaching for my empty glass, he asked, "Has your failed marriage affected how you view sex?"

I stood up to stretch my legs. "Why do you ask?"

"I was wondering if you enjoy sex."

I felt the heat rise up from my toes into my thighs, stomach, chest, throat, and cheeks. He gave me a slight smile and before I knew it, we were wrapped around one another. I felt I was having an out-of-body experience. His lips brushed my ear as he said, "I like sex — the smell of a woman, the taste of a woman."

Good God, I thought, *this guy is great! I'm just getting myself out of a marriage and now this man—this married man—shows up and all I want to do is stay here, be with him, drink every word that pours from his mouth.*

Hours later, when I got ready to leave, I knew that I would see much, much more of him.

As we said our goodbyes, he put his lips close to my ear and said in a low voice, "I'll be calling you this summer."

My feet barely touched the ground as I left, anticipating an exciting future I felt ready for. *Don't see a movie,* I thought, *be a movie.*

Chapter Two
The Principal and the Professor
1979

WAITING FOR THE PHONE to ring was not my idea of time well spent. It was too much like being sixteen again. There was no doubt in my mind that he would call, but *when* was the question.

This was a summer of hard choices and difficult decisions. If I was to end my marriage, many decisions needed to be made. I'd need to consult a lawyer, discuss finances with my new financial advisor, and decide what to do about the house. I wasn't quite sure that divorce was better than a legal separation, but I still felt ambivalent. Why, I don't know. I seldom saw Harold. For all practical purposes, he had moved on, just dropping in occasionally to see what I was up to, I suspect.

Jimmy called regularly, mostly to see how I was doing. He invited me to join him and his girlfriend, Ginger, to spend a few days at his cabin in Wisconsin. But then I'd be away from the phone, and what if Fred called? So I renewed my friendship with Clem (short for Clementine), who was one of my colleagues back in '69 when I first moved to St. Paul. Since Clem lived near me, I often dropped by her place for walks and talks.

Clem had a keen intellect and wide interests. She introduced me into her world of women friends. St. Paul is said to be a clannish Catholic town, hard for a newcomer to find acceptance. Because of

Clem I met many impressive women. Clem was one of those rare people who actually retained most of what she had learned. One was cautious to challenge her facts; they were invariably accurate. I've never been known to have a great memory. People say they like me because I'm fun. They liked her because she was wise, asked probing questions, was a good listener, and was everyone's best friend, including mine.

"Clem," I once said, "You look and act like a nun. It seems to me that more of that Catholicism than you realize has rubbed off on you." This primly dressed woman wore her short attractive white hair in a conservative cut, carried herself with a solid, confident posture, and referred frequently to the ethical system that guided her.

She responded, "I'm not Catholic, but I married one and brought up my five kids as Catholics. I preferred them to challenge their religion rather than me when they each reached their teen years."

She spent hours in her kitchen conversing with me about Harold and the unknown Fred. She had met Harold when she first worked with me years ago. She never liked him. She'd say, "I have a good shit detector and he is full of it." Not surprisingly, that view was held by many. Only I seemed unaware of his roving eyes and flirtatious ways with women.

But it was the new guy, Fred, who now interested her. "What is it about him that has you so attracted to him? You were with him a day and yet you are convinced that he is 'your future'?" Clem asked.

"Clem, I don't know how to describe it, but part of it is his honesty and part his acceptance of women. I know, I know…you're probably about to ask how I could determine his honesty."

"Well, you must admit, you didn't do too good a job of knowing when Harold was lying and when he was not," Clem said as she drew the ashtray close to her and lit a cigarette.

"I have never been more impressed with a guy's honesty than Fred. He just ups and says, 'I'm a married man; I don't plan to ever divorce my wife, but if she ever divorced me, I'd never marry again. I'm not the marrying kind.' Now does that sound like the typical line of a guy trying to get a girl in bed?"

"Well, I don't know much about pickup lines anymore, but it could have been his way of letting you know he was available *only* for the night." Clem took a drag on her cigarette and blew out a trail of smoke.

"That's the point. He was telling me what kind of guy he is. He likes sex, doesn't believe in sexual fidelity, and he's not about to change. That seemed darned refreshing to me." As I watched the smoke swirl around us, I thought back to that night with Fred. I thought about his sincerity. "I'm just too old to play games, pretending to be what I'm not. And so is he. I liked the way he cuts to the chase by saying, 'I am who I am and if that suits you, then we can get together.' That seems much more honest to me. Clem, I'm just so tired of all the men who've led me on—I married three of them—only to find out they didn't mean what they said."

Clem got up to get a couple of beers. She handed me one, then asked, "Shirley, are you saying you just want a series of one-night stands?"

I took the bottle from her; the summer day was so hot that the bottle was already sweating. "No, that's not what I'm saying, though there may be nothing wrong with recreational sex. I haven't told you the main thing we discussed: and that is what we want to do in our middle years, before it's too late. We each talked about our love of travel and how important it was to us. And our concern that life was passing us by. I don't know—it was like we were sharing our dreams with one another and in doing so, discovered they were similar." I took a drink of beer, but somehow a gin and tonic sounded better right now. "We also shared a bit about our respective marriages. He knows mine is drawing to a close. His isn't. But the fact that I'm considering getting divorced doesn't scare him off—seeing me as 'trouble,' 'bad news,' 'toxic'—like most married men might. In fact, he advised me to remain single at least ten years if I do decide to be divorced."

"Hum. That's interesting," Clem mused. "In other words, he's saying he's a contented married man hunting for a woman to have fun with." Clem looked me dead in the eye, "Is that what you want?"

I got up, stretched, helped myself to one of Clem's cigarettes, then replied,

"I don't know exactly what I want. I guess I know more what I don't want. I did ask him if he was into long-term relationships and he said 'reasonably so.'" I lit the cigarette and blew smoke up into the air. "You see, he wants to travel all over the world — kinda re-live the expat world of the '20s in a more moderate fashion. He digs adventure. And I realized that is exactly what I want. I think that without even saying it, we saw ourselves as perfect traveling companions. It doesn't hurt that there was a strong attraction between us."

"Well, Shirley. You had quite an evening. Don't be too fast into jumping into another relationship," Clem cautioned.

"Clem, he's gone for the summer. I don't know when I'll hear from him. I just know for a fact that I will. I'm hoping he'll call before he takes off, but it wasn't discussed and he may wait until he's back from wherever he's going. So I'll have lots of time to explore my options. For sure, I'm seeing my lawyer first and getting the divorce started. I just hope you don't mind my bending your ear."

"I'm here for you, kid. It's a long, hot summer so you'll have much time to sort things out. I do agree that divorcing Harold is what you need to do first."

I hugged her for dear life, then left with a bit of a tear in my eye.

I was startled awake by a sound. *Is that my alarm clock?*

Or the telephone! I jumped out of bed and got to the phone after several rings. "Hello?" I yelled as I grabbed the phone, my heart racing at the thought of hearing Fred's voice on the other end of the line.

It was Jimmy.

"You sound disappointed," he said. "I thought I'd drop by your place with some coffee and donuts. Is Harold there? I'll get enough for all three of us."

I looked out the bedroom window, but I didn't see Harold's car. "No. Why don't I just throw some clothes on and meet you at Bread and Chocolate on Grand Avenue?"

"You're on. See you there."

Jimmy was sitting at a window table. It was the perfect place to watch shoppers and people strolling around for a morning walk along Grand Avenue while we got lost in conversation.

"What's the occasion?" I asked as I scooted into my chair. Jimmy had coffee and donuts spread out. They looked good. "This is sweet of you."

"Just thought you might like some TLC and nourishment. I talked with my girlfriend and we think you ought to join us this weekend — get you away from sitting by the phone in a hot house."

"How sweet of the two of you. It does seem pathetic, doesn't it? A forty-six-year–old-lady waiting for a forty-eight–year-old Mr. Wonderful to call." I took a bite of a sugary donut. "You know, I think I will join you."

I encountered Harold while packing a few things to take with me to Jimmy's cabin. He wondered where I was going and, surprisingly, he said he just might join us later. I thought, *Why would he care?* Was he wondering what I was up to? I'd told him I'd seen a lawyer. We'd had the "division of worldly goods" talk and agreed on a November divorce.

In the meantime, this was his legal residence. He was planning to move to Arizona with his girlfriend as soon as the division of assets occurred.

On this occasion, Harold managed to stay until Jimmy and his girlfriend arrived and whisked me away. I knew he had no intention of joining us. He probably just wanted to check out Jimmy's girlfriend.

Jimmy's rustic two-bedroom cabin was near the cabin owned by my good friends, Don and Barbara, where I had frequently visited. Voyager Village was a favorite spot for Twin Citians to have a cabin. Located in acres of wood, surrounded by lakes, it was a private village surrounding a massive recreation center with tennis courts and an eighteen-hole golf course, complete with a small landing area for small planes.

On our last day at Jimmy's, the three of us sat around the outdoor picnic table, finishing off the remains of breakfast and launched into a discussion of how I would handle being "the other woman" in Fred's life. Jimmy also wondered if I were interested in ever marrying again. Would I be wasting my time with Fred when I would finally be free to seek a more appropriate partner — one with no strings attached?

These were good questions and made me think.

I was dropped off at my home early afternoon. Harold was at the door. "Welcome home," he said. "Did you have a good time?"

"It was fun and very restful," I said as I waved goodbye to Jimmy and Ginger.

"By the way, you had a phone call from a Dr. Reese." Harold remarked. "He said he'd call again."

I tried to look nonchalant as I said "Oh, thanks. Do we have any food for supper or should I go pick up something?" But inside, my heart was screaming, *Oh my God, he called! I knew he would!*

One of my pleasures was sitting on my patio, enjoying my garden and the birds at the feeders. *That pleasure would be greatly enhanced if Fred called today.* I thought. *Will he or won't he?* The loud sound of the phone ringing was like a jolt of electricity coursing through my body. *Could that truly be Fred?* My heart was beating a million miles a minute. *Ring, ring.* It felt like an hour before I reached the phone and finally picked up. Fred's voice said, "Hello! You're back."

"Harold said you called," I tried to play it cool.

"I thought you said he was never home," Fred said, chuckling. I felt myself blush but didn't say anything. "I was wondering if you would like a little outing and, if so, what kind of outing would you like?"

I couldn't believe it. Things picked up right where they left off. It was as though no time had elapsed since I last saw him. "Okay..." I decided to ask for the moon. "I'd like to spend several days with you, maybe on the North Shore?"

"How about a very romantic six-day outing to Michigan instead?"

Even better. "That sounds great! How soon?"

"I was thinking about day after tomorrow. I could meet you in the lobby of the Holiday Inn at 8:30 in the morning."

Heart be still, I thought to myself. "Yes, I'll be there!"

I packed a suitcase while Harold was out and put it in the trunk of my car immediately, then got up ridiculously early the next morning to avoid detection by Harold. I was parked and in the hotel lobby an hour early, anxious and on pins and needles. I sat in the lobby and picked up the paper. I opened to the second page and the third. I started reading some article on I don't even know what. My eyes glanced up to the clock on the wall, then back down at the paper, where I started the same article again, trying to focus. Trying to play it cool. *Would I even recognize him?* After all, it was two months ago.

My eyes went back up to the clock, then back down to the beginning of the article again. Finally, a tall, handsome man walked into the lobby. My heart skipped a beat when a smile broke out across his face. He reached his hand out to me and wiggled his fingers, "Let's go!"

As I settled in his jeep, strapping on my seatbelt, I told him I wasn't sure I would recognize him — and that I couldn't believe I was taking off with someone I barely knew. An insouciant grin crossed his face, "There are whips and chains in the back." His sense of humor immediately put me at ease.

"By the way, how did your summer go?" I asked.

"Let's see — I spent a week with Sonia on a trip we had planned to Vancouver, then a week with my son in California and finally a quick trip to see my mom in Ridgetown, Ontario. I try to see her as often as I can."

"You must be traveled out."

"The best is yet to come, my dear."

As we drove along the rolling hills of Wisconsin, I brought Fred up-to-date on my summer decision to meet with a lawyer and start procedures aimed at a November divorce.

"Is Harold okay with that?"

"Much to my surprise, we had a good discussion with mutual agreement on all aspects, including how to divide our property. There wasn't much to quarrel about: our kids are grown, we each have our own assets, and our property isn't worth fighting over. And we're splitting the lawyer fees. So it was all very civilized."

"As well it should be. You do good work." He reached across and gently put his hand on my knee. "Now you can enjoy our time together. Tomorrow we'll be taking a ferry across Lake Michigan from Kewaunee to Ludington in our own private stateroom. Tonight we'll stay in a motel on the way. We're on our way to Big Rapids, Michigan, where I'll be giving testimony at a court hearing."

"You sound well organized." *That's what I like—a take charge guy.* "What kind of testimony?"

"Oh, it's the results of psychological testing — something I do frequently."

After parking our car on the ferry, we hurried onto the deck in time to watch our ferry leaving land. It was hard to believe that my first date with this remarkable man was a trip of six days that included a ferry ride across Lake Michigan in our own private cabin.

Gentle breezes wafted in upon us from the porthole window. Fred whipped out a bottle of wine as well as cheese, crackers, and fruit as we began our four-hour trip to Ludington. *This man thinks of everything!* As he tipped the edge of his wine glass against mine, I felt like a damsel in one of those MGM movies being toasted by a debonair man of the world. "Here's to many good times," he said.

I clinked my glass with his and said, "You really know how to make a woman feel appreciated." I raised my glass to my lips and took a sip, my eyes locked on his.

"The moment I saw you enter the room in St. Paul I was hooked," Fred replied as he put his finger in his mouth, pulling his lip to the side like a hook catching a fish. "I had to meet you. Strong, attractive independent women are like catnip to me."

"Meow..." I replied as he pulled me into the awaiting bed. The gentle waves caressed us as we embraced one another, alternating between passionate love-making and gentle sleep. Too soon, we showered, enjoying the feel of the breezes on our damp bodies as we toweled one another dry. Finishing the last of our cheese and crackers, and the last of the wine, we stepped out of our stateroom looking refreshed as we joined the crowd lining up to disembark. *I could take a lot of this*, I thought to myself as we left the boat.

In our hotel in Big Rapids, we spent day after day talking until the sun came up, swapping stories from our respective lives. Some were funny, some idiotic, some tragic, and some full of wonderment.

He had me in stitches over stories he told about the people who lived in his little village of Ridgetown, Ontario. There was Peckerbeck, the minister's kid, who was the idol of all the little boys, including Fred. They got their sex education from him. And Mrs. Morgan, his mom's best friend, was Fred's "Mrs. Robinson" in his senior high years. She taught him well. I'll be forever grateful to her. Not even her son, who was Fred's best friend, knew about their secret life.

"Hey, I just tried to keep up with my brother who was far more successful than me in getting away with anything. I'm the one who always got caught or who the police brought home saying I'd wrecked the car or something. My mom kept saying, 'Buddy, why can't you be more like your big brother.' But none of them ever knew about Mrs. Morgan."

We laughed at the many dumb things we had done, amazed to still be alive. "There is so much I want to do," Fred continued.

"You mean all the sailing trips, scuba diving, hiking, skiing, and biking isn't enough?" His sophistication impressed me. I felt he was experienced in extramarital affairs and most capable of handling two love relationships in a responsible way. A wife has a different set of expectations for a husband than "the other woman" has for a lover. It was apparent to me Fred was not about to let a secondary relationship with me interfere with his primary relationship with his wife. I was okay with that. She was the one who had history with him and was responsible for being concerned about his economic and physical health.

Having been married for twenty-five years to three different men, I felt ready to strike out on my own, particularly when I had this charming, sophisticated, and adventuresome man as my guide and mentor.

In my childhood, I was influenced by women like Marlene Deitrich who once said that she spent every Christmas with her husband and the rest of the year with others, and she and her husband were married many years; and Ingrid Bergman, who once said that a strong independent woman needs a different man for each decade of her life. Perhaps I was unduly influenced by non-conventional lifestyles because it seemed to be my life. I felt I might discover that I was just not the marrying type — that there was much to be said for "the occasional man."

Much time was spent discussing our marriages. Fred shared how his marriage to Sonia was his second. He was single for ten years after his first marriage ended.

We were lying in bed, I was snuggled up to Fred's neck as he talked about his first wife Sally and how he had married her after he got out of the Army. "Being ordered about by stupid guys was not my idea of how I wanted to live. Sally came from money and her Dad offered me a job in his corporation, but being a corporate man was not a good fit for me either. So I decided to try the university lifestyle." He rubbed my back and said with melancholy, "I met a

Greek gal named Georgia who turned my world upside down. I became addicted to her. My marriage ended and Sally never got over it. She and our two kids moved to Arizona to live on a ranch that Sally's parents got for her."

"How old were your kids when you moved out?"

"About 4 and 6. I didn't feel good about it and felt responsible for causing Sally's unhappiness. Needless to say, her parents were not very pleased with me." Fred paused for a moment and took a deep breath. "She started drinking. The kids took turns running away from home. I saw them as often as I could. Georgia and I had a long relationship, but I finally realized that we came from two very different cultural worlds that could not be reconciled. She was an orthodox Greek and I was a WASP atheist. So I left Ohio to attend the U. of Iowa, partly to separate from Georgia."

I gave Fred a small kiss on his neck and said, "Isn't it amazing that we were both single while at the U. of Iowa?"

"Well, it's probably best we didn't meet because we might not have been ready for one another then," Fred commented.

The sun was just beginning to rise. The sky was turning from black to pink and purple. "Where was Sonia during this time?"

"We met and eventually married about ten years after my divorce from Sally. Sonia took on the responsibilities of being a stepmother to my two difficult kids. When their mother died of alcoholism, they moved in with us. Sonia had a successful and demanding career of her own and I was proud of how she handled both her career and my two kids. She did not want children of her own and I certainly wanted no more."

Tom was Fred's oldest child. When his daughter Sharon was thirteen years old, they learned she had leukemia. "I always thought it was unfortunate that Sally died before she knew Sharon had leukemia. Had she known, it might have given her a reason to deal with her alcoholism and a reason to live," Fred said.

Fred was also concerned about Tom's poor school performance. He had been failing most of his high school classes, spending more time with his Dad's graduate coeds than on his studies. "I wondered if maybe Tom was retarded so I had both kids tested. Much to my surprise, both kids tested high on IQ tests. Eventually Tom pleaded with me to let him drop out of school and join the Navy. He was just seventeen at the time. I told him, 'I don't think you are cut out for military life. You lack discipline and have a poor attitude about working hard and accepting responsibility. The long hair and beads will have to go. If you go AWOL, don't expect any help from me. I'd turn your ass over to the authorities in a New York second.'"

"Your son sounds like quite a handful."

"Well, both kids were. They seemed to take off at different times and just disappear. I remember once I got a call about one in the morning from a sheriff someplace in Arizona asking me if I was the father of a Tom Reese. I said I was. He then said he picked up my son hitchhiking on an Arizona highway and asked me what I wanted done with him. I said, 'Put him back on the highway.'"

Being psychologists, we both laughed.

The sun was slowly rising in the sky and I was starting to realize just how hungry I was. I grabbed a bag of pretzels from the dresser and climbed back on the bed. "That was tough love, behaviorist style, you dished out to Tom."

Fred dug into the pretzel bag. "Well, Tom went on to have a successful Navy career, got his GED, and after his discharge, eventually enrolled at the University of Arizona, and got a degree in Engineering. He now designs radar systems for Stealth aircraft for the Navy in California. And we make a point of spending a week together each summer engaged in some adventurous activity. This last summer we were dropped off by a helicopter in the Canadian wilderness with only basic backpacking equipment and were picked up a week later."

"I'm impressed. Your son has done remarkably well," I bit into a pretzel. "He does seem to be a bit like his Dad."

Fred leaned back on the headboard and arranged some pillows behind him. "Actually, he got his math skills from his Mom. Not me. I'm zilch in that area. The rest he has done all on his own. I'm very proud of him."

"What happened to Sharon?" I asked.

He looked out the window. The sky was red. "She'd take off on brief adventures only returning home when she needed more treatment. She was a wild child, dressed in hippy attire, looking like she could use a bath," Fred gave a little laugh. "When I was working in Washington D.C. in the Education Department, she decided to come check me out at my office. So, one day she comes, dirty and barefoot with loads of beads hanging around her neck and out-of-control wild hair, and tells my secretary she wants to see me. Well, here's the secretary, dressed in a crisp, black suit, wearing high heels, looking like a model for 'how to dress for success' — absolutely bewildered. 'Who shall I say is calling?' 'I'm his daughter,' Sharon replies. When I confirm that indeed she was, the secretary tried to hide her astonishment. But, and here is where it gets interesting, the very next day Sharon returns. I didn't recognize her at first. She was wearing a beige suit with hose and heels. Her hair was clean and pulled back in a discrete roll. And around her neck was a string of pearls accompanying the small pearls on her ears! I don't think my secretary recognized her until I said, 'Why, Sharon, come on in. I'll take you out to lunch.' That was the introduction of the new Sharon. She quickly found her way into a more conventional life of work and marriage."

"That is an amazing story! Did she just decide, after entering your work world, that it was time for a change?" I asked.

"That's exactly what I think happened. She was just ready to be grown up. But her marriage was anything but ordinary."

I put the bag of pretzels on the nightstand and leaned back against the headboard next to Fred.

"My daughter was still a very sick girl who needed expensive drugs and treatments from time to time. And if she married, she'd loose her medical benefits. She literally could not afford to be married. But the two of them desperately wanted to be married — or appear to be married. We finally found a Unitarian minister who would pretend to marry them. It was a secret carefully kept from all but immediate family. And none too soon. With each remission, she got a bit weaker. But she is a strong, gutsy woman, who continued to endure pretty painful treatments following each remission."

I wrapped my arms around Fred's arm and leaned into him. I expressed sympathy for what all of his family must have been enduring. Sharon sounded like a remarkable young lady.

Interspersed among time spent enjoying the whirlpool and dining were more endless conversations about our former lives. We spent much time discussing our respective marriages. Ironically, Fred, Sonia, and I were all psychologists. My first husband, Ron, was also a psychologist and the father of my only child, Linda.

One night while we were sitting in the hotel bar, Fred asked, "Why don't you tell me more about your marriages? There were three of them, weren't there?"

"I'll give you a condensed version of the three husbands. In the fifties, Ron dominated my life. Our paths crossed when we met on a blind date at the U. of Iowa. We were both immature, naïve kids from small Iowa towns. He was a Missouri Synod Lutheran. I was a First Methodist. He reminded me a bit of James Dean — he was a confused, idealistic, vulnerable man from a dysfunctional home seeking redemption." I stopped talking for a moment as the bartender set down two gin and tonics in front of us. I wrapped my hand around the cool glass. "Most the folks I knew seemed terribly boring and predictable including my family and me. Visiting his family was like being immersed in a soap opera full of drama. Ron, his brother who was also a student at the university, and I would spend hours analyzing his family, particularly his mother who was extremely erratic." Fred picked up his drink and swirled the glass around, then took a sip.

I took a drink as well and then continued, "She was a great cook who served each meal with aggravation, complaining about each of us, often accompanied with tears, eventually running from the room, locking herself in her bedroom. Ron's Dad would caution the boys to take it easy on her, 'she's going through the change, you know, and I have to live with her when you leave.'

"I am sure it is why all three of us were attracted to the study of psychology, particularly abnormal psychology."

Fred propped his leg on my barstool and rested his arm behind me. "What, you, interested in neurotic people?"

"For many years I was never bored, being a part of that crazy family. It was like sitting in the front row of an O'Neill play. We were both equally naïve, true believers in our respective religions."

"Now I do find that hard to believe." Fred leaned back. "My mother was a devout Christian Scientist, but my dad, brother, and I were always non-believers." Fred shook his head dubiously. "How long did that last?"

"Long after our marriage. We were mediocre students, spending our junior year drinking, smoking, and playing bridge with friends. The military draft for the Korean War was breathing down our necks. Neither of us knew what we wanted to do our senior year so we decided to get married before Ron was drafted. I was convinced my love for Ron was all he needed to become a confident man, successful in his endeavors. I was astonished to learn on my wedding night that both Ron and I were virgins. It would be hard to find two people less ready for the responsibilities of marriage. Neither of us had a lick of common sense. He ended up at Fort Dix where I joined him, working at a local real estate office in Trenton, N.J. until he was discharged."

"How did that affect you, knowing that neither of you had any basic skills for sex or marriage?"

The bartender moved back and forth down the bar, but I didn't care whether or not he heard any of our conversation. I was just so thrilled to have these deep, meaningful, honest talks with Fred. "Quite frankly, I lacked confidence in Ron's ability to make love and I suspect I was pretty much frigid throughout our marriage. It was like having said 'no' so often while dating, that I became unable to say 'yes' physically and emotionally when married. But we both thrived on the exciting intellectual lifestyle of beatniks in the '50s that led us to question our former religious and political beliefs. Ron led the way, encouraging me to continue earning my degree after our daughter, Linda, was born. He also encouraged me to start graduate school, showing me how we could arrange our classes so that one of us would be home with Linda. I couldn't have asked for a more supportive husband."

"What was the straw that broke the camel's back?" Fred asked.

"After making a straight 4.0 grade point on his M.A. degree, becoming the 'golden boy' of the department, he simply fell apart when starting his doctorate program. It was as though he feared success; that too much would be expected of him and he wouldn't measure up. I, along with some of his professors and best friends, were concerned that he would continually be his own worst enemy in failing to achieve professional success. He was the classic man against himself. By about the seventh year of our marriage, I was finding the crazy behaviors of Ron and his family to be as predictable and boring as I had found my family and life in Marshalltown. Our immaturities resulted in each of us going our separate ways."

"But what about Linda?" Fred swirled the ice around in his drink. " Where did she fit into all this?"

"I just figured that if Ron couldn't be my Prince Charming, I'd become my own Prince Charming. I'd pick myself up, dust myself off and start all over again—this time as a doctoral candidate. The 'Big U' was to me like Tara was to Scarlett O'Hara in *Gone with the Wind*. It was the place where I had most experienced success. And where I would most likely find another 'daddy' for Linda.

"I was determined to provide for her the kind of home and life I had hoped Ron and I would be giving her. It turned out to be a good decision. Ron provided no child support payments after I remarried. Linda was in first grade at that time. I really liked being in graduate school. Even more, I liked being 'Doc Shirl.' Now I felt assured I could give Linda and me a good life."

"You're really something!" He put his arm around me and squeezed my shoulder. I leaned into him as he kissed my forehead. "So, how about the next husband?"

"I met Ben at the U. He represented solid respectability to me, coming from an educated, successful family. His older brother was a research professor at the U, married with three kids. Ben introduced me to the world of social activism in the '60s as we confronted Civil Rights issues and Vietnam War protests that were occurring on the campuses across the nation. All of us were involved in politics—even the kids. They ran off protest or election notices on the mimeograph and distributed them in the neighborhood. Together Ben and I collected signatures from whites on their willingness to live with blacks, which I presented before a hostile crowd of realtors at an Iowa City council meeting. Together we gathered clothing and canned goods to send to Holly Springs, Mississippi, using the block politics that had helped us do our part to elect L.B.J. Ben was consistently hawkish on Vietnam whereas I wavered back and forth between hawk and dove.

"After getting my Ph.D. in educational psychology at the University of Iowa, Ben, Linda, and I moved to Independence, Iowa. When Ben began work on his Ph.D., he commuted between Iowa City and Independence. Walking our talk was important to us. Ben wanted to be a military historian living abroad. I didn't see how my career could fit into that lifestyle. We were stepping on one another's career ambitions. And so we went our separate ways."

Fred raised his glass to me and said, "And now we get to Harold."

"By this time I was teaching at the University of Northern Iowa at Cedar Falls where I designed their first classes training teachers how to manage behavior of disruptive children in the classroom. With Harold in the '70s, I explored the world of relationships—all kinds of relationships: black/white, male/female, parent/child, boss/staff, and friend/friend. We moved to St. Paul in 1969 where we both began working for the St. Paul Public Schools. During our ten years there, I learned the inadequacies each of us brought from our respective backgrounds. He came from the black working class and I from the white middle class. From him, I acquired awareness of racial and cultural issues and the need for me to refine and update mine. If initially I had admired his independence, his belief in his 'rightness' in how to parent, be a husband, be an employee, and treat his friends, I eventually saw that that confidence was based on his inability to tolerate any views but his own."

"In other words, his independent behavior was based on his need for others to believe totally in what he said and did," Fred remarked.

"Well put. As you might imagine, there would come a time when others, initially charmed by his confident manner, were unwilling to accept his 'rightness' in everything. It was as though he saw my 'whiteness' as enabling and I saw his 'blackness' as controlling. Our differences in how to be a family and rear children were irreconcilable. Eventually he left, taking his blackness with him and I once again wrapped myself up in whiteness."

Fred stirred his gin and tonic and took a drink. "By God, you really took those civil rights issues seriously!" He set his glass down on the bar as if it were the exclamation point to his sentence. "You certainly gave it the old college try. But you couldn't change from being a WASP." Fred motioned to the bartender for another drink. "You want another?" I nodded and he indicated two to the bartender. "You're a WASP. I'm a WASP. That's who we are. We come from the same stock, the same kind of families. Why, even our Dads are remarkably similar. Both of them businessmen, leaders in their communities. And you and I are so much alike, it's scary. Talking with you is almost like talking to myself."

That's it, I thought. It was our compatibility that so attracted us to one another. That's what I lacked in my marriages. I was looking for differences. But our differences were too great. In that moment I wondered if that was true for Fred's marriages, but I decided to leave that observation for another time.

Fred leaned into me, lowered his voice, and said, "Now, where do I fit in?"

I let out a small giggle. I hadn't giggled in years. "Well, what I've learned from those three men has prepared me for you and life in the '80s." I set my hand on his knee. "From you, I think I'm going to learn a lot about autonomy and independence and about the joys of being an independent woman. It may sound strange, but I really feel we'll be spending several decades together."

Fred put his hand on mine. "We certainly do good things together." The bartender set the drinks in front of us. "Here's to our future," Fred raised his glass to a toast. "Fuckin 'A, as we say in Canada. Life is good!"

I clinked my glass to his and I swear I saw sparks!

My infatuation with Fred had been immediate and hot, hot, hot! As I so lacked ability to understand Harold or predict his behavior, I was "on the money" with Fred. Immediately, I knew my passion was reciprocated and I never doubted that I would hear from him again.

I looked out the window of Fred's jeep as we drove home from Michigan. As the green fields passed by, Fred started telling me about two of his dearest friends, Sam and Susie, who truly lived a hippie lifestyle. "Sam and I taught at the University of Wisconsin at Oshkosh. He got involved with Susie, one of his undergrad students. He was married at the time but found Susie to be a kindred soul who dug his dreams to be a self-sufficient guy living off his own labors. So he procured several hundred acres of land, mostly trees and rocks, near Oshkosh, and with Susie's help began building a rustic wooden house in the middle of the woods. Eventually, they added a garage with an outdoor john attached and began living off the land. They've reduced their expenses by generating their own electricity, raising their own food, grapes for wine, and good old Wisconsin green—" Fred looked over at me with a spark in his eye, "Marijuana. And to top it all off, they built this wooden hot tub ready for guests or themselves."

"I'll bet they read *Mother Jones* magazine." I said with a laugh, "I'd love to meet them."

"They are different, but I think you'd get along with them real well. Maybe I could arrange a three-day weekend around Labor Day, after we're back at work in the fall? "

A shot of adrenaline ran through me. *Another trip!* "I'd thoroughly enjoy meeting them," I said enthusiastically. I reached over and gave Fred a big hug while he was driving. He gave me a little laugh. I thought to myself how quickly we each assumed we were headed for a long-term relationship. I suddenly felt that I could trust him to keep me in his life on a regular basis, and it felt like he could trust me to honor his marriage. *This occasional man thing might work out after all,* I thought as we continued our drive home.

The rolling hills created a peaceful pastoral scene that would normally create a calming effect on me. But the further our jeep sped through its beauty, the sooner we would be reaching the Minnesota border — I was definitely not ready to leave Fred and reenter my world with its issues.

As we approached the border, I cried out, "Fred, I'm just not ready for these six days to end."

Looking over at me, with a big grin on his face, he suddenly swerved off on a side road and got out of the car. He opened the passenger-side door and grabbed my hand. Without saying a word he started running towards the cornfield. Entering one of the rows of corn, he kept holding on to me as we ran out of sight of the road.

He came to a small pocket of a clearing in the cornfield where he took off his jacket, and spread it out on the ground. "A place for you to lie." He slid in beside me for one last romantic moment. I felt such peace as I lay on the ground surrounded by tall corn, while looking over his shoulder at the blue sky with its puffs of white cotton balls floating above us.

"Darling, you are giving me such wonderful memories. I do so thank you."

A week or so later, Fred called again, suggesting we spend our last few days of summer hiking on Lake Superior's North Shore. After agreeing to the trip, I soon realized that becoming an intrepid hiker requires a certain skill set. I quickly became an avid learner.

Our initial forays into the hiker's world required proper equipment and clothing. "Get your credit card. We're going shopping!" Fred announced as we headed for REI. "You're gonna need waterproof hiking boots, a backpack, a bedroll and mattress, layered clothing for all kinds of weather, a hat, and water canteen—for openers." He left me in the clothing section as he headed towards the camping-gear section.

This guy clearly means business. I'd never been in such a store before so I could see this was going to require much thinking and decision-making on my part. I weaved my way through the store, stopping in the shoe section, the sleeping bag section, clothing, camping supplies. My mind spun with all of the choices. I talked to the shoe salesman and tried on low hiking shoes, hiking boots, heavy hiking boots, and waterproof hiking boots. *Did I really need waterproof ones?* That's what Fred said, so that's what I got. I tried on all sorts of clothing, which felt much less foreign to me, but then wandered aimlessly in the camping section until a nice saleswoman helped me sort everything out. Canteen, hat, backpack, mattress and bedroll, I was set.

Fred and I arrived at the cashier's at the same time; then we went out to the parking lot and started loading up his jeep. Fred had already packed some of the necessities for our trip: a box of books, a box of booze, a box of boots, a box of CDs and books on tapes. His taste in books revealed his love of history, mysteries, and biographies. And of course, he had items such as paper towels, Windex, basic tools, snacks, and a two-man tent.

Our first hiking trek—he assured me there would be many more—was on a muddy trail heading towards the Canadian border on Minnesota's North Shore. It was a cool day. The woods were thick with tall trees surrounded by underbrush. Fred took his wallet and car keys and hid them among the brush. "What did you do that for?" I asked.

"Helps me travel light," he remarked as he strode ahead of me, beginning his trek up the gradual hill.

"I can see why you insisted I get waterproof boots," I yelled, trying to keep up with him. The mud was oozing up the sides of my boots, splattering thick black blobs on my pant cuffs. Fred kept a fast pace that kept me huffing and puffing. I clearly was not used to such exertion. After what seemed like hours (but was probably an hour and a half at most), he spied a clearing. As I looked across the landscape, I saw a small waterfall and a river rippling over slabs of rocks. The cool spray speckled my face.

"That's Canada over there," he pointed. I looked out across the tops of trees, flanked by rolling banks of high bluffs. We'd worked up a lot of body heat. Fred began stripping off his outer garments, then all his clothes and boots and headed for the water, plunking himself in it.

"Come on in! The water's warm. Get yourself cleaned up."

"But what do I do to get dried off?" I asked. That was me— always worried about the logistics.

"Not a problem. Just pick yourself a big, hot rock to lie on. When one side is dry, turn over and dry the other," he said.

OK, I thought. *So this is how you do it.* We splashed each other for a while—me playing modest as Fred reached for my "private parts" — and I taunting him, calling him a naughty boy. After we got out, we laid back on the hot rock to absorb the sun's heat. It was so peaceful and relaxing—better than any day at any spa. As the sun warmed my front and the rock warmed my back, I drifted off into a nap. The wind was creating a slight breeze and the trees rustled in response.

Suddenly, Fred jumped up and announced with a loud clap, "Time to get going! Get your clothes on and feet moving!"

The slog back through the slippery mud was exhausting me and I gave up trying to keep up with Fred. But I kept him within visual range. Dusk was moving in. Fred went right to his hiking place in the brush and dug out his wallet and keys. I dragged myself into his car, my legs aching and my feet sore.

We reached our cabin overlooking the mighty Lake Superior and I headed for the kitchen stool. While I pulled off the heavy, muddy hiking shoes, Fred made me a gin and tonic. I was so thirsty, I nearly gulped it down. It was so refreshing.

Fred opened a can of chili, put a saucepan on the stove, and poured in the chili.

The next thing I remember was waking up in the middle of the night with all my clothes on, in bed. I screamed out, "What am I doing in bed? How come all my clothes are on?"

Fred rolled over and looked at me. He quickly came out of a dream. "Huh?"

"I'm hungry! Where's my bowl of chili?"

"I ate it all," Fred laughed. "You fell asleep on the stool! Luckily, I caught you before you fell on the floor. Guess I shouldn't have given you Tanqueray gin in your drink. It's pretty strong stuff."

And that was my initiation into hiking the North woods. It was only the beginning of many hiking and tenting trips with my new occasional man.

Chapter Three
Endings, New Beginnings, &
Rules of Engagement
1979

I<small>T FELT GOOD TO</small> be back at work, to catch up on school and faculty news and gossip, and to prepare for the new school year. I loved my work and knew I was good at what I did. The amount of attention and reinforcements I had typically received from work associates on a regular basis made up for the lack of praise or attention I got from Harold over the years. My faculty and I felt ready for the new school year.

My lawyer informed me the divorce was on the docket and assets were divided agreeably. Harold was not contesting the divorce (since it was his idea) and we were splitting the modest cost (since the lawyer was a friend of mine).

My new life had begun.

But my joy quickly turned to a sense of gloom every time I walked into my house. I would open the front door and enter my home, which was in a bad state of disrepair. Some rooms had cracked walls and peeling paint. Some rooms had age-old wallpaper wilted and ready to retire. Doorknobs rattled, floors creaked. In addition, the house's unkempt look, with housework piling up, seemed to accuse me of neglect. Walking into the kitchen, I saw dirty dishes stacked high, food that needed to be thrown out, a refrigerator lacking any basics, and a floor that needed mopping. I wanted to flee from this house that was no longer a home; maybe buy a nice clean, new condo.

My financial advisor, Dennis, gave me the many reasons why that would not be a good decision. He had carefully explained to me, in the way a teacher explains to a young child, that it was not the time to sell when interest rates, inflation, and gas were so high and many people were desperately trying to sell the homes they could no longer afford. It was going to require hard work on my part to bite the bullet and use the resources available to me to eventually turn "this old house" into a cared-for, loving home.

I was only just finding out that the house needed insulation, storm windows, a new roof, improved wiring, and new copper water pipes, for starters. But Dennis assured me it could be done in possibly three years. Then I could begin the cosmetic improvements. Together we came up with a plausible plan.

I wasn't accustomed to making decisions about fixing up the house or handling money issues. That had always seemed to me to be "man's work"; the thought of it terrified me. I tackled the problem head-on and hired Brian, a young man with carpentry and repair skills, to aid me in the many fix-up years that stretched out before me. We would tackle one or two projects a year. Now, I was beginning to see the work on the house as a challenge rather than a curse to bear. Life was beginning to feel exciting once again.

Fred had been calling weekly. With Labor Day approaching, he called again to arrange our three-day outing to Wisconsin to meet his dear friends, Sam and Susie. The weather was ideal. Fred had just purchased a new jeep and was eager to show it to Sam and Susie, so we took off for another adventure.

I sometimes wondered how Fred's wife felt about him leaving without her, but the fact was, it was none of my concern. I had Fred for the weekend and that was good enough for me.

Fall was in the air. Bits of red and yellow peered out from the edges of leaves but the sun was hot and the breeze welcoming as it wafted through the jeep's open windows, caressing our faces. We drove through small Wisconsin towns that sat neat and tidy along the highway. They were tucked safely between fields of corn, soybeans, or rows and rows of trees. Each town was orderly and well-kept (unlike my house); little storefronts lined the highway through town.

Fred told me to keep a lookout for a little gravel tractor road with an old farmhouse on one side and field after field of tall grasses and weeds on the other side. This seemed easy to miss, but we actually did find it.

We drove about a mile or so to the path leading to their rustic home. It was surrounded by oak trees, tall and plentiful, that encircled their home, totally shading it from the bright day. But all of that faded into the background because all I could focus on were two bare bottoms sticking up from the big garden. Our hosts stood up, grabbed their clothing and greeted us with huge smiles. "So you're Shirley," Susie said as she welcomed me into their home.

While the guys were examining the new jeep, I assisted Susie in getting some cold brews for the four of us. When we came back with ice-cold beer, Sam casually said in his understated way, "We'll just have to try out that new jeep of yours in our woods to see what it's made of. The muddy paths should provide a good test of its endurance."

"Good thinking," agreed Fred as he clinked bottles with Sam.

Somehow, this didn't seem like a good idea to me. "But Fred, your brand-new clean car will get filthy muddy in these woods. And probably get stuck in the mud as well."

"All the more reason to get started while it's still light out," Sam said with Fred readily agreeing. Before I knew it, we were all climbing into the jeep and heading off to the woods. I had decided to go with the flow.

Sure enough, the jeep got stuck in the mud as soon as we got down the slippery hill and into the soggy woods. That mud was like quicksand; it looked like it had a permanent hold on the tires.

"Fred, you start the motor while we start pushing. You gals get behind each rear wheel while I push from this side." Sam braced himself and Susie and I did the same. "OK, Fred, rev her up!"

We pushed and shoved and pushed some more with mud kicking up and splattering our feet, our clothes, our faces. After rocking the car back and forth for some time, the former clean car inched its muddy exterior out of the mud with the guys roaring their shouts of victory. Apparently the new car had passed their endurance test.

Once we were literally out of the woods, covered in mud from head to toe, Sam ran toward the lake, beckoning us to follow.

"And you've gotta see our new dock we built since you were last here." said Susie. She then grabbed my arm, leading me toward the lake and said, "We try to have something new to show Fred each time he comes here."

Fortunately, some of my Norwegian friends had acquainted me with skinny dipping many years before. So we all whipped off our muddy clothes and dove into the water. "You've gotta watch out for foreign fish in this lake," Sam warned. "It's full of cocksuckers and pussysharks!"

"Oh," I screamed. "I'm being attacked right now!" A great water battle began with us fleeing or chasing the invading fish. Finally, I climbed up on the dock to escape those pesky pussysharks. As I laid my newly clean body facedown on the hot dock, I suddenly felt something slushy and gooey all over my back and rear. Fred, with juicy red tomatoes in each hand, was leering at me as he squished me with more tomatoes. The attack began in earnest among the four of us, squealing and shouting and ending up back in the lake. Such was my introduction to this trio of good friends.

Everything on "their estate" had been built, created, or done by the two of them, with an occasional helping hand from a neighbor. Their clothing consisted of overalls, sweatshirts, boots, and wellies in cold weather. All ordered from L. L. Bean; but on hot summers they often worked in the nude. They did everything together—from skinning a deer to fixing a tractor or canning vegetables.

Eager to show us the changes they had created since the previous year, we followed them around to see the new tractor or an addition to the garage or the huge new garden. We ended up in the hot tub with a glass of their homemade wine where we listened to them catch up on local gossip.

Later we enjoyed another glass of wine in the slightly elevated greenhouse attachment that served as the living room. It was filled with plants on one side and partially open to the kitchen so that I could hear the guys laughing while I kept Susie company as she fixed supper. The small table where we dined was in a lower area that included a few more chairs, a floor lamp, and a TV that showed only a few channels because of the rural location. On one wall hung a deer's head with an impressive rack. Susie was a mighty fine cook who prepared food largely raised by them.

Susie and Sam at their Wisconsin estate

After a few days of enjoying this amazing getaway, we were in a joyous mood as we hugged them, then waved as we drove out their gravel road to head home.

"So what did you think of Susie and Sam?" Fred asked with a twinkle in his eye as he anticipated my positive response.

"I hope we can see more of them. They are a couple truly living their dream," I observed. "Kind of like we hope to do."

"Fuckin' A", Fred said in agreement.

Fred continued calling weekly. He had been periodically visiting his daughter in Ohio, who was back in the hospital. He was very concerned that after each procedure, her remissions were briefer and she was weaker. He said, "She yells at her doctor, telling him to keep his fuckin' hands off her." By this time Fred said her body held many scars from the various surgeries.

My own daughter called one day to tell me that she and her live-in boyfriend had just broken up. She didn't know where she was going to go or what she wanted to do next in her life. She was pretty upset. I suggested she move in with me until she decided what she wanted to do; she was relieved and made plans to do so the next weekend.

It seemed both strange and comforting to be living with Linda again. She seemed fragile, so like a butterfly emerging from its cocoon while still perceiving herself as a caterpillar. All she said about her boyfriend was that he preferred drinking beer to being with her.

Looking about the big empty forlorn house that had once been her home, she could probably see that I would have much work to do turning it back into a home. The large bedroom she chose for herself remained filled for weeks with stacks of her unopened boxes, which she appeared to have no interest in opening. The only change she sought was to get a cat to catch the many mice who also lived with us in our very large Queen Anne house.

The next day we went to the Humane Society where Linda found a grey-and-white-striped kitten that had lunged upon her chest, holding on for dear life. Holding it tightly on her lap as we drove home, she decided it should be named Jasper. We now had another member of our family.

Each morning we would head out the door for our respective cars, driving off to work. Gradually we fell into a pattern of having breakfast and supper together, engaging in small talk while sharing a bottle of wine in the evening.

One night Fred called to inform me that his daughter had died. I felt so sad for him, knowing how much he loved her and feared she was losing her battle—a battle she had been fiercely fighting. His conversation was brief. He was too choked up to talk further. Saying he would call later, he hung up. I just sat there for the longest time— too stunned to move until Linda came over to find out who called. She knew all about Fred, and I had briefly shared with her a bit about Fred's daughter. She was very comforting to me as she sat with me and held me.

I couldn't call Fred, for obvious reasons, so I had to wait for him to call me. Two weeks went by. Not a word from him. I was so worried about him. Where was he? More importantly, *how* was he?

Then one day at work, he called me. "I'm in Ontario. I'm all right. I just had to be alone. So I came to a place where we used to downhill ski and that's what I've been doing every day, all day. It keeps my mind focused on just skiing—staying upright, mastering the moguls; a contest of me against the slopes."

I was so relieved to hear from him and asked when he would be back.

"I'm ready to return. I'll call you soon." With that, he hung up. He was never one to talk long on the phone. I was just glad he was finding a way to deal with his extreme grief.

Several weeks later, Fred visited me and met Linda for the first time. Linda was about the same age as his daughter. It was amazing how naturally Fred and Linda got along.

During the holidays, we fell into a pattern. Fred would visit every other week for several days. The three of us would have breakfasts and family dinners, often followed by bull sessions lit by candlelight. Conversations often continued deep into the night. Fred and Linda each had a great sense of humor and loved throwing zingers at one another. Challenging one another at chess was one of their favorite pastimes. Linda looked forward to his visits. She felt the three of us were the best family she had had. Fred was like the Dad she never had. She often wondered if she somehow helped Fred deal with his loss of his daughter.

Fred wondered about Linda's relationship with her father. He was shocked to hear that Linda had no contact with Ron in many years—not even a birthday card—and she was his only child. "Linda is a beautiful young lady. What I don't understand is Linda's father. She is just a delightful, intelligent girl. How could he show so little interest in her? It is certainly his loss."

"It had been surprising to me too. He was an attentive father during my pregnancy, her birth, and her first six years of life. She even lived with him and his second wife for a few months while I was just starting my doctorate. But then one day he showed up at my duplex with her and her suitcase and simply said, 'She's her mother's daughter.' That was it. When we moved to Minnesota, he made one visit. The other contacts were when he was back for his parents' funerals in Iowa. Linda drove down to join Ron, his wife, and brother. Linda said he paid little attention to her on those occasions. She had brought her scrapbooks to show him the various trips she had enjoyed, but she said he showed little interest, talking only about his dogs and big-brained people. Go figure!"

Linda's disconnection with her father certainly saddened me, but Fred brought her a new kind of connection, and for that I was grateful.

With the holidays over, I looked forward to winter, snow, and skiing. I was fortunate to live near Crosby Park, a rugged wooded area of acres of tall oaks and pine trees surrounded by wild grasses nestled between Crosby Lake and the Mississippi River. One could get lost hiking along the many trails. It was hard to imagine this rugged piece of wilderness was located not more than a mile or two from downtown St. Paul and my home. It had been my refuge for years – hiking its many paths in the fall, cross-country skiing in the winter, and biking in the spring.

Though Fred said nothing about how he, Sonia, and Tom were dealing with the death of Sharon, I sensed this was a winter he needed to stay close to home. His son generally spent three days with the two of them each Thanksgiving and Christmas. The days would grow long after his son left. Yet Fred could take quick trips to visit me and get in some skiing at Crosby. We'd get home from these robust outings to enjoy the warmth of cocktails by the fireplace with Linda often joining us for dinner.

Fred had become friends with Don, a social worker at my school, who had a cabin at Voyageur Village in Wisconsin, about a three-hour drive away. Don offered us the key to his cabin since he and his wife Barbara didn't use it often in the winter. Now that their kids were grown and on their own, the cabin was used even less. We found it much to our liking so it became another convenient spot to get away and enjoy nature.

As our relationship developed, we found more places to ski and explore near St. Paul. With good snow, we could ski through March.

How frequently we saw one another was determined by Fred. I respected the efforts he made to include me in his life and he, in turn, shared no frustrations incurred by him in doing so.

Occasionally, he'd let a week or two go by without a phone call. These were the days before call waiting and answering machines and voicemail. I'd let him know that I didn't like sitting by the phone waiting for "the call." He'd often remind me to not wait. "I'll keep calling until I get you. Just live your life." I understood from the beginning not to call him.

I'd keep explaining that my need to hear his voice was so great, that I could do nothing until I heard from him and know when I might next see him. It took him a while to understand why I felt the way I did and why he did not. He was in control. I couldn't make plans comfortably until I knew what time, if any, he might be available. He then apologized and said, "You're right. I will call weekly."

No more was said. No more needed to be said. If I had learned nothing from my marriages, I had learned the art of timing. One had to know what issues were important enough to discuss and when was the best time to discuss them, then let appreciative silence rein.

Quite often Clem or Tib, another close girlfriend, would want to know more about how Fred and I related to one another. They saw no evidence of any relationship issues when around us. They asked me, "How do you avoid arguments?"

I told them, "I say to myself, 'is this enough of a difference to make a difference? Really? In the long haul?' And usually I decide it isn't."

Clem had remained highly interested in watching our relationship evolve. Tib, who had been widowed at age forty-five, had tried out many relationships, often fraught with drama. The three of us were married when we first met ten years prior; we were now single and had a close friendship. Clem was the judicious one who avoided risk situations. Tib was highly impulsive with changeable moods, and me — I'm not sure how they might have described me. But we fiercely liked one another and spent much time together, including travel.

The interesting fact is that Fred and I got along amazingly well.

One spring day, Fred and I headed for Don and Barbara's cabin to spend a few days. It was one of those slushy days with the remains of wet, dirty snow underfoot. We unloaded the jeep and carried our supplies into the rustic, log cabin, plunking them on and around the kitchen counter. Fred hooked up the electricity and turned on the water while I put groceries, books, and clothes away. Fred started a fire in the fireplace. I checked out the neat wooden porch that wrapped around the front of the cabin overlooking a small pond. We pulled out a lawn chair or two and set them on the porch so we could smell the freshness of the air and feel the gentle wind in our hair.

Fred handed me a gin and tonic. I set out some ashtrays for Fred's cigar and my cigarettes. He'd usually have only one a day and did not inhale. It would be late afternoon and evening when I'd smoke my seven for the day. Fred told me how smoking had become quite a divisive topic in his household. Sonia was critical of his drinking and he of her smoking.

He drank too much and she smoked two packs a day. Neither were willing to change. But Fred made a point of saying, "At least I don't drive when I drink. That's why I stay home nights. But you," he pointed at me, "I'd like to see you quit. I notice you have quite a cough in the morning when you first get up"

"True," I said, "but I only smoke seven a day starting at cocktail time."

"Yes, but I notice you smoke those ciggies down to the last half inch. It hurts seeing Sonia smoke so much, especially when it affects the flow of blood from her heart to her legs. That's why she has trouble walking much further than a couple of blocks without needing to rest. She's already had one procedure. That's why I'd like you to stop."

"You know, I did once in 1956 for five years, but after marrying Harold, who'd smoke while taking a shower, I started in again. But I'll work on it. I really don't want to smoke and I know it's bad, bad, bad."

Just then a chorus of frogs rose up from the pond. Fred and I both stopped talking and began to listen carefully. The tones were easily recognizable: alto, contralto, and sopranos — each chimed in.

"It's positively wondrous!" I said as I got up and started leading the chorus. "I just love it here!" I cheered.

"Ideal living conditions," stated Fred. "We must come here every spring at this time — when the frogs perform."

Our little outings were as satisfying as those more elaborate. It was just being together, enjoying Nature's gifts, that made me, at least, feel at one with the Universe.

Chapter Four
Smooth (and Not-so-Smooth) Sailing
Another Summer—1980

IT WAS EARLY IN the morning on a warm summer day when I looked out my living room window and saw Fred's jeep out front with a small sunfish sailboat attached to its hitch. "Come on," he said. "Let's go sailing." With school on summer break, I was free to go.

This was a new experience for me. We took off for a small marina on the St. Croix River where Fred carefully backed his boat in the water, then climbed up to the dock to attach the boat. I watched as he patiently got his small boat ready to sail.

He put up the pole first, securing it with screws he took from a small glass jar. Then he began attaching the ropes to the pole and mast, again searching out the right-sized screws for each task. Occasionally, he asked me to hand him some kind of equipment, but otherwise he worked in a quiet, meditative manner. Then up went the sail with the breeze capturing it before he skillfully attached and strung it up in the proper place. Fred used the nautical names for everything that had to do with the boat. A rope was a sheet, "port" and "starboard" were terms for right and left. I was quite sure the nautical names would be difficult for me to remember.

Fred seemed unperturbed by the amount of time spent on just getting the boat ready to sail. Next he fastened on the motor and attached the various sheets to different parts of the small boat. I looked at my watch. At least a half-hour had gone by. Apparently this laborious process was part of the fun.

Finally, he backed up the jeep and parked it. After he hopped on the boat, he motioned to me to do the same. He helped hoist me up and I moved cautiously, trying to balance myself as he took the helm. I couldn't figure out where to sit without getting in the way of a sheet or sail, or getting a clunk on the head from the mast suddenly swinging about.

There was barely room on this small sunfish for two slender people. I seemed to be constantly leaning back over the water, hanging on to something for dear life, or leaning far forward to avoid the swinging mast.

From time to time Fred uttered something like "coming about," which meant I should duck my head somewhere. There was no time to check out the scenery. I was much too busy ducking or leaning. When we picked up speed, Fred began to do something he called "tacking," which seemed to coincide with "coming about." He referred to the wind as "quirky," which must have been the reason my hair was constantly blinding me as it was blown into my eyes. Whenever I looked at Fred, he was grinning from ear to ear with what appeared to be sheer pleasure; I gathered that we were now having fun.

During a rare quiet moment between tacks, Fred assured me that I need not learn the nautical terms. He would just motion to a rope and tell me to hand it to him or hold it tight against me until he'd tell me to release it. As we skimmed along at a fast pace, I saw Fred hold his head back, taking in the sun on his face and the breeze on his back. He yelled, "Fuckin' A'! This is great fun!"

As we headed back to the dock, it took him another half hour or so to dock the boat and undo all that he had done to ready it for attachment to the jeep. So all in all, it took an hour of prep time to sail for an hour. "You were great!" he said, as we climbed into the jeep. "I'll make a sailor out of you yet."

So I shouldn't have been surprised when a few weeks later he informed me that he had just leased a friend's thirty-six-foot sailboat for a week's cruise on Lake Superior. His friend Dick would be joining us. When Fred asked if I had a girlfriend who might also like to join us, I immediately thought of a friend of mine who was an excellent sailor; she lived in Duluth and had her own small boat. She was recently divorced from the psychologist who worked in my school.

We eventually all met for drinks and she hit it off well with Fred and Dick. "Count me in," she said. By the time we departed from the Superior Harbor, Pat and Dick had become comfortable friends.

The Reckless Sailors on Lake Superior

As I stood on the pier looking across the top of the thirty-six-foot boat and the seemingly endless waters of Lake Superior, I asked in awe, "So now I'm going to become a sailor?"

Fred just smiled at me with that charming grin he had. He decided to give me a tour of the boat while we waited for Pat and Dick to arrive. I was surprised at how spacious it was, partly because of the creative use of space. Two bedrooms—I mean galleys—a "head" (their word for toilet), and a combination kitchen/dining area with steps going up to the front deck. The kitchen was adequately supplied with dishes and such.

"Ahoy!" Dick and Pat greeted from the deck. They, too, were impressed with the size and creative use of space. The deck was good sized—plenty of room for us to spread out and take in the rays. Captain Fred took his position behind the impressive wheel. We stocked the kitchen—or is it a galley?—with enough food for the week.

The three of them examined the nautical map while Fred traced our route from Superior Harbor on the Minnesota border to the Apostle Islands in Wisconsin. I felt in safe hands. The three of them were experienced sailors and Fred had his Captain's license.

The sky was sunny and blue without a cloud in sight. The water was gentle with a perfect wind guiding us towards the Apostle Islands. The sun felt good on our pale shoulders as we looked forward to being bronze in a day or two.

"Now what did you say these ropes are for?" I joked. Actually, I wasn't sure I could remember. I was the novice on this voyage.

After an afternoon of smooth sailing, Captain Fred said, "I tell you what, why don't we take turns going down below." He offered a wink and a wicked smile. "You and Pat can go first. Then, our turn, and then you two can fight over who captains the ship."

"Sounds like a plan," Dick said as he grabbed Pat's hand. Smiling agreement, she and Dick quickly left. *Well*, I thought, *they seem to be getting along very well!*

And so a ritual was established.

After a delicious chicken dinner prepared largely by Pat—I was the inept sous chef—we enjoyed gin and tonics while watching the blazing sunset. Starting as a fiery, red ball, it expanded and expanded, until its rays covered the sky. The four of us stood wordlessly, watching the magnificent performance of the huge red ball as it began its descent, ever so slowly behind the horizon, with its rays spreading so far and wide that their colors began fading. Finally the red ball itself disappeared, leaving us in an unaccustomed darkness.

After an evening of congenial conversation, we each sprawled out on the deck to better watch the stars that were now demanding our attention. I had never seen a sky so full of fat, chunky stars, all packed together so tight that for a moment I felt they might crush us. We all agreed that it was quite amazing.

Later Fred dipped a pail over the side, filling it with Lake Superior water. We used that water for drinking, teeth brushing, and the guys used it for shaving. While sipping a nightcap, we luxuriated to the motion of small waves gently lapping on the sides of the boat. None of us could think of a better place to be.

The days flowed on, barely distinguishable from one another, as we experienced a serenity too often lacking in our usual daily lives.

"It'd take an awful lot of this to upset me," I said. The other three agreed.

One day we docked at one of the Apostle Islands and explored its grounds and the lighthouse, still in operation. We chatted with the couple manning it and climbed to its top. "I wouldn't mind spending a summer here, running the lighthouse," Fred said.

"As a matter of fact, it would suit me too. A great place to read and read and read," I said.

That night during the cocktail hour, as the sun sank and soft pinks and purples swirled in the sky, the conversation turned serious. Dick asked Fred how he was handling the grief of his daughter's death. Fred's voice quivered as he said, "I should have done more to keep her alive—maybe insisted on that last operation. It isn't fair that I'm still alive and she is gone. She had so much to live for. She was so strong, so courageous, and bright. A parent isn't supposed to bury their kids."

Dick wrapped his arm around Fred and said, "Fred, you did all you could to save her and when that was no longer possible, you supported her in the decision only she could make."

Pat added, "When one of my daughters died in her teens, I was grief stricken. She had a long and lingering illness. I agree, Fred, there is nothing worse for a parent than to bury a child."

Fred added, "I only hope I have her courage when I face death. She was really something...." I was so appreciative of the support Fred was getting from Dick and Pat.

The day came when it was time to head back to Superior. Pat and I fixed a breakfast of ham and eggs with blueberry croissants and steaming hot coffee, which we ate on deck while listening to the ship radio give the weather news. It looked like a great day for sailing. Not a cloud in the sky. I wasn't paying much attention to the radio because it spoke a nautical language unfamiliar to me. The guys agreed our boat could easily make it back before any possibility of bad weather could occur.

Pat expressed her doubts.

Off we went, thoroughly enjoying the boat gliding swiftly through the waves, leaning first to one side, then another. Heads thrown back, we were enjoying the feel of water on our faces and wind in our hair as our boat carried us swiftly through its waves.

After an hour or two of great sailing, the wind picked up. Pat noticed the door to the galley was open and rushed to close it as waves suddenly splashed into the boat. I was on the other side of the boat as it raised far up, then came crashing down.

I looked at Captain Fred, bracing himself solidly at the wheel. He yelled out to me, "Fasten yourself in, now!" I felt a moment of panic, but Fred looked calm and confident as he yelled the same command to Pat and Dick, who were holding on tightly to the railing. They looked like they were vomiting over the side.

Fred ordered me to climb up and reef the ripped mainsail. He still looked confident, so I figured we were having another one of our adventures. As he shouted orders to me — the only crewmember ready for action, I was determined to measure up to his expectations. As I pulled the ripped sail down, the beam broke, crashing onto the deck near Fred. Aggressive winds looked determined to upset us. I could feel the cold spray of the waves against my face, making it difficult to keep my eyes open.

The boat lurched from one side to the other. With great determination in my war against the force of the wind, I yanked down the ripped sails, somehow securing them. I could barely hear Fred as he yelled to us all that we had to find a safe place to land the boat. We were in real danger of being blown over.

Shirley at work

Both Dick and Fred spied a dock that looked feasible if we could only slow down the boat enough so it wouldn't crash into the dock or, even worse, the craggy rocks. Fred ordered each of us to man a position with rope in hand. He had devised a plan that he thought would work. We all steeled ourselves to carry out the plan. Fred and Dick jumped off the boat and onto the dock, pulling on the ropes, desperately trying to slow the boat down. Pat and I abandoned ship and jumped onto the dock on the other side of the boat, also pulling. The wind and water were trying to take the boat away from us, but we dug in, pulling harder than ever before. The hull crashed to a stop. The four of us dropped our ropes, rubbed our rope-burned hands, and looked at one another in relief.

"That was terrific wind and a son-of-a-gun- storm!" Dick yelled over the waves.

"We're fortunate we made it to Port Wing," Pat said to me as we met the boys on land.

"I thought we were goners," Fred told us. "Especially when I saw that door to the galley open." He put his arm around Pat and gave her a squeeze. "Thanks to you, it was closed in the nick of time. I should have seen that was closed when we first took off."

Dick pointed out a bar up the hill. "Let's go get cleaned up and grab a bite to eat."

Fred at the helm

As we entered, the old salty fishermen at the bar were amazed when Fred told them we had just crash-landed our boat at the dock. They couldn't believe our stupidity. One said, "Oh, Jesus Christ, no, we get offa the water in such a storm. No, no, you don't find us out there, don't 'cha know."

Pat was not amused. She had cautioned Fred and Dick at breakfast about heading out, feeling uncertain that we could beat the storm to Superior.

She and Dick got a ride to where their cars were parked, but Fred and I took the crippled ship back when the wind died down. We used our motor to finally get us back to Superior Harbor. Fred's friend, who had leased him the thirty-six-foot sailboat, was said to have never leased it again. Fred, of course, paid for all the repairs.

"That was a little more adventure than we bargained for," Fred said as we walked to the car. "You did really well—you hung in there and helped us get safely to land."

"I have to admit, Fred, I had such confidence in you because you seemed so calm, that I wasn't afraid. Even when we headed for shore, you seemed to know what we had to do to land the boat." I clicked in my seatbelt. "Did the bow look very damaged to you?"

"It could've been worse. I know a place where I can get the sail repaired, but the mast and beam and bow—well, that's gonna cost some. But I'll take care of it—it was my responsibility and I still can't believe I didn't check that galley door to see it was shut when the wind began to pick up. That could've been a disaster. One big wave could have swooshed water through the galley door and sunk the boat."

I really had no idea of how serious it all was until it was all over. But Fuckin' A, was life ever good!

Chapter Five
Penelope and Ulysses
1980

IT WAS MY HABIT to be at the front door awaiting his arrival, unable to contain my joy and enthusiasm at seeing him walk up to the front door. This excitement at seeing Fred remained consistent with each visit. As did the grin on his face as his eyes met mine and he gently bit his bottom lip. I would say, "I'm so excited to see you! I have everything you like waiting for you."

And he'd reply, "As well you should."

This was our "Penelope welcoming Ulysses home" bit.

It was also my way of letting him know I understood and accepted his need to ebb and flow in and out of my life on his schedule, no questions asked. Surprisingly, I had no curiosity about what he did when he was not with me. I was quite satisfied with the time Fred spent with me. He came into my life as he felt comfortable and stayed as long as he wished. And because of that, I knew that he was with me because he wanted to be. I knew he needed to make time in his life for Sonia and others.

Likewise, Fred knew I needed time with my family and friends to pursue my other interests. I had no need to ask him for what he couldn't give because I had so many other people to see and places to go. The same was true for him; he didn't ask me to give what I could not give.

I found the whole arrangement "heady" and exciting. It was more love and acceptance than I had ever before experienced. I was truly digging this newly found "personal freedom" that accompanied "life with Fred."

I loved Fred's teasing. It was so good-natured. I could be busy fixing a magnificent feast while he sat on a kitchen stool, smoking a

cigar, and sipping a gin and tonic. Then suddenly he might say, with sheer mischievous joy in his voice, "I wouldn't do it that way." That turned out to be one of his favorite "all occasion" expressions.

I'd often tease him about his frequent use of about fifteen phrases he'd utter to handle a variety of situations. He'd pepper reassurance into possible unpredictable situations such as "not a problem," or "not to worry." And as a way of encouraging another, he'd say "good thinking" or "it's permissible." If our plans or accommodations were above expectations, he'd say "ideal living conditions."

But he had a way of letting a person know they were about to tread on troubled waters by cupping his hand to his ear and saying, "I think I hear my mother calling," or "Oops, it's time for Vespers."

The amazing thing was how effective his system worked. These expressions could be used in a playful situation or to avoid a conflict. In the conflict situation, it would give me a chance to pause and reflect on whether or not the subject was worth pursuing. Fred often said he could not and would not abide loud arguments. It was civil discourse or he was out of there.

Linda and my friends would often tease him about his reliance on these frequent expressions. His expressions were used so often that I'd tell him he could type the phrases up on a card and use them in almost any situation—like the words on a card an inexperienced therapist might use with patients in therapy such as, "I see," or "could you tell me more."

On one particular day, we went hiking at O'Brien State Park. The park beckoned us to explore the winding, up and down hills. The once-green grass was beginning to show the wear and tear of a long hot summer. Fall was in the air. Tips of leaves were beginning to turn yellow—some red. A few leaves were falling. The air was crisp and cool—just perfect for brisk hiking.

As usual, Fred led as we climbed up the hills. I found it necessary to stop from time to time to catch my breath, but if Fred turned his head to see where I was, I'd pretend I had stopped to look at a particular bird or something. He, of course, was onto my ploy.

But when it came to going down the hills, I handled them with a running step, shifting my weight quickly from one foot to another as I would often do when downhill skiing on a slope. On one downhill I was far ahead of Fred. The path curved and there were lots of bushes. I looked back and couldn't see Fred, so I decided to hide in the bushes and wait for my prey.

He rounded the corner. I could see it in his eyes that he was trying to figure out where I had gone. I should have been in eyesight. As he got closer, I leapt out of the bushes. Fred lost his balance and we tumbled on the ground together, giggling and kissing and hugging. He rolled on top of me and bit my earlobe. "Fred," I cooed in a sugary Scarlet O'Hara voice, "You naughty boy. You let me up this instant."

With reluctance, he stood and pulled me up. After a few more kisses, we continued on our way. After some more challenging hills, we came upon an old bench. We were ready for a rest, so we stopped for a while. Fred got out his buck knife and sliced an apple from his backpack, handing me a wedge. I offered water from my canteen. We stretched out our legs and arms, enjoying the stretch, each thinking our own thoughts.

"Penny for your thoughts?" I finally asked.

Replying slowly, choosing his words with care, he said, "I see

Sonia and myself drifting apart, largely due to each of us being in different stages. But her career interests may take her to Washington D.C., and my lack of career interest may take me adrift."

This struck me as interesting information. "How does that make you feel?"

"Well, it's probably necessary, even desirable, considering where each of us is. I do recognize a deepening bond occurring between you and me."

"Does it occur to you that you are rather like Alec Guinness in *The Captain's Paradise*?" He looked at me quizzically. "It's the movie of a man with two wives in two separate places."

He laughingly acknowledged that it had occurred to him. He knew he was becoming more a part of my life and it seemed to be what he wanted. He added, "I value you very much and I, too, assume we will be partners for a very long time. But you must remember that my independence is my top priority."

Well, I thought to myself, *he remains consistent in the way he defines our relationship.* "I like that, when a guy says what he means and means what he says. It creates precise boundaries. I can't tell you, Fred, how delightful it is to be with a man who is with me because he wants to be, who thinks I'm okay just the way I am. With Harold, I could do no right. With you, what I do is permissible."

"I just enjoy the companionship of a woman. I never tire of the smell of a woman, the taste of a woman, the time spent in taking you on an out-of-body-ecstatic journey." He snuggled his face into my neck and said in a low voice, "It's a real turn on for me to turn you on. Remember, *you* are like catnip to me."

I giggled as his breath raced across my skin. "And I love it!" My god, all these women fighting for equal rights, but Fred's acceptance of my sexuality was a true gift of equality. I brushed my fingertip across his thigh, "You are simply the greatest lover ever."

"Hey," he said as he reached out for my hand, pulling me towards him. "I embrace the feminist movement and take pride in your achievements — and Sonia's. I strongly believe that a nation cannot reach its full potential until its women have equal status with men."

I hugged him tightly and said, "You're too good to be true."

I came back from a post-Christmas skiing trip with Fred with a sad heart. On our last night in our friends' lovely cabin in Voyager Village, we had settled down before the roaring fireplace. We had lifted our wine glasses in a toast to good skiing and savored the taste of good wine while absorbing Bach's Brandenburg Concerto. Fred shared with me what his first Christmas was like, with his daughter no longer with them.

He was feeling remorse and confusion from her death and had confided that he felt he has only a decade left of vigorous, highly physical living. "I want to spend that time doing what I like with whom I like," he said. "I know that sounds selfish but I find myself withdrawing more and more from university life and national and world events. I want to spend my time living simply: skiing, backpacking, sailing, pursuing my favorite activities. I'm considering taking a year off from the university to maybe visit Toronto or London, two of my favorite cities. Maybe I could arrange for you to be with me. But I'm really not sure what I will do. Maybe it's a passing moroseness, but I doubt it."

The conversation had me feeling down and when Linda came home I told her I needed to talk about it. She handed me a glass of wine as she sat down on the sofa, pulling Jasper on her lap. "What's up?"

"Fred told me he doesn't expect to live more than into his mid-sixties, and he's now almost fifty." The thought of living without Fred in my life...it was unthinkable.

Jasper purred contentedly as Linda held him gently against her chest. "Do you suppose he's going through a mid-life crisis?" Linda replied.

"I just don't know why a guy, so full of energy, joy, and a zest for living, is so preoccupied with death." It worried me. On the other hand, his dad died at age seventy-two, his brother at forty-four, his first wife also at forty-four, and now his daughter at twenty-one.

Linda and I speculated that maybe he was fearful of losing the physical ability to continue his present lifestyle. Skiing, hiking, sailing...all of it was important to him.

"It may be a stretch," I said, "but Ernest Hemingway chose to end his life at sixty-two rather than live longer without being able to continue writing and maintain his vigorous lifestyle."

Fred and I had been together almost two years. We had many future plans together. When he was with me, he was not with Sonia. I was glad he spent much time and all holidays with her. To me that was the honorable thing to do. I'd made a point of practically insisting he spent time with her. Lord knows I had enough to do, keeping up with the demands of my life. And I didn't want him regretting he ever got involved with me. I didn't want him to regret anything in his life.

"I'm sure Fred will sort it out, Mom. He has a good head on his shoulders."

I hoped so. I certainly hoped so.

Chapter Six

Whee eee!!!

1981

I WAS RELIEVED TO hear Fred's voice several days later. He was excited when he called. "I've got us a cabin on the North Shore. It's about twenty-five miles from Grand Marais off the Gunflint Trail, booked from mid-January to mid-February." Fred had told me that he wanted to get away for a month and do some skiing. When I protested that we'd be back at work he said, "Well, I know you principals have rigid work schedules but we professors need much time away from teaching 'to think'! We need lots of 'blue sky time.' So I'll be up there more than you, getting things ready, becoming familiar with all the trails. But you have some three-day weekends and a day or two off for national holidays that you can drive up. It'll work out beautifully!"

"Humph, you professors hardly work. We principals have a real job to do," I murmured. "Well, you better have that cabin in top-notch shape."

That was the beginning of what I hoped would be many winter ski outings on the North Shore. He called me before I left home to tell me there was tons of snow and the trails were great. He spoke with such enthusiasm, like a little kid at his favorite place, that I could hardly wait to join him.

The day I drove up, the year's worst blizzard was predicted to arrive late in the day. I loaded up the car with a shovel, sand, candles, and extension cords for plugging my car into electrical outlets plus loads of food, a crockpot, and warm clothing. It was a five-hour drive if I didn't stop to eat. I hoped to beat the storm.

As I left Duluth on Highway 61, the sky was clear. Rich pristine snow was piled up high on both sides of the road, flanked by lovely birch trees and an occasional deer. Not many cars were on the road. As I reached our meeting place at Highway 61 and Gunflint Trail, the day was beginning to darken. Fred waved from his jeep, gesturing me to begin following him as he backed out and started up Gunflint Trail.

It was beginning to snow; lightly at first, with small flakes gently drifting to the ground. I felt a bit insecure driving on the snow-packed road, trying to keep up with Fred who was way ahead of me. As he turned onto the side roads, it looked like I was driving into a tunnel. The narrower roads, more like paths, had been shoveled frequently, leaving tall banks of snow heaped up on each side.

The falling snow changed into big, fat heavy flakes that stuck to every surface of my car. I turned on my windshield wipers and focused my eyes on Fred's taillights. The roads became narrower, with just enough room for one car. I had a white-knuckle grip on the steering wheel.

We finally got to the cabin, and I released my aching hands from the steering wheel. Fred jumped out of his jeep and rushed over to my car. He had a big grin on his face and said, "Isn't this great?!?"

Less than an hour after our arrival, the blizzard hit, leaving us with a new foot and a half of snow and temperatures of 20- and 30-below zero. We snuggled up in front of the fireplace and watched the new snow pile up. There was no radio, no tv. It was perfect. We had everything we needed—food, drink, and a never-ending fire.

After a few days, we were finally plowed out and able to hit the trails. Pines were draped with ermine fur coats. In the high country, snow was too deep for the deer and wolves so there were no animal tracks—just miles and miles of diamonds shining off the snow's sparkling surface.

We skied along the magnificent Lake Superior with its waves angrily slapping against the icy, snowy shores, leaving coats of ice on its boulders. I was maintaining a "plodding" ski, causing me to

Zen out—probably to get my mind off the aching arm and shoulder muscles required to do the heavy poling. As we neared the end of the trail, I decided there were five kinds of skiing:

1. plodding

2. gliding

3. escalator

4. whee eee!!!

5. Oh my God!

We did the first three that day.

As we dragged our weary bodies into the cozy cabin, the magnificent odors of a beef meal greeted us. There is much to be said

for crockpot cookery. I'm a mediocre cook, but Fred thought I was absolutely gourmet. And I owed it all to my crockpot with simple recipes of meals made for hungry, famished skiers. I threw the ingredients into a pot around 10:00 a.m. Arriving home in the dark, after an exhilarating but exhausting day of skiing followed by running a few errands, we would stride into the darkened cabin smelling the mouth-watering odors of one delicious meal after another. "Wow, Shirley, it smells great and you are the greatest!" yelled a very pleased Fred.

My reply was always, "I have to be, to deserve a great guy like you."

Following a shower, a little lovemaking, and the cocktail hour, we would sit down to another great meal with wine, candlelight, and jazz. "A perfect way to end another perfect day in Paradise," said a contented Fred.

We seemed to get up later each morning. But as Fred said, "who cares? It's whatever time we want it to be!" And that's a luxury few have.

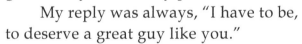

The next day we were skiing Deer Yard loop. I suddenly found myself careening down the steep slope with my legs frozen into a "hot dog" stance. I was out of control, heading for a brushlike tree. I couldn't stop. I landed on my back and my head bounced off the snowy trail as I slammed into the small tree. The tips of my left ski were trapped in the deep snow below.

All was silent for a moment as I lay sprawled on the ground. *Am I even conscious?* I took a moment to assess myself. I was looking up at a crisp blue sky. *Yes.* I tested my legs to see if they still functioned. Toes wiggled in hard boots. *Nothing broken.* With a sigh of relief, I tried to figure out how to get up. Fred skied next to me and, once he was sure I was okay, gave me a helping hand. We both laughed as he pulled me up from my ski-snow-tree-tangled position.

It was a three-hour ski of plodding, gliding, escalator, "whee ee" and "oh my God" all wrapped into one outing. We were pleased we could still move our bones that night.

On those too-cold-to-ski days, we stayed in the cabin and sat in front of the fire reading. Biographies, histories of various wars and events, political and sociological books and mysteries — all of our trips included much reading. We were never short on conversational material.

We would never tire of skiing on the North Shore of Minnesota. Skiing in those woods was like viewing art in the greatest museums. Not only is Nature the greatest artist, but the sanctity of the wilderness left me feeling blessed to be surrounded by its sacred beauty. Well-groomed paths with long gentle hills offered us thrilling glides. On below-zero days, the frozen snow underfoot and snow-covered tree limbs above would create noise so loud that when I stopped, the noise would stop. The coldness of the snow made the movement of skis and poles against its surface sound like the crunch of glaciers glancing off one another as they collide.

One day it was even colder, about 30-below zero. The added noise of the roar of the wind against the frozen trees sounded like the forest was about to split open with trees crashing down upon us at any moment. "Where else could one experience such wonders of

Nature?!?" shouted Fred. "It's a privilege to ski in these woods." Ice formed on his eyebrows and tiny icicles protruded from his nostrils.

For every long graceful hill down was one to climb up. Where Fred used his legs to master these hills, I used my poles to give me leverage. We would arrive back at our cabin knowing we had earned the good food, music, drinks, and books awaiting us by the roaring fire as darkness again enveloped us.

On driving home after these awesome retreats in the snowy wilderness, I felt this remarkable man who knew how to commune with Nature helped me connect with as good a meaning as I know — for why we exist.

That spring, we just hung out more around the house. My house remained forlong-looking as the many improvements I had made since my divorce were the kinds that didn't show — such as plumbing, rewiring the house, insulating the attic, installing new storm windows throughout the house. Still, we had a steady stream of Linda's friends and mine traipsing through the house. Fred enjoyed them all, particularly some of Linda's friends.

If I suggested going to a play or a social event, Fred would usually say, "oh, you just go on. I'll finish my book and watch some TV." Sometimes he'd have one of the neighbors over for cigars and gin on the patio or a chili dinner and beer and guy talk. When I'd get home, he'd ask, "How's my socialite lady doing? Did you wow them at the party?" He'd want to know all the details. This happened so frequently that I once jokingly suggested, "you just come to visit my house. It doesn't matter if I'm here or not." Actually, I was pleased that he felt so comfortable.

Summer 1981

Fred decided to lease a condo in Steamboat Springs for a month in the summer. They were a bargain. He explained that we'd use it as a home base for overnight outings elsewhere. Being equally frugal, we'd split the costs on everything.

During our stay at Steamboat, we spent many days and hours hiking, getting ourselves strong enough to hike Goldcreek Pass, an altitude of 11,000 feet. The day finally came when we hiked ten miles up and down the mountain in seven hours. "Fuckin' A!" Fred yelled as we approached the top. The sky had threatened rain but as we raised our heads to look about us, the sun returned, giving us a spectacular view of Gilpen Lake.

"Do you feel as victorious as I do?" I asked Fred.

"We've really done something." Fred observed. "How many people our age do you know who could have done this?"

"Not bad at all for a couple of folks pushing fifty," I replied.

Jumping into the whirlpool upon our return home felt unbelievably good on our achy, creaky muscles. This trip had been good for me. Fred was good for me. Driving my body, my legs, up rugged rocky terrain for hours and hours was good for me. Fred required that my reach exceeded my grasp. He expected me to find my own solutions. Because of him, I found I could do more than I had ever dreamed possible. He confided, "You know, I find your strength and your 'ruddy good health' extremely appealing. Sonia's heart condition makes it impossible for her to engage in most physical activities."

"My gosh, that has to be hard on her. Didn't you say she was much younger than you?"

"Yes, twelve years younger—that would make her thirty-eight. She tires easily, even when walking more than a couple of blocks. She does work out on a treadmill at the house. But it is discouraging. That's why my vacations with her have to be highly sedentary, such as train trips or cruises. But even my college buddies shy away from taking any trips that include stuff like kayaking or skiing. I miss not having more guys to do physically active things with."

This helped me understand Fred's attraction to me. Again, he repeated, "Look at us. We both have ruddy good health!"

Not only did we hike the many mountain paths surrounding the village of Steamboat Springs, we explored the town itself on rainy days or took day trips to surrounding areas. One such place was the village of Marble where Fred's father had tried his hand at mining gold and silver about seventy years before.

Colorado was unbelievably beautiful. The mountains were breathtaking—so much greenery of all shades—with valleys tucked here and there. The village of Marble was in one such valley, surrounded by steep mountains, some with river streams plunging down the rocky surface. We were standing on a gravel road that was flanked by a series of terraced stone walls on top of one another that finally disappeared into forests of birch and oak trees. A man wearing cowboy attire; work pants stuck in beige leather cowboy boots, beige shirt worn over red underwear partially hidden by his white beard, topped by a cowboy hat, looked like he was cast by MGM. Striding towards us, he extended his hand in greeting and introduced himself as Ira. "Can I help ya?"

Fred told Ira he wanted to find the Black Queen Mine his dad had owned and mined. Ira became quite excited, saying he had seen an old map in a local store showing various mine locations. "I can take you up these mountain paths now to where I think it begins, but it may take me some time to find the right map with the exact location showing its opening. Any chance you might be back in these parts another time?"

"A good chance." Fred's face lit up. "I'd like to bring my son. But you say we can see part of it now?"

"Sure. Just follow me to my jeep up this road." The two men strode off, me scampering along behind them. I could catch part of their conversation. It was easy to tell they were both excited. Apparently Ira saw Fred as a major find—a person actually connected to one of these old mines, especially when Fred said he had his dad's old deed of ownership he'd bring with him next time.

Upon reaching the jeep, Ira motioned us to get in. We climbed in the open back. Ira backed up, turned around, and then started going straight up the perilous gravel road. It was apparent the road had been washed out in places; only one vehicle could pass at a time. Looking down on the driver's side—way, way down—we could see the creek that had once carried slabs of marble to

Ira and Fred

be harvested by workmen below. "Look Fred, there's a broken truck or two way down there that couldn't manage to stay on the road. Come to think of it, we don't have seat belts on. In fact, there aren't any on this vehicle!" My life flashed before my eyes as I imagined us plunging over the side.

"Steady, girl. You're going to be just fine." Fred reassured. Then he pointed out the remains of the Black Queen Mine. "It was named after a black Madam in Leadville," Fred said. "She loaned my Dad money to start the mine."

"How do you suppose that ever happened?" I wondered. "Did he ever say?"

"Dad didn't talk much about those days. I guess he and his buddy hung out at her place in the little town at the base of the mountains. Probably weren't many places to get a drink and a bite to eat. Business must have been good and the money flowing so the Madam had plenty to lend until WWI started. That's when the military confiscated use of the trains the mining business relied on — as well as the workers."

I like to think your Dad charmed her and said he'd name the mine after her if she gave him a loan," I suggested.

I tried to imagine what kind of man his dad must have been to seek out such a place so different from his origins, what sense of adventure and hardship he must have endured, to live in the rustic shack he and his partner devised. It had to have been especially harsh living in the winter. No electricity or plumbing. I could better understand Fred's love of adventure, his almost addictive need for adventure.

And wasn't his son cut out of the same cloth? The more Fred told me about Tom, the more remarkable his son seemed to me. Tom seemed particularly attracted to extreme pursuits like doing acrobatics in his plane or piloting glider planes or operating a two-man submarine off the coast of Maine used in scientific pursuits or leading rafting trips in the Grand Canyon. This trio of men fascinated me: grandfather, father, and son — all so alike in the need to live their adventuresome dreams.

Fred added, "Tom had some inherited money from Sally's family when she died, but he has lived very frugally, and other than splurging on an airplane, he has spent little. You should see how he lives. He rents a modest two-bedroom house full of unpacked boxes. His bike is parked in the living room with guy stuff everywhere. He doesn't even have a TV. Doesn't want one." I was getting more interested in one day meeting this remarkable young man.

It was an exciting experience for Fred to share this piece of history involving his departed Dad with me. I felt honored.

The next summer Fred and Tom returned to spend more time absorbing the mine area that had been such an important part of his Dad's life. In fact, they hired Ira to be their guide. As luck would have it, Ira got a copy of the original mine, making it possible to explore the remains of the mine in great detail. I was thrilled that father and son could have such a remarkable experience together. No one could be prouder of his father and of his son than Fred.

In the fall of 1981, Fred and I were scheduled to read papers at a psychology conference in Tucson, Arizona. Fred learned that his son would be there at the same time visiting a girlfriend. At last, I was to meet his son. At our hotel, Fred had just mixed me a drink when our room phone rang. Fred answered, "Tom!" He looked at me with a wide grin on his face. I was motioning him not to invite his son to our room when he continued with Tom, "I'll meet you in the lobby in twenty minutes. OK? See you then."

"Fred, what have you told him about me?" I suddenly felt a bit apprehensive. I hadn't thought this through.

"Not to worry. I'll introduce you as my colleague."

And so he did. His son saw Fred immediately as we got off the elevator. Like his Dad, he was tall, slender, and well built. Wearing a big smile, he approached his Dad, beckoning his girlfriend to join us. In a matter-of-fact manner, Fred introduced me as his colleague and Tom introduced his girlfriend Joy to both of us. Motioning to the front door, Tom said, "I've got my truck outside. Come on, we'll figure out the seating arrangement." I saw what he meant after seeing that the truck sat two in the front and had an open bed in the back.

"Dad, you drive and Joy and I will climb in the back. I'll direct you to my favorite restaurant." I could see he hadn't expected his dad to bring along a colleague. Only I seemed to feel uncomfortable with the seating arrangement. As we drove off, Tom and Joy were gaily holding a conversation with one another, with Tom shouting directions at his dad through the open window. Joy seemed to be enjoying herself as the two of them laughed, moving their heads from side to side, catching the gentle evening breezes. And so we joined in the laughter as we pulled into the parking lot. It was the kind of restaurant that invited a college crowd, serving loud music, Tex-Mex food, and lots of margaritas. It was amazing how quickly we were absorbed by the atmosphere, ordering several rounds of drinks and laughing at whatever was said.

Later Joy and I went to the restroom. She immediately told me how crazy she was about Tom and how glad she was to see him. Apparently they had been "an item" before he moved to California.

We put on fresh lipstick and rearranged hair, then rejoined the guys. After more laughter and a few more rounds, we left. The guys had fun lifting Joy into the open truck. Back at the hotel, Tom leaped out of the truck to shake my hand good-bye and give his dad a hug. They then both climbed in the front and quickly drove off.

"Well, that was quite a surprise," I said. "So you think your son wondered about me?"

"No, not a chance. Why would he?" Fred shrugged his shoulders in a nonchalant way as he unlocked the door to our room. So I shrugged my shoulders back as I entered. "Not a problem, I guess," I murmured as I wondered how they could lack such curiousity about each other's lives.

Chapter Seven
Nobody's Perfect
1982

BY THE END OF 1981, Linda and I were both looking forward to another Christmas in Winter Park, Florida. When our plane landed in Orlando, we saw the smiling faces of Mom and Aunt Edna, who could hardly contain themselves when seeing us. Mom drove us the short distance to Winter Park where we enjoyed the company of their friends, vying for our attention.

The weather was warm enough that we could spend much time in their swimming pool. As Linda and I frolicked in the pool, taking turns swimming under the water so that we could toss one another, I heard Aunt Edna say to Mom with pleasure in her voice, "They are more like sisters, aren't they Cynthia." They had a lovely apartment filled with the English antique furniture my aunt and her husband Dale had acquired when in England.

My aunt had a distinctive voice. Although she grew up in rural Iowa, she spoke with an English accent and dressed much like the Duchess of York. My mother was the youngest of eight children and the only one to graduate from high school. Edna was the second oldest. My mom was always Edna's favorite sister. Edna had the distinction of "marrying well." Her husband had a doctorate in mining engineering and made a small fortune with his inventions.

When Edna's beloved husband died, she begged my mother to move in with her, offering to pay many of her expenses and take her on trips around the world. Mom agreed to take care of her older sister in exchange for being the administrator of her estate. They got along well and were having a good life together.

Mom seemed to be the only one in her circle of friends who had any children, so Linda and I were shared with many. We truly enjoyed all their friends. We all had a marvelous Christmas dinner at the Langford Hotel.

After we got back from Florida, I was ready to join Fred for more skiing up north. This time we stayed at a different cabin, equally modest in size and non-winterized. I stood before the sink and turned the handle. A great moan came out from the pipe; it felt like the whole cabin rattled. I quickly turned the handle back and tried again. Once more there was a moan and a rattle, as if Bob Marley's ghost was making a visit. I twisted the handle back into place. I was not amused. Fortunately, there was a phone in the cabin and Fred called someone to tell them about the water, but it didn't sound to me like he was getting good news.

"Fred, I'm not staying here. There's no heat and no water. They better have another cabin for us," I said in an angry tone. Fred motioned his hand towards me in an attempt to silence me. So I started taking stuff back out to the car. I heard him say, "Shirley, they're sending someone out here right away to fix the water so hold off."

He then began putting wood in the pot belly stove. I thought he was overly optimistic as I had visions of us staying in some dumpy motel on the highway.

A truck pulled up in our snowy drive and a plump middle-aged lady got out. She was wearing brown overalls and a bulky cap. A few medium-sized curlers poked out from the edges and strained the fabric all around. She introduced herself as Nancy and said she was going to get the water going. She then headed for a heater by the kitchen and pulled out a hair dryer.

Was she going to do her hair before she fixed our water situation? She headed toward the sink and then I realized what was going on. "*That's* your tool?" I asked, stunned.

"Works every time," she replied as she blew hot air across the pipe. She then went outside and opened up some container, again applying the hair dryer. I was skeptical, but sure enough, the water began flowing,

"Good work!" Fred cried out in amazement. I was astonished.

"Just call me if you have any problems," she said as she climbed back in her truck. Nothing for me to do except unload the car again. At last the cabin was warm and cozy, groceries and clothes were put away and I put some ribs and potatoes in the oven.

So what could we do but have a gin and tonic while waiting for dinner? Pulling out our trusty boom box, we put on some Duke Ellington tunes. "Did you notice Nancy had curlers on her hair under her cap?" I asked.

"Yah, I did," Fred said. "Now that was a can-do woman."

"I guess you have to be to live up here in the boonies in the winter." I moved over to the window and looked out on the pristine snow and naked, snow-touched trees. "Gosh, I do love it up here. I don't think this cabin is too far from the one we had last year."

Fred moved up behind me, put his arms around my waist, and gave me a soft kiss on the neck.

By the time dinner was on the table, we were listening to "My Fair Lady" with Fred singing along with Rex Harrison. That just confirmed my love for this place, for these times, with this man.

The next day, we decided to do one of the longer ski loops. To do this, we needed to have a car at each end of the trail so we could ski the trail end to end. So we dropped my car off at one end, and together we drove to the other end, parked, and started the long trek. Somehow the trail had a different feel to it. Fred thought so too. We were used to seeing deer and wolf scat, but on this day we approached something a little bit different.

Blood was soaked into the once-white snow and big clumps of what looked like deer meat and fur were strewn about the path. The unmistakable footprints of several wolves surrounded the blood-stained snow. My heart was in my throat. "Do you think we scared them off?" I asked in a hushed voice.

Fred nodded and suggested we move out sharply, his tone quiet and sure.

About a half hour later, an uneasy feeling came over me. I felt like we weren't alone…like eyes were following us down the snowy path. "Do you have the scary feeling we're being watched?"

"Could be," he responded. "Isn't it strange that in all our skiing we've not seen wolves? But we often see deer, even a moose once or twice."

"Somehow I don't feel they would attack us." I hoped I was right.

"No, I don't either."

I continued leading the way, hoping that those following eyes stayed a good distance away. There were few hills, but the path involved a lot of plodding, which I found boring. Even the snow was not too inspiring. It was old snow and needed touching up to give it that magical look. After a very long trek, all of my extremeties were crying for relief from this constant plodding. Finally, I spotted my car ahead. We wearily removed our skis. My legs and arms felt like rubber.

When we got to the car, Fred wiggled his fingers as he stood at the trunk. "Keys?"

I reached into the pocket that usually held my keys. Nothing. I reached into another pocket. And another. And another. I was starting to panic. I looked in my fannypack. Again, nothing. "Did I give them to you?"

"Oh, no," Fred groaned. "You really don't know what you did with them? You didn't leave them in the ignition of your car, did you?"

"Even I wouldn't be that stupid." I ran to the front passenger side and looked in. The ignition was empty. No keys. "Are you sure you don't have them with yours?"

"I do not." Fred stayed calm as always. "Think. Did you have them in your hands when you got in my jeep?"

Suddenly an image flashed in my mind; my heart sank. "Uh oh. Maybe I did. I might have put them in the cup container while I got myself a drink of water," I confessed in a somber voice.

"Well, we've got no time to waste." Fred handed me my ski poles. "It'll be getting dark before long. We've got to get back on that trail now. Hurry up!" he ordered as he quickly put his skis back on and headed back to the dreaded trail.

"Oh, Fred, I'm so sorry." I felt like I could cry. "Are you as tired as I am?" He was already making tracks, so I wearily put my skis back on and trailed him all the way back. We had no choice.

It was hard work. Neither of us spoke a word. As we plodded down the trail, pushing rubbery legs, backs aching, the element of fun had all but disappeared. I felt horrible. *You're in the army now*, I thought to myself. *I wonder what Fred thinks of me now.*

After a couple hours of plodding, Fred suddenly stopped and motioned to me to hurry. He wanted to show me something. As I approached him, I realized this was the deer-kill spot. "Look," Fred said, "See how little is left. Just some little strings of fur."

"But a lot more scat," I pointed out. "How many wolves do you think were here? And, where *are* they now? Still watching us?" It was a stilled atmosphere as we stood looking at the few remains, realizing we had interrupted a big feed the first time around.

"Well," Fred said. "*They're* no longer hungry. But *I* am. Let's move!"

We both knew we were reasonably close to where we started the trail, which gave us the energy to persevere until Fred spotted his jeep. We were even more relieved when we opened the jeep door and found my keys. Thankfully Fred said nothing and we had a silent ride back to my car, then on to the cabin.

Opening up our cabin door, the smells issuing forth from the beloved crockpot smelled even better. "Fred, I love you for being so kind to me," I said as I hugged him tightly and left kisses all over his face.

"You have your crockpot to thank for that," he said with that charming crooked smile of his.

After a delicious beef stroganoff dinner with wine, our energy restored, we eagerly sought out the pretentious humor of the loveable Nick and Nora Charles movies. I remembered them with great fondness from my high school days and was delighted to learn they were also favorites of Fred. We were perfect foils for one another and enjoyed slipping into our pretentious party-loving behaviors. Other times our Professor Henry Higgins know-it-all behaviors tangling with the impatient Eliza Doolittle's demand of "don't talk, show me, show me now!" played out. Or the "all that jazz" couple who liked their jazz hot and their gin cold.

Actually, our ongoing Ulysses and Penelope enactment of the continual good-byes and hello of life with "the occasional man" was most greatly enjoyed by both of us. Whenever I'd see him drive up to the house, I ran out to greet my Ulysses with an over-the-top big hug and kiss.

These were all silly, fun rituals that we never tired of playing. Sometimes we'd exchange roles of chef and sous chef while preparing dinner together, dancing in place to our favorite jazz tunes.

We didn't need to *see* a show. We could *be* a show.

Fred suggested we take a Sabbatical together in England. He proposed I call a contact of mine in England, Sue Jenkins. We could plan a visitation program there and in neighboring Cheshire to learn about their special education programs. It was his intent to then place some of his St. Cloud students as assistants in some of their classrooms. I was interested in learning how the Brits delivered special education services to children in both special settings and mainstream classes.

We then submitted proposals to our respective Human Resource Directors. It sounded like a huge undertaking, but we were hoping for approval by 1986.

By this time Brian and his crew had done major interior

decorating on the house resulting in a kitchen with newly painted walls, woodwork, and counters. All cupboard doors and drawers now operated perfectly, no longer hanging askew. The entire first floor had fresh paint and sparkling white woodwork. Old curtains were gone, replaced by blinds. It was amazing what paint and wallpaper could do. I began dreaming of the entertaining I might engage in. Life was definitely getting better.

Chapter Eight
Creative Ways to Get Around
1983 and 1984

THE COMMITTEE HAD GATHERED! Brian Walters from North Wales called Fred to confirm that he was bringing twelve special education teachers from North Wales and Cheshire, England in March for two weeks. My friends and I (aka "the committee") quickly determined which guests would stay with which host the first week. We also planned their visitation schedule. Fred planned all second-week activities occurring in St. Cloud.

Fred met the group at the airport on a cold March night. He delivered them by taxis to my home where they would meet their hosts and have dinner. It didn't take long for the group from overseas to discover the liquor cabinet. By the time each met their host, the liquor was nearly all gone! We all realized we were in for a "jolly good week."

Again Linda and I spent the holidays with Mom and Aunt Edna. By this time they had moved into a luxurious facility that offered different levels of service from independent living, to apartment with meals provided in the cafeteria, to nursing home care. Mom felt she was just too old to handle apartment living any more. Aunt Edna reluctantly agreed to the move. All their friends at Sutton Place were also moving into the same facility. As usual, we had Christmas dinner at the Langford Hotel with all their friends, who by this time were also ours.

We were back in time for me to join Fred up north skiing.

One hot summer day of 1984, with schools again closed for vacation, the phone rang. I answered to hear a voice say, "Any hot ladies there looking for fun?"

"Fred," I said, "Where are you?"

"Well, I'm here at a snazzy hotel in Washington, D.C. and need some company. Why don't you fly here tomorrow and I'll meet you at the airport."

"I'll get right on it and call you back," I said, and I did. Fred greeted me at the airport and took me on a quick tour. He knew the area well since he had once worked near the White House.

Approaching the front entry of the elegant hotel near the George Washington Bridge, I saw about six men, all dressed in similar suits, milling about the front door. The plush lobby was filled with well-dressed business folks, some registering at the front desk, others at the bar, and a mixture of ladies with hats and children with grandparents seated at various tables for tea. Taking me by the elbow, Fred rushed me to the elevator. We had it to ourselves as he said in a sexy, low tone, "I've gotta get you to our suite. We have things to do!"

"What can that be, oh, what can that be?" I asked in all innocence.

We got to the fortieth floor and entered the honeymoon suite. Bestill my heart! I was stunned by the vastness and luxuriousness of the suite. Its tall ceilings topped huge wrap-around floor-to-ceiling glass windows with the sun streaming in. A very large living room opened up to a spacious bedroom and bath.

"A drink?" Fred asked as he mixed two gin and tonics.

"Just what the doctor ordered," I said as I reached for the glass, eagerly sipping its coolness; I bit my lip as I looked at Fred.

"Welcome to Washington D.C." he said as his glass tipped against mine.

Almost in unison, we each said "What shall we do, what shall we do?" I stepped up to Fred and drew my fingertip down from his neck to his chest. I undid his top button slowly. "It's good to have you here," he murmured as he drew me against him. He began unbuttoning my top with increased fury. Soon we were in bed together.

After a shower I wrapped myself up in one of those thick luxurious white Turkish towels. I strolled over to the floor-to-ceiling window and looked down below. "Fred," I said, "Those men I saw out there when we entered are still there, milling about. Do you think they are secret service men? Casing the joint?"

Fred said, "I wouldn't be surprised. President Reagan is out of town, but I think Vice-President Bush is attending a conference in this hotel today."

"Do you think they can see up here this high in the air?" I asked.

"I wouldn't be surprised."

"Well, I think I'll check them out. Yoohoo...boys..." I wickedly said as I pushed my naked body against the cool glass. To my surprise, a few of the men looked up at exactly that moment. More followed. They all started waving. I couldn't believe my eyes so I rushed over to the next window and peeked down. Their heads swiftly turned as they continued waving. I quickly jumped away from the window and wrapped myself back up in the towel. The phone rang, startling me. Fred answered. It was a quick call. I heard him give his name. He hung up and chuckled as he said, "The desk was just checking."

"Now why do you suppose the desk called?" I asked.

"I dunno. Maybe just checking to see if the guy who answered had the same name as the man who was registered. They can't be too careful, you know," he said as he slyly winked at me.

Fred decided to show me Georgetown, at the foot of the hotel across the bridge. As we left the hotel, strolling past the agents, I tried to act nonchalant. Fortunately (or unfortunately), none of them paid any attention to us.

It was a pleasant evening. We crossed the bridge and found a cozy place to dine. On the way back, Fred pointed out the canoes nestled on the banks of the Potomac under the bridge. "This is where we start our day tomorrow." I was amazed at Fred's creativity in planning such excursions and was excited for another adventure.

The morning started out hot and the day quickly became both hot and humid. Dressed in shorts and sandals, we got in a canoe and began paddling. Fred said, "It's much easier to see the sights of Washington by boat than by car. No problem finding a parking spot." I really admired Fred's approach to dealing with parking issues.

As we neared a museum, we hopped out of the boat and pulled it onto shore and up the bank. Fred then hid the oars in a bush and we were on our way. We spent the day getting in and out of the canoe and seeing the sights. We saw the Jefferson Memorial, the Lincoln Memorial, the Washington Monument, and the Vietnam Veterans Memorial. Tears rolled down my cheeks as I saw families huddled around a name, or a woman taking a photo of a name, or a tired-looking man with an artificial leg, gently touching the name of a comrade. The endless rows of names, all precious to someone, stretched out glistening in the hot sun. Its simplicity of design made it so moving.

By the time we got back to the Georgetown Bridge and checked in our canoe, we were hot, sweaty, tired and ready to relax.

Our room had a table for two nestled in a window cove with a great view of the city and the multitude of planes flying over in about two-minute intervals. Fred decided to order room service. By the time we were cleaned up and finishing our first drink, the porter came with our dinner. He placed a linen tablecloth on the table along with flowers and a candle, then set the table and served the food. "This is so what I'm used to, Fred" I said in my most pretentious way. "You are a dear."

"Yes," he said. "That is so true." Then we counted planes coming in for a landing. That's what you do when you come from the Midwest, better known by New Yorkers as "fly-over country."

The next day we explored the surrounding areas of D.C. by car then we began our drive home, taking the Canadian route back. We decided to tent through the beautiful woods of Ontario.

Our tent was easy to put up and take down, which came in handy whenever we were caught in a wind or rainstorm. No matter where in the world we were, the pattern of our days followed a similar routine: Upon arising at a civilized time of day, we would devour a hearty breakfast, read for several hours while listening to Bach or Beethoven on our boom box, then take off for our physical activity of the day around 11:00 a.m. We'd generally spend about four hours on that activity, run errands, and arrive home in time for showering or skinny dipping, followed by our cocktail hour, dinner preparations, and a late meal by candlelight and jazz.

When tenting, we'd spread out our mat on the ground, using our rolled-up bedroll as a pillow, and enjoy our morning reading. I was impressed at how easily Fred could find comfort by making multiple uses of our few simple supplies. Showering would occur in the river or lake and a candle stuck in an empty wine bottle would provide us with ambiance for our cocktail hour and dinner, then chat time by the campfire until bedtime. These simple activities produced magical moments when performed in this magnificent wilderness. We liked lying on our bedrolls in the tent with our heads stuck out the tent flap so we could enjoy the starry skies until we fell asleep.

I put on my best impression of Meryl Streep from *Out of Africa* and said, "Hemingway could not produce a more romantic environment with his bounteous supplies from which to draw when dining at a table covered with a linen tablecloth, fine china and silver, a candelabra, and music playing from a record player."

"Ideal living conditions can be created anywhere, my dear," Fred replied.

We spent many days in the bush, getting a little gamier by the day. The further northwest we went, the more exhilarated we felt. The scenery was dramatically different from the lushness of the bush—sandy, rocky soil, some burned-out birches and surprisingly hot weather.

I pointed a sign out to Fred advertising the Polar Bear Express. I thought it would be a great excursion and without any hesitation, Fred drove right into the parking lot of a train depot. We both decided to get on the Polar Bear Express and go wherever it took us. So we left our jeep behind, taking with us only our backpacks.

We ended up at the town of Mosinee on James Bay, a saltwater bay fed by Hudson Bay, which in turn was fed by the Arctic Ocean.

Jumping off the train, Fred yelled, "By God, we're in a wild Western town of yesteryear. I'd hate to drive a car on these rough dirt and gravel roads!" The town of 600 was home to Cree Indians and very little else. What little we saw of the town was the big building containing the restaurant and rooms. Across from it was a one-floor building with some kind of tin roof housing the liquor store. Across the pitted, dirt road was a one-story Hudson Bay Company that sold Hudson Bay blankets and other woolen goods. The other buildings were nondescript sheds, garages, and huts. The only way to get there was by train or plane.

On another island was Moose Factory, a fur trade post established in 1673 by adventurers from the Hudson Bay Company of London, England. About 2,400 people live in Moose Factory now. It was Ontario's first English-speaking settlement. The land was rich in valuable furs that caused years of bitter skirmishes between French and English traders. The English finally won. The population of the two towns was about 79% Cree.

The streets were unpaved, rocky, dusty, and hot. The temperature was in the 90s. The sky was hazy — getting more so as the day progressed due to vast forest fires in Manitoba, which caused all airports on the Hudson Bay shores northwest of Mosinee to shut down. The heat was almost unbearable.

"Let's find a canoe to rent so we can row over to James Island," Fred suggested as he pointed over to an old rowboat lying near the bank of the water. "This one has an empty coffee can in it, which doesn't inspire confidence," Fred commented. After searching around, there were no boat rentals, so we went back to the rowboat with the coffee can. The owner, an old Indian man, was willing to rent it to us. It had no life preservers.

"We'll take it," Fred said.

We set out across the bay, with me in the front and Fred in the back. I asked, "Why do I always end up the one rowing?" Fred was spending his time steering and scooping out water with the coffee can. "I'm rowing like hell and the boat is hardly moving," I complained. In fact, it seemed to be going backwards.

"It's tidal water," Fred yelled. "We're rowing against the tide."

"Are we having fun now?" I asked.

"Row on woman! Row on!" Fred commanded as he kept scooping water.

It was hard work getting to the island, but we were instantly restored when we saw the incredible beauty. Mosinee consisted mostly of camping spots and hiking trails. We quickly put up our tent on a grassy spot overlooking the beach and Mosinee. We jumped into the bay and had a refreshing swim.

Suddenly it began raining—hard. We took a water taxi to Mosinee to eat at the lodge. "Where was this water taxi when we were hunting for a boat?" I asked.

"I think it only runs at night," Fred said.

Only two places in town served sit-down meals and only during meals could one buy a beer. Alcoholism was such a problem in Mosinee that its sale was restricted to the two lodges at mealtime—with a meal—or by paying a high price at the only liquor store. After dinner we took a water taxi back to our island and slept well. It remained stormy with the temperature dropping about 15 degrees.

We woke up to a hell of a storm and it was still cold. We got much use out of our warm clothing and rainwear. When the rain subsided, it left behind hot, sticky weather. We went from one extreme to the other! We paddled our canoe to Moose Factory—a much different ambience from Mosinee, though equally rugged and primitive. This time we were prepared for it, wearing only shorts and t-shirt because of the heat and the possibility of being caught in another storm while paddling home.

We spent some time at the island of Moose Factory, but our visit was cut short by the looks of an impending storm. We no sooner got in our aluminum boat than Mother Nature unleashed her full fury on us. We paddled desperately with lightening cracking all around us. The force of the wind made going forward exhausting work and I found myself ducking whenever a lightning bolt shot from the sky. Boy, was I eager to get out of that boat. I was paddling frantically to the shore in this God-awful aluminum boat with lightning blazing closer.

Finally, we pulled onto the sandy beach surrounded by cliffs. We grabbed our things, and ran like hell to seek shelter. We began to scale the cliffside, knowing that there must be somewhere to get out of the lightning and pouring rain. The surface was muddy and my hands kept slipping down; I couldn't get a grip on anything. The lightening sizzled closer than ever. Fred reached down to pull me up to the top and I grabbed his muddy hands. There we huddled, under the eaves of a locked building, soaked and freezing, as the wind seemed intent on blowing us off the face of the earth.

"Are we having fun?" I shouted to Fred.

He yelled back, "Ideal living conditions!"

We both laughed as rain pounded around us and thunder boomed above. It was still windy as hell. I was so relieved to be out of that boat.

When the wind and rain finally subsided, we ran to our tent, took it down in short order, broke camp, slid back down the muddy slope, ran down the beach to our canoe, and paddled back to Mosinee during the brief lull. We made it to the railroad station with an hour to spare. I used that time to clean up and change into dry clothes. Fred just sat with great dignity in his wet clothes — reading — oblivious to all going on around him.

I envied the way he could shut out the world by picking up a book. By the time we reached Cochraine, he was completely dry. It was just another day in the lives of the middle-aged intrepid travelers.

Summer 1984

The following summer, Fred and his son, Tom, visited James Island on Hudson Bay. Fred had remembered reading a book by Eric Sevareid, first published in 1935, about his high school adventure with a friend, canoeing from Minnesota on many rivers that eventually reached the great Hudson Bay and sea beyond. They had just finished their senior year in high school and were ready for a great adventure. Their canoe trip in a second-hand, eighteen-foot voyageur-style canoe covered 2,500 miles.

Fred and Tom's canoe trip was considerably shorter. Yet they experienced the hazards of canoeing the rapids, living off of fish caught en route, finding places on shore to put up a tent, going through storms and finally arriving at Hudson Bay.

That same summer, Clem and I found ourselves in Maine in a seaside restaurant. She had a bib around her neck and a beautiful, big lobster on her plate. She thought she had died and gone to heaven. This was my birthday gift to her. I had given her a card treating her to the meal of her choice in the place of her choice. Clem was a gourmet cook and a "foodie," which I lightheartedly defined as "a person who lives to eat." Immediately she said, "I know exactly what dinner I want: A lobster dinner in Maine." So there we were, staying in a quaint B & B and exploring historical spots.

I had been making weekly calls to my mother because she was having health concerns related to surgery she had had seven years before at the Mayo Clinic. At that time she had nasal polyps removed that had grown over her right eye, distorting her perception. For instance, she would have difficulty judging where the rim of a glass was so she could drink from it. The difficult surgery was successful, but the doctor had informed us that the polyps would grow back in about seven years because he had to leave a tiny piece on her optic nerve or she would lose vision in that eye. He knew she loved to read and since she was seventy-five years old at the time, it seemed like a realistic gamble. She was now 84.

During my trip with Clem, I called Mom and learned she was to undergo surgery the next day and wanted me there. Clem was very understanding and left me at the local airport headed for Boston. From there, I would fly to Orlando.

I gave Clem a big hug of appreciation, then found a seat in the gate area as I waited to board the plane. A stately well-dressed gentleman, with a beautiful head of shocking white hair who looked remarkably like Tip O'Neil, approached me and politely asked, "I just paid another gentleman five dollars to sit next to you. May I?"

How could one refuse such a charming line? As we chatted, he asked me where I would be staying in Boston. I indicated I would be catching a plane from there to Orlando. With that information, he stood up, bowed, and said, "Nice meeting you"; he sauntered off to try his line elsewhere.

Flying down the eastern seaboard of America was breathtaking. I looked out the plane window the entire trip as we followed the coastline.

At Winter Park, Aunt Edna was distraught. I would have preferred taking Mom back to the Mayo Clinic but knew I couldn't handle both Aunt Edna, whose short-term memory problems made her difficult to manage, and my mother's needs at the same time. Aunt Edna was insistent on being with her beloved sister and she was a woman used to getting her way. I stayed with them both until Mom was back in her apartment. We made arrangements for her to get nursing care while remaining in her apartment. I was able to return to Minnesota knowing that both Mom and Aunt Edna would be well cared for.

Fall was a busy time. Brian was working on the second floor of our house, restoring the original engraved glass in the bedroom transoms and redecorating every bedroom. Linda and I were delighted with the results. Our previous forlorn, unloved house was becoming an elegant home. The ugly green tile was removed and the beautiful parquet floors restored. Transoms that were previously painted white had been scraped to reveal amazing etched glass with peacock details. All of the closets had been modernized. My new library had an exposed brick wall in it that gave it a certain eloquence and charm. There were even sparkles in the new ceiling that reflected light like a diamond. It was all very suitable for "ladies of distinction."

Mom's lawyer called me. Mr. Winslow was a dedicated, caring lawyer who took excellent care of his clients, many of whom lived at the Towers. What my aunt had most feared happened. She fell and broke her hip and was now most unhappily in a private room in nursing care. Mom would spend much time with her during the day. But Mom was also enjoying her freedom to be with friends.

Mr. Winslow was encouraging her to take a single room in the building where she lived with Edna since Edna was to remain where she was. It would be an enormous savings.

Mom had long had her eye on a single apartment that had a superior view of the lovely grounds. So I flew down to help with the move, work out details with Mr. Winslow, visit my aunt, and help Mom throw a cocktail party in her new digs for her favorite friends and Aunt Edna in her wheelchair with her private aide.

Work kept me busy as we moved into winter and the holiday festivities. Fred visited frequently, but he, too, was spending time visiting his mother, family, and ailing hometown friends. The weekends we spent skiing were welcomed and appreciated. Linda and I again flew to Florida for Christmas.

Upon my return home, I shared our concerns about Mom's and Aunt Edna's health with Fred when he called. Neither seemed to be doing that well.

Fred dropped by to cheer me up. We were both involved with

long-distance care of aging mothers. I observed the way he kept in regular contact with his mom over the years and tried to do the same with mine. I asked him what role Sonia played with his mom and her own. Fred shared very little, only saying that she had no strong relationship with his mom and had been estranged from her family. I didn't feel it was prudent to enquire further.

Instead he preferred to talk about several of his close friends who had died recently and how he had been asked to speak at their funerals. With a kind of gallows humor, he said, "I've given so many talks at both family and friends' funerals these last few years that I'm becoming a bit of a pro. Another college friend of mine who lives in Washington D.C. is dying and I'm in close contact with him. Whenever I'm in the area of Columbus, Ohio, I visit the graves of Sally and Sharon."

Fred had had many good years since the sad year of his daughter's death. But now his main concern was his mother's inability to die as she turned ninety-nine years old. He had called and visited her regularly ever since I had known him, but he was now concerned on her insistence that she remain in her own home in Canada. He had arranged for caretakers to visit her, but when she had several falls resulting in broken bones, he was forced to carry her screaming out of her beloved home to an assisted living apartment where she was most unhappy.

With no other living relatives since his brother and father died years before, he had been caring for her. They had been very close. He had been saddened to witness her grief and her decline. I was thankful I had Linda to aid me in the care for my mother.

But enough, I thought, *it's too beautiful a day to stay inside.* "Let's go ski Crosby!" And we did.

Chapter Nine

Transitions

1985

OUR MOVEABLE FEAST, FRUGAL-STYLE, would soon be a reality! Fred and I learned that our Sabbaticals were approved. We were to take off the next year, in March of 1986, and be back the end of July. That would give us lots of time for our spring sabbatical in the UK, followed by backpacking and U-railing across Europe.

Around February, I began getting calls from both Mom and her doctor, concerned that her nasal polyps were rapidly returning. The doctor was recommending radical surgery or radiation. I was so upset that I asked Linda to listen in on the telephone conversations in order to help me ask the doctor appropriate questions. I was overwhelmed by the gravity of the situation. Linda was amazingly cool and focused as she asked a series of questions I hadn't thought of, like where might either procedure be done and who might do it. It took a series of phone calls with doctors and mother before Linda and I became convinced that Mom's best option would be radiation therapy by a renowned specialist at Gainesville, Florida. Surgery was simply too horrid to consider. It would necessitate rebuilding her face. But radiation was no walk in the park, either.

Linda and I would each have to take turns spending a week with

Mom in Gainesville during the four weeks of treatment. I would go the first week, driving her from Winter Park to Gainesville, getting her settled in a nearby hotel, and helping her understand and adapt to the treatments. Linda would take another week and I would take the last few weeks, including driving her back to Winter Park.

Both of us had talked with the radiologist, who was convinced Mother was an excellent candidate for the treatment. It was a complicated process, but Mom, Linda, and I all felt hopeful. It was hard to see Mom with all of the purple stuff they put on her face prior to treatment. It was like some crazy radiation roadmap.

Both Linda and I received support from our respective bosses. I was proud of how capably Linda handled being with her grandmother when undergoing radiation, and how skillfully she found fun things for them to do late afternoons and evenings. She confided that she frequently ended up crying in the shower so Grandma wouldn't hear her. Equally upsetting to her was witnessing the number of young children also undergoing radiation. The doctor continued sharing his optimism with us.

The day finally came when I could drive Mother home. She looked so much better with all the awful purple stuff off her face and with a visit to the beauty parlor. Her friends were all outside the front door of the Towers waiting for her when we drove up. They were all eager to hug and kiss her. And her beloved sister, still in a wheelchair, had tears running down her cheeks as she tried to get up. It was near Mom's birthday so I decided to throw a quick birthday party for her and her close friends.

I was helped out in the party plans by the aides that Mr. Winslow had hired. We all assembled in Mom's new apartment with the view, complete with cake and champagne, and colorful balloons floating about. It was a happy occasion for Aunt Edna to see her sister so happy and looking so well.

Mother and Mr. Winslow wanted me to take home copies of her will and Edna's trust information as well as contents of their safety deposit box for security reasons. I was quite baffled by all this information because I had carefully kept myself out of Mom's and Aunt Edna's affairs. That both Mom and their lawyer were insisting on involving me gave me a strange feeling of being the last to know what was going on.

ersisted as I sat on the airplane, with a
nd safety deposit contents, thinking to
vn, all the family jewels and money go down

when I left," I told Linda and Fred. "She's
I hope she has time left to enjoy living
it."
" Linda explained to Fred. "Mom and I
e with grandma. Aunt Edna insisted on

nd aunt," Fred said.
eep sea scuba diving with Tom went.
ccount of how skilled Tom was in scuba
eye on his old Dad. He certainly knows

from one another, but it was also great
up on one another's adventures. Even

In May I got another call from Mom's lawyer. He said she lacked
the energy to spend much time in her apartment. The two aides
arranged for the sisters to visit one another in their nursing home
rooms. Consequently, he recommended that I fly down, dispose of
their unnecessary items and close the apartment.

"How do you feel about that, Mom?" Linda asked.

"I feel it is the end of an era. It means neither of them will be
able to live the lives they have been enjoying. Linda, it means he is
preparing us for their deaths," I said as I started crying. "I'm not
ready for Mom to be going. We haven't taken our cruise of Alaska
yet. She always wanted to go there. I'm just not ready! This must be
what I was feeling on the plane. When Mom and Mr. Winslow both
kept insisting that I take all the documents, the income tax returns,
the family jewels. I couldn't figure out why. Mom seemed on the
road to recovery."

Linda hugged me and said, "Mom, both she and Mr. Winslow must have known she wasn't as well as she let on."

So off I went to Florida again. I was shocked to see my mother's condition; she was suddenly weak and could no longer get out of bed, brush her own teeth, or go to the bathroom alone. I was pleased that Mr. Winslow had hired Mary, the full-time aide to be with her.

It seemed so strange to be sleeping in Mom's apartment with the wide windows open, listening to the strange sounds of crickets, frogs — whatever was out there making tropical-sounding noises all night. The heaviness of the moist air blowing in through the open French windows contributed to the oddness of being there, alone, in hot weather.

Mr. Winslow showed up the next morning and gave me a list of things that needed to be done. "Now Shirley, you just decide what furniture you want and mark it, along with other items you might want. I can recommend two different furniture movers to you. The estate will pay for their services. You need to go through all the clothes and determine what to do with them. The aides can assist you. Then you can meet me at my office and we can go through your mother's and aunt's documents."

Both Linda and I were so impressed with Mr. Winslow, a true southern gentleman who always referred to my aunt as Miss Edna and made known his affection for my mother.

Both Aunt Edna and I could see that Mom was not well. Mom had always said to me, "When I can no longer play bridge, I'll be ready to leave this earth." She was a very matter-of-fact woman whose approach to life seemed to be, "it is what it is." I was so proud of her and so not ready to agree on "it is what it is." Nor was Aunt Edna, who in her wheelchair sat so anxiously at her dear sister's bedside, crying and asking me, "Is she dying?"

It wasn't supposed to be this way. I felt so sorry for both of them, for all three of us. I said my good-byes to Mom and Edna who seemed sad to see me leave. When Mother and I were alone, she said to me, "You take care of Edna." I promised her I would.

Upon my return home, I was grateful that Mary, Mom's aide, read my letters to Mom, played the tapes of Mom's favorite music from her childhood, and helped Mom talk with me on the phone each day. When Mom was no longer able to converse, Mary talked with me. We grew very close. She also gave me progress reports on Aunt Edna.

I was back at work preparing staff for the first day of school when I got the call from Mr. Winslow. "Your Mother died this morning." It was Labor Day. How like her, I thought, to die on Labor Day. It was so like her to not want to inconvenience anyone. I called my boss and Linda. Once again, we were on our way back to Orlando later that morning.

All of Mother's closest friends huddled about us as we entered the front door. Linda and I planned, with the Methodist minister, an intimate memorial service for Mom, complete with sandwiches and tea and flowers galore. As we were leaving for the church, I was informed there was a phone call for me. Fred's caring voice came from the other end, "I was sure I could figure out where you were," he said. "Tell me, what happened and how you are?" I was so grateful for his call.

Linda and I then arranged for a stretch Cadillac to pick up those dear friends still remaining. Unfortunately, Aunt Edna was not able to attend. Afterwards, before we left for the airport, Linda said, "Mom, let's leave a bouquet of flowers from the church, on the doorstep of each friend." They were such precious people. It gave us great pleasure to leave the flowers, then run like kids leaving May baskets on neighbor's doors.

Eventually, old routines and patterns returned and work and home continued on. Now that Aunt Edna was permanently in the nursing home, I was to take all of her furniture. Linda wondered what to expect the day the furniture truck would arrive. "Oh, Linda, I was torn in so many directions; I think I just told them to send all the furnishings here. I figured our huge Queen Anne house was so large that it could easily absorb all Aunt Edna's lovely Queen Anne antiques."

"I remember, Mom, how Aunt Edna would touch, even caress, her furniture with such loving care. Her furnishings were like the children she never had. Don't you think she would be pleased her lovely things would find a new home with us in our Queen Anne home?"

I agreed saying, "She was such an Anglophile. How ironic that I ended up choosing this house fifteen years ago when all I was looking for was a cheap house big enough for our blended family."

Chapter Ten
The Frugal Man's Moveable Feast
1986

FRED'S EYES WERE FILLED with excitement as he basked in the surrounding history. We were standing in the middle of his favorite city about to begin our Frugal Man's Moveable Feast.

After the past year, with mother's death and all, the timing of this sabbatical could not have been more perfect.

"Fred, we're really here! London! I can hardly believe it!"

I stepped out into the crosswalk. Fred suddenly grabbed my hand and pulled me back to the curb. "Careful, dear. You're about to get hit." Traffic rushed past me from the direction opposite of where I was looking. I had barely avoided getting hit. I forgot about the whole "driving on the other side of the road" thing. You catch on quick or you die.

Big Ben, Tower of London, Trafalgar Square, Buckingham Palace. I couldn't believe the beauty of the unbelievably old, stone buildings with turrets of varying sizes, intricate stone carvings encircling them. In front of the buildings were many statues of historical figures and gargoyles. How could anyone afford to build such magnificent buildings nowadays?

We Americans don't have a concept of old. My house was over 100-years-old but many of these impressive buildings had been around for centuries. They looked remarkably well for being 600 or more years old. Stability, tradition, and resoluteness were concepts that came to mind when I looked around at all these remarkable buildings.

That night we ended up dining at a Greek restaurant that became a favorite of ours. Good food, good wine. But before dinner we heard some sad, stunning news. A bomb had exploded on a TWA plane en route to Athens earlier that day. Four were killed. A man named Kadaffi was blamed.

At breakfast we read more about the bomb. "It sounds like President Reagan plans to retaliate by firing on Libya if he finds that it was Kadaffi's fault."

"Yes," Fred replied as he took a sip of coffee. "I see the newspaper's editorial is pro-USA."

"What a time to be in Europe," I said as I brushed toast crumbs off my fingers. "I'll bet our kids are concerned."

"Well, there is nothing we can do but see the sights. And wait to learn more," Fred replied in his unflappable way.

Hyde Park was fascinating, full of people milling about, looking at artwork that lined the streets where vendors hoped to make a sale, or listening at the Speakers' Corner to anyone who felt like getting on a podium to passionately argue a cause.

Striding on, we observed strikers protesting "wapping" at Trafalgar Square. We never did figure out what "wapping" was.

We spent the afternoon at Westminister Abbey, an amazing edifice steeped in history that held the tombs of royalty. Queen

Elizabeth I and Mary Queen of Scots were buried there. Sir Walter Raleigh was buried next door at St. Margaret's Church, the commoner's church, all across the street from Big Ben and the House of Parliament. The atmosphere reeked of tradition and religion.

I enjoyed seeing the joy on Fred's face; his love of history was serving him well.

We stayed to watch Evensong; it was a treat to hear a Cambridge choir in a 900-year-old church. Their beautiful voices echoed in everlastingness, culminated by an organist gone wild. I'd heard Fred talk about Evensong back in the states, but I had no idea what it was.

Dressed way too casually, we were soon seated in our own ornate pew. I was seated next to an elderly man dressed in velvet religious clothing of some kind, holding a prayer book. Again, I looked down at my khaki clothing and boots in chagrin. I could just hear my mother saying, "Can't you ever look halfway decent?"

"True roots," Fred reminded me. "This is the center of WASPism. This is who we are."

I'm glad he knew. Whenever folks had asked me back in Marshalltown what my roots were, I'd usually say, "Oh, I'm like Heinz 57 ketchup — a little bit of everything." I'd shown little curiosity in my roots and I didn't recall my folks talking much about it.

That night when we returned to the hotel, I called Linda. She was very concerned about the bombing incident and about us being in Europe. "All the talk and news here is about the bombs and whether or not Americans should travel to Europe this summer."

It was an academic issue for us since we were already there. And quite frankly, we both liked being where the action was.

The next morning we heard news about a bomb going off in West Berlin at a nightclub frequented by U.S. military. No one claimed responsibility. Two were killed and many injured.

———————

We strolled to Buckingham Palace, but the Queen was not in. We did, however, watch the dramatic changing of the guards.

It was so easy getting around the city, which seemed unusually safe day or night. We envied their transportation system of buses and tubes that worked so efficiently. Even though the population was highly diverse, everyone looked good, except the punks, and everyone seemed to possess a sense of style—even the punks. London's citizens appeared to be a tolerant people who could accept almost anyone, any lifestyle, any eccentricity of dress—their behavior remaining civilized. I found their footwear fascinating, too, especially the women who wore Nazi storm trooper boots with black hose and long black skirts or tight black pants.

I was surprised at the many bicyclists—obviously middle-class workers—amidst the horrid city traffic. Men and women of all ages were biking to work. No wonder so many were slim and trim. Also, it seemed everyone smoked. No evidence of anti-smoking campaigns here.

Thanks to the superb tube system that Fred had mastered on previous trips, we were able to see many far-flung sites during our week in London. The British Museum, one of Fred's favorites, was a must, as was the National History Museum and Science Museum. We lingered over the Royal collection of art at the National Galley at Trafalgar Square, and a favorite of mine was the Tower of London with its colorful guards protecting the home of the crown jewels. Another must for me was Shakespeare's Globe Theatre.

The marvelous hospitable pubs offered us easy access to comfort and comfort food as well as good people-watching.

Every day seemed colder and rainier than the previous day. One night we saw Bernard Shaw's play, *The Apple Cart*, starring Peter O'Toole, which was a fun satire on manners, morals, and relationships. We loved it. Another miserable rainy day was saved by Yo-Yo Ma's evening performance with the Philharmonic Orchestra at the Royal Festival.

Our next destination was Cornwall, a Provence located in the southern tip of England. We picked up a new red Ford Fiesta at the airport and took off for Lyme Regis, a true English coastal town where the movie *The French Lieutenant's Woman* was filmed. Much of the town curved along the shoreline next to the sandy beach, undoubtedly inviting in the summer.

We anchored in at one of the smaller Cornish fishing villages — Mousehole (pronounced mous-sell), three miles south of Penzance. There we found a charming B & B called Tavis Vor, which had direct access to the sea through its own grounds, providing us with a marvelous view overlooking the harbor and St. Michael's Mount. With Fred recovering from a bout of flu, a more idyllic spot for reading and convalescence could not be found.

A knock on the door brought us not only a bowl of soup for the recovering Fred but news from the waitress. "Your president has had a go at Kadaffi and is warning all Americans to avoid travel to Europe this summer. Apparently your fighter planes bombed Kadaffi's home, killing one of his children as retaliation for the TWA plane bomb explosion."

Fred grabbed my hand and said, "It's going to be an interesting trip, especially when we leave the UK and head out for European countries."

"There's talk about you Yanks getting Canadian lapel pins to wear," the waitress mentioned. Evidently, people thought we would be safer if we identified ourselves as Canadian. Fred reminded me he was raised in Canada as he smiled at me in a roughish way.

"Well," I said, "We wouldn't be having a Hemingway-type experience if a hint of danger or excitement didn't exist." I squeezed Fred's hand. "We're going to have a real adventure."

"Quite right," Fred agreed. This was part of the Nick and Nora Charles affect we occasionally donned.

It was hard to remember the world events as we dined mornings and evenings in an elegant room overlooking the sea that we shared with another couple from Oxford on holiday. Our affable host served us his wife's culinary delights. After dinner the four of us would retire to the living room for conversation in front of a warm fire set in the fireplace.

Each day we hiked on footpaths over rugged terrain on the shoreline. Meadows and meadows of golden daffodils blinded us on these walks as the wind whipped about us trying to toss us over the craggy cliffs into the sea below. "There is a bit of a blow out there," our host had warned us. We just loved the Brits' use of understatement.

Our last two days there were our first acquaintance with sunshine since leaving the USA.

The Sabbatical Begins

We once again entered the world of constant rain as we journeyed to the home of our Welsh hosts, Tony and Sue Jenkins.

Though both were born in England, North Wales was their home. They were eager to welcome us into the next chapter of our great adventure.

We examined their "estate" in Mold, Clwyd, North Wales. It was five acres of wooded land featuring a broken-down very old stone building—more than 600-years-old—surrounded by a sea of mud. At the other side of the property stood two very small caravans—also surrounded by mud, where Tony and Sue lived.

With great excitement, Tony and Sue showed us the blueprints for a future, when the old stone gatehouse they had bought with the fruits of their own hard labor would one day become a manor suitable for a Lord and Lady. It looked like an enormous undertaking, but as we came to know them better, we became admirers of their "true grit."

They housed us in the caravan with the bedroom and bath and they stayed in the caravan with the kitchen and living room.

On their television, we watched Prime Minister Maggie Thatcher getting quite worked over by the men in the House of Lords, who seemed rude and interruptive. I couldn't imagine our President being treated by legislators in a similar fashion.

Ms. Thatcher's response was icy steel, controlled and unflappable. I could see how she got the title of "The Iron Maiden." She was most impressive. There was much to discuss.

I knew little about English politics. It was eventually apparent to me that Sue highly respected the Queen and the role she played in maintaining traditions, keeping the UK a sought-after tourist destination that brought wealth to the island. Yet I knew some of our other English friends were critical of Maggie Thatcher's party and some of the monarchy as well. However, I maintained a hands-off attitude. It wasn't my country and I felt I'd never have adequate data or take the time to get it, in order to come up with a point of view of my own. In truth, I had enough difficulty trying to figure out American politics.

Fred said, "You Brits have much to be proud of. Without the Brits, English would not be the international language. That has had a profound influence on the world." We had noticed in our travels that some Brits felt second-class in the world because of the shrinkage of their empire. "How many conquerors of previous empires have left such a lasting effect when the sun has set on their dominance?" Fred asked.

Each day, upon returning home from work, our remarkable host and hostess put on the clothes of day laborers and began their second job. Wading through the spring mud in their wellies, they gathered their tools and continued work on the building that was to become their dream home. What a remarkable team they were with the vision, skills, discipline, and determination to achieve their dream.

This young couple was in the beginning stages of their journey. We greatly admired their vision and determination as they worked together to build the nest they hoped would one day include a child or two. But Fred and I had raised our children and were now near retirement. We were ready for less responsibility and more adventure.

Each night Tony and Sue would wine and dine us while discussing news of the day. Reagan had shocked us all: American flighter planes were taking off from British-based airports (including the air force base where Tony worked as an engineer) and striking at Libyan targets. "Your planes take off from our base to attack Kadaffi. That certainly implicates us," Tony said. Headlines of the Welsh paper stated: "Back Off, Reagan." We agreed that international opinion seemed to be highly negative for both their leader and ours.

Arab terrorists in Beirut and Morocco had killed several British teachers, a Welsh couple, and two news correspondents during the last two days. We met an Australian traveler at a nearby pub who was concerned about his wife's safety. She was flying on an Air Britain plane over Middle Eastern terrain. He advised us against going to Morocco.

It was hard to know where we would be once we started backpacking Europe and riding the rails with our U-rail tickets.

"Is it exciting enough for you, Shirley?" Fred asked, draining the last dregs of beer from his glass.

"I was just thinking how much this situation reminded me of a book called *Winds of Deliverance*. The heroine, Madeline, seeks adventure by flying off to Europe during WWII without even a suitcase of clothes, saying she'd buy some when she got there." I stabbed the last bite of food with my fork. "That, I thought was pretty impulsive. But this seems a safe version of it," I replied as I finished off my meal.

"Just what I was thinking. The odds are highly against us being where the danger is."

"As Churchill once said, or was it Roosevelt, 'There is nothing to fear but fear itself.'"

I reached out to take a bite of the food he had on his plate. Even though my stomach said full, my taste buds said eat! Fred grabbed my hand, preventing me from attacking his food and said, "Good thinking. We aren't the kind to over react or under react to events around us." He put his fork in his mouth and gave me a wicked smile as he swallowed the last bite.

We were happy to see our friend Brian Walters again; he was the Director of Special Education for Clwyd County. He fashioned an excellent observation schedule for us and introduced us to members of his staff who would be with us the next few weeks.

The county served approximately 85,000 students from birth to the age of nineteen years through their county nurse programs for all new "mums." About 20% of the students were seen as having special needs. At that time, legislation was in the House of Lords requiring programming for handicapped youth over the age of nineteen. I felt we Yank educators had much to learn from our British colleagues. The new mums program especially impressed me. It seemed evident to me that the earlier help was given disadvantaged families — while the mother was pregnant with her first child — the healthier the child would likely be when born. This was not a service offered newly pregnant mothers in poor American families at that time. We anticipated learning a great deal.

Our host Sue worked at Ysgol Bryn Offa, a comprehensive secondary school in Wrexham, Clwyd. She served as their assistant principal. The school held over 1,300 students, ages eleven to sixteen. Older students interested in the top levels went to a school nearby.

Shirley with students

We were kept busy viewing their special education programs in both Mold and Chester. Fred, being Welsh, particularly enjoyed visiting the Welsh immersion school where children were taught in the Welsh language — a language that seemed to consist of mostly consonants and few vowels. These were popular programs with parents and were only just beginning to pop up in St. Paul and St. Cloud where Spanish and French immersion schools were starting.

I watched Fred talk with the children about our country and its schools, using the maps he had brought with him as teaching tools. He wisely made no attempt to speak Welsh. Fred was a "natural" as a teacher. He knew how to draw students into the discussion by asking them questions such as, "How many of you know where the United States of America is on the map? Who can show us?" The kids were clamoring to answer. Then, "Now, this is a harder question, who knows where Canada is?" And from these questions, he would draw their attention to the midwestern part of America, then Minnesota that borders Canada. By this time, they were circled around him, eager to be involved and asking him questions.

Fred teaching the children at the school

Our last day with the Jenkinses was festive, topped off with a walk in the windy but sunny meadows. The high hills surrounding their five-acre estate were so beautiful that we threw ourselves spread eagle on the ground and luxuriated in our closeness to nature. Standing high on a hill on their property, we could see Liverpool on the far horizon. Tony told us how a wealthy slave trader had stood on that very spot to watch the arrival of his ships coming into Liverpool laden with slaves. A flag would go up on his office tower when they arrived. That was his signal to ready the horses for the trip to Liverpool. With money from the sale of slaves, the trader built his estate, which included the buildings on Tony's five acres. This was astounding news to

Fred, Tony, and Shirley

me. I had been unaware of the UK's involvement in slavery and the slave trade.

That night we dined at their favorite spot in Mold, indulging in great wine and never-ending courses of food, desserts, and after-dinner drinks. Reluctant to part from one another, we kept having another round of drinks or telling another story. The four of us had become fast friends.

The next morning we headed to Ruthin Castle to spend the weekend. Sue suggested we take a room there before leaving for Lancashire, England. Tony quite agreed the castle was an experience not to be missed. Founded in 1281, it still contained relics of its past, including a fireplace from Henry V's time in one of its many gracious drawing rooms.

The well-groomed grounds were filled with strutting peacocks involved in a highly stylized mating ritual. The four-poster bed in our room was adorned with silken sheets and a spread of pink flowers that matched the drapes, making it look like it had been part of an MGM movie depicting life of the Royals. The room also featured a dining room table flanked by four chairs in front of a huge marble fireplace. A huge suit of armor stood on the landing of velvet-clad steps, posed as if waiting for battle. When I reminded Fred that, according to Sue and Tony, his last name (spelled Rhys) in Welsh meant Prince, he then stood erect, holding his slender cigar at shoulder height, and imitating the royal wave, said, "Well now, these royal quarters in a castle are my birthright."

We then went on to Chester where we spent time visiting Sheila and Mike Gore. They had been my houseguests during the invasion of the Welsh and Cheshire educators "to the colonies," a term they enjoyed using when referring to America. We were overwhelmed with their hospitality. They served all kinds of delicacies, including scones, coffees, salmon flanked by a marvelous fruit assortment, wine popped open and sitting on the patio to breathe, along with all kinds of dessert cheeses. There seemed to be a different kind of liquor — whiskey, sherry, or wine — available any time during the day or night. In the evening they would invite friends over to meet the Yanks. Guests included their Director of Education, who had also been among those Brits who had invaded us several years earlier. He brought his wife and teenaged daughter who were quite excited to meet some real Americans.

With great reluctance we left their neck of the woods, promising them we would be seeing much more of them in the future. And indeed, we visited one another many times, not only in our respective countries, but in the British Virgin Islands as well.

I could tell Fred was eager to be off on his own. He was clearly a man used to traveling alone. Nonetheless, he shared how pleased he was that we were having such good times together and confided that he had not spent as much time with any woman as he had with me. But since he needed to visit Alnwick Castle in Northumberland where he had collegial contacts, he left me at a B&B in Hexham, Northumberland. "I'll be back in about four days," he said as he got in his car.

Actually, I, too, was looking forward to being on my own. I viewed it as just one more adventure. At the B&B I was introduced to my new roommate—a cat. Each room came with a cat.

Global crisis number two surfaced during my stay in Hexham. A Kiev source on the telly said 2,000 people died in a Soviet nuclear plant disaster at Chernobyl. Sweden was the first to inform the West after noting high levels of radioactive clouds in their country. All kinds of precautions were to be put in place in neighboring countries. Sheep were to be slaughtered, fruit and vegetables to be washed and eaten with care. All were closely monitoring the radioactive cloud. It was now moving towards Austria and Switzerland.

This was definitely not the year to travel abroad. One could only hope that first reports were exaggerated possibilities of how far the radioactive clouds would spread. I wondered what Fred was thinking about this last crisis as I spent a day hiking to Colbridge and back—about twelve miles—to view the remains of an old Roman town that housed the famous Roman Sixth Legion. This had been the supply base for Hadrian's Wall, which Fred long wanted to hike. I knew Fred was steeped in Roman history and this was my chance to learn a bit more about this aspect of time before the two of us began tackling Hadrian's Wall. Unfortunately, my long hike was taking its toll on my lower back.

When I got back to Hexham, I first joined the other people staying at the B & B who were clustered about the telly. One couple from Sweden was the most concerned. There was much speculation among the group on whether radioactive clouds would spread into this region. I thought to myself how it would be more than ironic if being where I wouldn't normally have been resulted in my being exposed to something cancerous. But it wasn't my nature to worry about speculations or things I couldn't control. As exciting as their conversation was, I knew the ache in my back demanded I take to my bed. The cat joined me. I must have slept about ten hours.

Once Fred returned from his business trip, we set off to hike Hadrian's Wall. It was a once-in-a-lifetime experience. The wall, built of thousands of pavers stacked in rows on top of one another, went on for miles and miles up and down hills, eventually stretching from coast to coast. Over the centuries many stones had disappeared, probably taken by people needing them to build their homes or repair their fences. We saw thousands of sheep and pretty much had the long wall to ourselves. It was such an exciting experience that we both wondered if anything else we would experience in the next few months could top it. To me, it was absolutely awesome.

At times we felt we could sense the presence of the Romans as we looked for signature signs on some of the stones. The inventiveness of the Romans was highly evident, not only in the remarkable wall, but also in their water system and the comforts it provided in the baths, latrines, and kitchens. It was even more remarkable when one realized it was built in 75 AD. It is questionable that it could have ever kept the Scots out, but it did keep a great number of Roman soldiers

and locals busy so they wouldn't have extra time available to get into trouble.

The Scottish Royal Air Force gave us a dynamic air show late one afternoon as we stood on the wall's highest crag. In fact, we both ducked as they swooped in close to our heads.

We became steeped in Roman British history as a result of visiting Chester, Homestead, Cholleford, and Vallehara, hiking under varying weather conditions, three to five hours daily for five days.

Fred at Hadrian's Wall

We returned to London in order to fly to Spain, hoping a bomb that had earlier exploded in front of the Air Britain Office — the very place where we had purchased our tickets a month ago — did not destroy our airline tickets. Stepping over all the rubble, we were relieved to find our tickets intact. "With the Irish problem," Fred said, "the Brits are probably used to dealing with occasional bomb explosions."

Benalmádena, Spain: *On the Costa del Sol*

LaRoca, the hotel where we were staying in Benalmádena, was on a high hill with a dazzling view of the Mediterranean Sea. By the third day, we were beginning to look and act like natives. We observed siesta during the heat of the day on the veranda of our poolside room. In the mornings, we would rent cabanas on the beach. It was a culture shock for me to view the ease with which the ladies would disrobe, walk around topless, and bathe in the sea. Vendors of all ages, including young boys, would sell food and drinks to these same ladies with no signs of embarrassment. I couldn't help but notice that men reading paperbacks in their cabanas were often holding them upside down.

We met many Brits and Scots there and enjoyed their company. Denis's Pub up the street from our hotel became a favorite watering hole for us. A Scottish couple joined us for drinks one night. Fiona, the wife, was effusive in stating how attractive she found me and how fortunate Fred was to be my companion. Then she stated, "But you're not married, are you?" Her husband was shocked by her statement that he deemed entirely inappropriate, until I responded that she was right, and Fred, giving me a wicked look, stated, "We like to live in sin." Fiona said she could tell we weren't married because we so enjoyed one another's company.

The UK, USA, and world problems seemed light years away as did the incessant rains, clouds, fog, and cold so typical of the England we experienced. We had shipped woolies back to the states and the summer wardrobe of thongs, bathing suits, t-shirts, and such had taken its place.

Of the various places we visited in Spain, Gibraltar was perhaps the most exotic. It was our first exposure to Arabs and Muslim women dressed in their black dresses and burkas. Yet on their feet were big American-type tennis shoes. They didn't seem too happy.

Fred hired a taxi driver to take us on a tour of the city. The Rock of Gibraltar has two distinctive geographical features: the way it rises from the sea to its high peak and the tiny strip of land that attaches it to the mainland. From a distance, it looks like an island. Strategically, it guards the exit from the Mediterranean to the ocean beyond. It is hard to believe the whole area is only two square miles.

Its strategic location has made it attractive to many countries, starting with the ancient Phoenicians. Its name came from the Arabs who invaded Spain centuries ago. Its architecture has been influenced by the Moors and it has been captured, lost, and recaptured, often by the Spanish. It eventually came under British control in 1713. Its present citizens are a collection of Moroccan Jews, Portuguese, Brits, and Spaniards. Gibraltarian society has acquired a character all its own—largely Mediterranean in origin, but it shows the influence of three centuries of British rule and one and a half centuries of English culture.

The Main Street was narrow and filled with traffic; it was dominated by tall Moorish-looking buildings on each side. It reminded me of New Orleans and Venice with its delightful charm,

At the Rock of Gibralter

strange languages, and tiny streets with its milling throngs of people. Our taxi driver took us to the "Rock" to see the world-famous Rock Apes. They really looked more like monkeys and were very mischievous, stealing anything—a billfold from a purse, keys, money—anything shiny. We kept a close eye on our possessions.

The airline runway ran smack dab through the causeway, linking the "Rock" with the Spanish mainland, tying up traffic for miles when a plane needed to land or take off. The short runway was like those on a carrier. It was fascinating to see the two countries working together, although the tension could be imagined. The many racial and ethnic groups that made up Gibraltarians seemed proud to be British subjects in a democratic nation.

Since we were going from winter to summer, we sent our extra suitcases back to the US. That left us with only our backpacks to live out of for the next two months. This was Fred's system and it worked great. We planned to take trains to wherever they went, letting serendipity play a major role in determining destinations. Our first-class train tickets assured us of sleeping accommodations. When Fred spied a Holiday Inn, he said, "Let's go in and reserve accommodations at the Frankfurt Holiday Inn for three days prior to our flight back to the states."

"What a great idea! I would never have thought of doing that. Obviously the mark of the experienced world traveler," I announced. Thus, two tasks were accomplished while in the Gib.

Backpacking Europe

After two weeks of fun in the sun on the Costa del Sol, we activated our U-rail tickets at Malaga and made train reservations for Barcelona, where we would switch trains to go to France.

"Protect my back," Fred ordered as he faced the ticket office. I was soon to find out the reason for his order. Many people were milling about, particularly around ticket-buying passengers. My back against his, I kept my eyes on a Gypsy woman holding a child in one arm while reaching out towards Fred as he reached for his billfold. I kept moving between the two of us until he had completed his transaction and had secured his billfold. This became a common practice at various railroad ticket offices. It seems that railroad stations were a source of ill-gotten gains for throngs of persons there for that purpose. Fred was aware of this practice from his former travels.

A whirlwind of activity greeted us once we left the leisurely beach-bum life on the Costa del Sol for the backpacking life of U-rail cardholders. I certainly learned how to get by when you don't speak the language. Fred was a natural at it; he'd simply point to our destination on his map, then using his watch, point to the time. Whenever I showed concern that we were lost or getting lost, Fred's frequent response was, "Not to worry." And invariably, he spoke the truth.

Learning to focus, then process environmental clues and cues quickly while in railroad terminals, became a necessity in order to make connections. My brain was much too slow in even figuring out where to look before the information on the station timetables changed. The same was true in figuring out which train, and which car on the train, was our car. When that was established, we had to scramble like hell to avoid being without a seat when the music stopped and the train started.

Learning to read a timetable, seek information from tourist bureaus and other tourists, figure out the new currency systems, get a map of the new town, while figuring out rapidly where to stay, how much to pay and how to get there, was the name of the travel game. And Fred was good at it.

For our first destination, Barcelona, we found ourselves in a compartment for four; it appeared there were no private compartments on this train. We would be on the train overnight. Another gentleman was already in our compartment. He spoke no English but we learned by watching him. As hours rolled by and others were considering joining us, we observed how he discouraged them from doing so. We also learned what levers to push to make beds out of our chairs.

No meals were provided, but at some stations, food vendors were available to sell us food as we leaned out our train windows.

Eventually, we arrived at Barcelona and learned we were in for a long wait before we could catch a train on the French side of the border. There was a train strike going on in France affecting conductors. While deciding what to do, we purchased some croissants, cheese, fruit, and wine to carry in its plastic bag so that we would have food for the next day on the train. We sensed excitement as fellow passengers waiting for a train into France began standing up, looking ready to go somewhere. By this time it was late at night. A train was arriving.

Fred suddenly said to me, "Wherever that train is going, we are going. I don't want to spend a night sleeping in the railroad station. Come on. Let's go!" We raced to the train. Somehow we managed to climb onto one train and jam ourselves into a compartment with two young ladies. Fred immediately slammed the compartment doors, not letting anyone else in. The young ladies were both Japanese but did not know one another.

Fred showed them how to make beds out of their chairs and we did the same, then used our backpacks to make it appear the compartment for six was full. The train pulled out while we were introducing ourselves to the ladies. When we glanced outside our compartment, we could see the aisles were full of passengers trying to find a place to prop themselves up for a night's sleep. The train restroom was right next to our compartment. We quickly shut our compartment door, frankly feeling victorious that we had learned the system of train survival so quickly. The young gals seemed appreciative that Fred was taking charge, assuring the four of us a good night's sleep to wherever we ended up. We shared some of our food with them before falling asleep.

I was first to wake up as I sensed the movement of the train going up, up a steep surface. Early morning was beginning to make its appearance. Outside the window was the most beautiful, breathtaking view of mountain terrain I had ever seen, covered with all kinds of greenery—trees, shrubs, birch, pine. In awe, I punched Fred and pointed to the window. His mouth opened up in amazement. Then one of the gals woke up and looked at where I was pointing and shook the other gal to do the same. We were obviously in the mountains going somewhere and, wherever it was, it promised beauty.

Soon we arrived at a station, the train stopped and all of us began piling out. It was 6:00 a.m. and we were the first passengers inside the station, just opening for the day.

Fred spied the sign first, "Welcome to Geneva, Switzerland!" The cafes and other shops were not yet open so we joined our fellow travelers finding spaces on the floor to sit, and we began exchanging travel stories and information with those who were English-speaking—mostly young backpackers from England.

After getting information from the Visitors' Booth, we set off for the Old Town to seek lodging at a nearby hotel. It was my first but not last encounter with hotel elevators the size of upright coffins. It was large enough for one person with a suitcase or two people chest to chest with backpacks.

Our room size matched that of the elevator. Its contents were a bed inside the front door, a chair, and a bathroom. A very large window, open to the world, gave us a view of our immediate area.

We spent the day exploring Old Town and dining in an outdoor café, watching birds sharing meals with customers. A very heavy elderly man sitting at a table next to ours was sharing food with a bird, who was eating it eagerly from the his fingers. They seemed to be good friends. Later in our stroll through a park, we noticed many needle exchanges occurring among young folks. It brought no notice from others. Later we hiked up the nearby mountains separating Switzerland from France, offering greetings in French to others we met on the gentle paths. We even saw many cows wearing bells around their necks, just as depicted on tourist postcards.

The next morning, we were awakened by a tap on the door. From the bed, I reached over to the doorknob, managing to open it, and in stepped a maid carrying a tray containing coffee and croissants. She handed it over to me, then backed out wishing us a good day in French. "Now that is what I call good room service," said Fred, as he took the tray from me, carefully setting it between us on the bed. Such was our first experience of breakfast in bed.

After exploring the city for several days, we left for Rome on a Swiss train where we actually had a private room and bath. Standing in the area outside our compartment looking out the window at the passing countryside, we encountered an interesting lady who ended up spending much of the day with us. She was highly upset with the conductor, who was requiring all passengers to give him their passports for his care until we reached our destination. But she very much took umbrage with that, saying she was a French citizen whose work constantly took her to Italy and this was a frequent battle she had with the conductors.

She had made a copy of her passport and told him he could have that, but he remained insistent. Apparently, she once had a bad experience with a conductor misplacing her passport. So she sought refuge from him by accepting Fred's invitation to join us for a drink in our compartment. She eventually returned to her compartment. We never did find out who won the battle of wills as we made our departure at Rome early in the morning.

Once again I guarded Fred's back as he sought housing

information at the Information Desk. Again he resorted to gestures, opening a Rome street map while pointing to the street. After a lot of head nodding by each, he then turned to me while going for the door to the street.

"So what's happening?" I asked.

"The gentleman referred me to a three-star hotel just down this street about four blocks." I was once again impressed with Fred's traveling skills as I watched him check us in and switch to Italian currency (this was before the Euro).

Our room was big and bare, providing only basics. We both leaned out the big open window with no screen. The sound of traffic, horns honking angrily, people shouting, was a preview of the night to come. But by then we didn't care. The man at the hotel desk gave us directions to a good Italian restaurant that was filled with excited soccer fans clustered around the TVs watching a match between Italy and Germany. It promised to be an exciting night—the food was excellent—and the wine bountiful. Somehow we found our way back to our hotel and our noisy bedroom—Rome seemed to be a city that never sleeps—but it didn't keep us from sleeping well. We were so tired.

Almost as amazing as its spectacular sights—Vatican City, the Roman Forum, the Colosseum, and circus, the majesty of its famous ruins and cobblestone roads—were the streets of everyday Rome: the traffic didn't move due to people leaving their parked cars in the middle of the street or parking on the sidewalks; the cacophony of constant horn honking surrounded us; the lights of street signs were merely a suggestion.

One day Fred spotted a Tourist Office and, grabbing my hand, entered and approached the man behind the counter. Fred said, "Let's get some information on how to get to Greece from here." The man extended his hand in greeting to Fred while seeking some pamphlets to give him. His English was good. After a brief conversation, Fred gave him his credit card. Fred called me over and they showed me how Fred and I would spend our next few days. Was I impressed! They seemed to have all the bases covered.

We first went to the train station where we saw a group of young backpackers sprawled out on the cement, some with backs propped against pillars, others sleeping with their heads supported on their backpacks. Since the train was late, we joined this young college-aged herd, making ourselves reasonably comfortable.

When the train arrived we were on our way to Brindisi, located on the heel of Italy in the Adriatic Sea. Once there, we made our way to a dock for an overnight ferry to Greece. All of us stood on the dock in a row, looking much like upright turtles, before we finally gained entry onto the ferry. We joked around with our fellow backpackers while enjoying the feel of the wind practically blowing us over as the boat sped through the water. When darkness came, the young folks sprawled out on the deck for a good night's sleep. We didn't tell them we had a private room. But when I went to the bathroom in the middle of the night, I found myself walking around or over sleeping bodies in the halls and on the floor of the women's restroom.

The joys of travel persisted the next day when we finally docked, then all caught the train to Athens. We were among the fortunate to find seats; the crowded train had no standing room or food or toilet facilities available and we were going to be traveling in this horrible humid heat for four hours. All the train windows were wide open, blowing in hot air. It had to be close to 100 degrees.

Arriving in Athens at midnight, we left the young backpackers behind and met another young couple from California on their honeymoon. They waited for a cab with us. The young gal said she had noticed me on the train because I looked so cool and crisp in my khaki blouse and skirt.

The cab driver threw our luggage in his trunk and asked us

where we were going. The young couple asked the cab driver for a suggestion, but we said we were booked at the Athens Hotel. Hearing that, he tossed our luggage back on the street and took off with the young couple. They called out they would get a hold of us the next day.

"Welcome to Athens!" Fred said to me as the taxi roared away. "Guess he had a deal with particular hotels and ours wasn't one of them." We finally managed our way to our plush hotel and Fred immediately ordered a sandwich and a couple of cold beers.

The best view of the Acropolis was at night from a rooftop café where we ran into our young California couple. We all squealed with delight when we watched the colored lights play on the various buildings of the Acropolis. Walking home, I began dancing Gene Kelly style off and on the curb, holding an imaginary umbrella while singing in the rain, with Fred close behind me, smiling at my goofiness and gently touching my back as I passed in front of him.

The next day I discovered that crossing an Athens street is a flirt with death. The traffic was speeding 50 or 60 miles a minute. I stood, terrified on the curb, when I noticed a little old lady dressed in black, cross herself as any good Catholic would do, then walk across the street, miraculously arriving safely on the other side. "Did you see that, Fred? That must be the ticket." So I crossed myself and hoped for the best. It worked.

We then hiked up the steep hill to the Acropolis in unbearable heat. Fred found shade for me and got me a cold drink. He said my face was deep red. I was even shivering from the heat. Fred quickly found a shady spot for me and got me some water. After drinking a lot of water, I started feeling better and we managed a guided tour of the ruins, then headed back to a Tourist Agency whose agent recommended and booked us on a trip to Skiros Island on the Aegean Sea for a week.

We loved the funky island with only horse-drawn carriages, quaint buildings and plenty of "limeys" (Brits) to join us for late-afternoon cocktails at our villa. The beaches were rocky, but the atmosphere of the island was amazing. There were many neat places to eat the great Greek food and the Greek music inspired us to start clapping hands and dancing like Zorba the Greek, with arms flung up high above the head.

One night we took a taxi (horse-driven carriage) to the far side of the island to dine at a highly recommended restaurant. The sides were open to nature and the inside was filled with long tables. A man dressed in colorful Greek fashion sat us at one of the long tables with other folks, providing instant intimacy with other diners. Drinks

for the group were served. The music got more and more intense. The waiter came back to check on us and seeing the many glasses, some empty, some full, he suddenly tipped the table. All the glass and dinnerware crashed to the cement floor, smashing into many pieces! We watched, stunned, as he wiped the table top clean with his billowing sleeves. We didn't know how to react, but as he brought more pitchers and clean glasses, we realized that this was what they did. We began toasting everyone. More dishes were thrown.

Then our waiter grabbed Fred, pulling him to his feet beside him and began the famous Zorba the Greek dance. He motioned to Fred to grab me, and then motioned to the others at the table to join in. Soon a whole line of customers were joining the waiters in attempting the Greek line dance as the beat of the music intensified, getting faster and louder. Those not dancing were clapping their hands to the beat of the demanding music. It was great! Nothing but smiles could be seen on everyone's faces as we danced on to eventual exhaustion.

We collapsed at our table, ready to eat and drink. By this time, Fred and the waiter had become great friends. He was inviting Fred to another party elsewhere. Fred, laughing and shaking his head from side to side, protested that he was too old. Let the young folks go.

Later our carriage arrived to take us home. It was quite romantic being rocked by the rhythm of the horse's gait back and forth, looking at the moon cast its glow on the ocean as Fred gathered me in his arms and I laid my head on his shoulder. "Can it get any better than this?" I asked.

"Ideal living conditions," Fred responded.

In our villa, our room in its cement dwelling was the first in a line of similar dwellings. It was the habit of the young crowd we hung out with to bang on our door when they came home from a night out and yell, "Good night, Fred! Good night, Shirley." On this night, we got home last.

After a week of so many delightful moments, we returned to Italy, taking the same route back and once again getting on the train going north.

"Where do you want to go next?" Fred asked.

In a heartbeat, I said, "Switzerland—someplace high in the mountains."

Finding ourselves once again in a compartment of six passengers, Fred was uncharacteristically annoyed that we didn't have our private room. We had paid for a private room and rarely had one. He went off to complain to the conductor. In a fed-up tone he said to me, "Figure out where we're going."

A pretty young blond from England, sitting across from me, asked "What kind of place are you looking for?"

I instantly replied, "Oh, a beautiful but quiet place surrounded by the beauty of Nature."

"I'm from England, but I work in such a place right now."

She went on to describe a ski village that was busy in the winter but quiet in the summer. "Kind of a one-street town but very quaint. Just a handful of hikers and some leftover skiers in the summer. It's a place called Zermatt, home of the Matterhorn."

"What?" I interrupted her. "Did you say Matterhorn? That's a place Fred has always wanted to see. Can you tell us how to get there?"

"Well, I'm returning to Zermatt from a weekend elsewhere. You just get off when I get off. I can take you there."

Just then, Fred returned, looking tired and disgruntled. "Fred, sit down. I know where we're going and it's the next stop. It's the home of the Matterhorn!"

It was exactly what we wanted. Taking a tram going straight up, we headed to a hotel recommended by the young lady. We were ready to start our week in Zermatt.

We could see the magnificent Matterhorn from our hotel room window. It was beautiful, with a crisp white peak reaching toward an endless blue sky. Early the next morning, a strange sound woke us up. Fred sat up abruptly in bed. "What's that?!?"

We rushed to the window. On the gravel street below were about fifty black and white goats with bells around their necks,

Boy leading goats through town

following a young shepherd boy, who was herding them through the main drag, their bells clanging wildly as they walked along. We were later told this occurred daily, early in the morning and again late afternoon when the goats returned to their barn.

After breakfast, we noticed a small cemetery nearby with about thirty large tombstones. The names on each were of young men who died trying to climb the Matterhorn. A pickax was affixed to one headstone with the words chiseled in marble stating, "I Chose to Climb." The young man, from New York City, was seventeen years old.

Fred got a map of the various hiking trails that went up to the base of the Matterhorn. It would take three to five hours to reach the base where one could continue on with picks and ropes, or return to the bottom by cable car or on foot. We fell in love with the home of the Matterhorn, climbing its mountains daily.

At the Matterhorn

Fred was once again going his own way. Long before we left the states, he had made plans to visit his nephew in Belgium. I was to meet him in Frankfurt a week later.

In the meantime, I looked forward to more hiking and spending time with Jadeen, the waitress at our hotel, and Michael, her boyfriend who was the chef. The day after Fred left, they took me on a picnic in the mountains and taught me how to climb up the rocks on a huge practice boulder, used frequently by mountain climbers as practice before scaling the Matterhorn. I looked quite professional in my harness and felt triumphant when I reached the top, then traversed down to the ground. They took photos of my feat so I could make Fred feel envious when he saw them.

Another day I strapped on my daypack containing the necessities for reaching the top at the base of the Matterhorn. I looked forward to tackling the mountain alone. It was necessary to reach the base in time to take the last cable car back down the mountain at 4:30. Fred and I had learned that most deaths from mountain climbing came on the way down, when climbers were careless, too eager to get down, or more exhausted than they realized. In fact, one lady in Zermatt had died while on the way down several days earlier.

I started my climb at 10:00 a.m., making sure to take rest breaks on my climb up. I took out my raincoat to lie on, using my pack as a pillow and ate an apple while reading my paperback. As I climbed above the snow line, it was interesting to observe the foliage change from abundant trees, to shorter trees and shrubs, to finally gravel and snow chunks. I stopped to put on my raingear for warmth as I spied the magnificent Matterhorn ahead. With no mountainside or trees for shelter, I felt the chilling effect of the wind and pulled my hood up over my head. I raced to buy a ticket on the last cable car down, then gobbled down a hot bowl of soup. Getting on the cable car minutes later, I felt most triumphant. Fred would be proud of me. Not bad for a fifty-three-year-old.

Shirley rock climbing

I was to meet Fred in Frankfurt at the Holiday Inn where we would spend the final three days of our Sabbatical before returning to the states. The Swiss trains were impressive with food and wine readily available. A porter kept careful watch over me, seeing that I got off the train at the right stop, which was tricky because the train stopped for only a second at each stop.

A taxi took me to my destination and I was flabbergasted. Our room was a luxurious two-story suite complete with kitchen, two baths, and an office, in addition to the living room and balcony. I was sure a mistake had occurred, so I hurried downstairs to check the price while striving to remain calm. Unbelievably, it was the cheap price we had agreed to when in Gibraltar.

Relieved, I reached for a cold beer from the fridge, turned on the TV to a tennis match, and then called my daughter on the phone that offered direct-dial service. I suspected she might be watching the same match. She was, so we talked tennis for about a half hour and I bragged about our cool digs in Frankfurt.

Later when I was taking a shower in the second floor of our suite, I heard a loud banging on the door. Wrapped in a towel, I gingerly opened the door a crack, peeked out—and it was Fred! I wasn't expecting him until the next morning. He said he missed me so he came a day early. I pulled him into the shower with me—clothes and all.

We spent the remaining days exploring Frankfurt. Fred checked out graveyards wherever we went because he liked the sense of history each one revealed. This one contained people who had died during WWII.

We took a ride down the Danube and marveled at the city's restoration. One could only marvel at the industriousness of the Germans. The city was neat and clean with no signs of any destruction from WWII.

When Fred returned from paying the hotel bill, he remarked, "The bill included a phone call for $225. What was that for?"

I couldn't believe that my thirty-minute call to Linda would cost that much. "Fred, I carefully read the phone information on calls from the room. It said there was no extra charge for long-distance calls."

In his typical unflappable manner he said, "Well, you didn't read the part in German stating their policy for additional charges for international calls."

I was truly upset. "How on earth could they expect me to read German! That information should have been in English too!"

"Not to worry. It's only money. But I'm going to have fun telling Linda when we see her tomorrow at the airport, 'Do you know how much your mother loves you?'"

Remembering to confirm our airline reservation a day early, we were at the station well before our 8:30 a.m. departure. The station was extremely crowded with long lines everywhere and soldiers patrolling with their Uzis, which had become quite common. I had frankly gotten used to seeing soldiers in UK airports and around government buildings in Italy.

The lines were so long that we could not make it to the counter to get our boarding pass before departure time. I was furious! So were other passengers. We were hurried to the departure gate without boarding passes, again finding ourselves in the middle of the long line of unhappy passengers. I was endlessly complaining, talking with other passengers, getting more fired up. We were there two hours early and now the plane was three hours late. I had had it!! Fred was trying unsuccessfully to calm me down. Suddenly we heard our names being announced on the loud speaker. We shoved our way through the crowd to get to the gate where officials asked us why we were so late responding. Apparently, they had been calling our names for some time. But that still didn't pacify me. Even when we got to our seats, I was still spitting feathers.

Fred finally said, "Shirley, what are you holding in your hand?"

"A glass. Why do you ask?"

"What's in your glass?" He asked.

Lifting it to my mouth to taste, I said, "Why, I think it's a mimosa."

"Now, look out the window. Where are we?"

"Why, we're on the tarmac."

"Now what did you say was in your hand?"

"Oh, my God, you mean we're in First Class?!?"

"Yes! So shut the fuck up," he said with twinkling eyes and an insouciant smile as he offered me a toast with his glass held high. "Bon Voyage!"

And thus, while dining on lobster and steak, we had a smooth, elegant flight back to Minnesota.

Chapter Eleven
Trouble on the Home Front
1986

LINDA'S FACE BURST INTO crinkled eyes and a great smile as she spied us at the luggage carousel. We met in a great group hug before taking off for her car. Right away Fred was letting Linda know how much I loved her through the pricey phone charge and we all had a great laugh about that. After getting us in the house, Fred said he had to get going. So I gave my Ulysses a big kiss and hug as he climbed in his jeep, and waving back to me, he drove off.

Once Linda and I were alone, I could see that Linda wasn't her usual self. "It's Steve, Mom. Something has happened to him."

"What do you mean?" I asked. She had been dating Steve for a year or so. They worked together at the State Employment Service. Although he had become an important part of her life, I had suspected she didn't see him as suitable marriage material. He had seemed a bit rough around the edges to me, but he had that same ribald sense of humor as Fred. In fact, the four of us had gone boating together on the St. Croix River once or twice.

"Since an old buddy of his started working with us, his sense of humor has become more crude, even hurtful to people at work." She picked up Jasper and pulled him close to her chest. "It just hasn't been fun at work for a long time. Our coworkers even try to avoid him."

"Is he aware of all this?"

"Oh, Mom, we've had many arguments about it. So many that he's now pretty much giving me the same treatment at work."

"What about your bosses? Doesn't anyone complain to them?"

Linda then sat on the kitchen stool and, with tears streaming down her cheeks, related to me that everyone at work, including her boss, was afraid of Steve. In fact, she learned that he was doing cocaine with his buddy Jake. The more she implored him to stop seeing Jake and using drugs, the more controlling he became of her. Finally, she said that when she tried to break up with him, he just went crazy and began calling up several of her closest friends, threatening them or telling them lies about her. It sounded to me like he was trying to isolate her from her sources of support.

I reached over and grabbed her hand. "Well, Linda, this is astonishing to me. I didn't see him as husband material, but I certainly didn't see him as any threat."

"What's more, Mom, he calls me *all* the time. The more I hang up on him or don't answer, the more he calls. Sometimes I just leave the phone off the hook. He's scary, Mom. The whole atmosphere of the office has changed. Everyone is cautious around him, even the supervisors."

I didn't really know what to do to help Linda. I even sought advice from a colleague at work. Then, a few weeks later, Fred called. Steve had contacted his wife, telling her about me and Fred's other life. My heart sank. I felt sick to my stomach. Even though Fred's voice was controlled and he showed no emotion, I hoped beyond hope that Fred could see this wasn't my fault.

Linda and I were stunned and shamed that we knew a person who would commit such an immoral act against someone who had done him no harm. There was nothing we could do for Fred other than pray he would forgive us, while doing what we could to rid ourselves permanently of Steve. Linda and I were both aware that my relationship with Fred might be over. Linda felt badly, that had she been more forceful with Steve, the incident might not have occurred.

I assured her, "Linda, I knew from the beginning that if Fred were in a position where he might have to choose between Sonia or me, his choice would be Sonia. I understood and I accepted his terms. I will honor his choice. What you and I have to do is decide how to handle Steve. You have to get him out of your life, no matter what Fred decides to do."

"What can we do? He's making my work life hell. He insults me and calls me names in front of the staff. They're all scared shitless of him. I don't see how I can continue to work there."

"Exactly. Your safety depends upon you being elsewhere. He has to give up on calling here countless times a day and threatening you." I suggested to Linda that now would be a good time for her to finish college. She had started at the University of Minnesota when she was fresh out of high school, but it was too big for her, so after her first year there she dropped out. I encouraged her to look at some of the small private colleges and enroll in one in the fall.

We also made a plan for her to visit her friend Tony in Ontario for a week to get away from Steve. "That's a great idea," Linda said. "And how about adding a second week visiting Sheila in Florida? That would really have him confused."

I agreed that being elsewhere for at least two weeks would be great. These were two good friends who would enjoy her company. She would be back in time to start college. For the first time in weeks, Linda began to look hopeful.

But then she said she was worried about me. "He's just so unpredictable, Mom. What if he comes over here? What if he gets violent? What if…?" She began to cry. To be honest, I had wondered the same thing.

It just so happened that a coworker of mine, Joe, needed a place to stay while he was getting a divorce. After I told him the situation and suggested he stay in the basement bedroom for a while, he was happy to offer Linda and I some protection.

Linda was enthusiastic about the plan. "It'll take me a while to decide on a college and let my boss know, then call my friends."

Things were getting so heated up with Steve that I told Linda not to answer the phone when he called. We also implemented a plan for our safety. We began taking different routes to work each day. Then Linda learned that Steve's buddy Jake had been in prison for blowing up his girlfriend's car when she tried to start it. So we even began checking under our cars before getting in.

Two weeks later, I heard from Fred; he said he would see me at the state principals' convention. I was so excited to hear from him, but I didn't know what to expect. I prepared myself for a good-bye scene.

As he approached me at the convention, my heart was pounding hard against my ribs. *Here we go,* I thought. I felt awkward greeting him, not knowing what to expect. We gave each other a European kiss on the cheek and he seemed like his usual mellow, unflappable self. "Shall we go to your room?" he said with a warm smile.

I thought maybe he wanted to break up with me privately, which would make sense. Even his calm demeanor didn't break my concern. But when we got to the room, he handed me a valentine card with a comic message. Then he graciously absolved me of all blame for the serious troubles he was now experiencing in his marriage.

"Sonia chose not to tell me specifics about Steve's conversation, but she was angry and felt humiliated." He sat down in the chair and leaned forward as he spoke, slowly rubbing his open palms together as he spoke. "I don't blame her. She has every right to feel injured. I have great compassion for her feelings. A code between us to do nothing indiscreet that would embarrass the other has been broken." He leaned back in the chair. "I know our marriage will not be the same and might not survive this assault."

I listened carefully and didn't ask questions. He said he wouldn't get into specifics with Sonia about us nor was he willing or able to change from the person he had been for fifty-six years. "Our marriage has been based, in part, on not knowing certain things about one another's lives when apart from one another. Now some facts are known. The marriage could endure when we each chose to remain ignorant about certain facts. But now that's not possible. This event is forcing us, particularly Sonia, to rethink the basis upon which our marriage had been consummated."

He gallantly said their problems did not concern Linda or me but were strictly matters the two of them had to work out. He let me know he planned to continue our relationship as long as I wanted it.

If anything, I was even more in love with this man. Our eight-year relationship was even stronger than I had imagined. I had braced myself to let him go and wish him well.

I had the feeling he did not relish the end of a relationship he valued, nor did he relish the continuing deception necessary to maintain his marriage. I'd suspected from the beginning that choosing to have two lives must have been an emotional burden on Fred, which he chose to skillfully conceal. It was why I seldom mentioned Sonia, and had been supportive of him spending time with her.

I was relieved that Sonia later decided to continue the marriage. My occasional man was the perfect situation for me.

Several weeks later Steve was out of our lives and Fred was back in. Even better, Linda was enrolled at Hamline University, ready to finish work on her degree. We never saw Steve again.

We had much to feel thankful for at Christmas. Linda had a successful first semester at Hamline, her friend Tony flew down from Ontario to spend the week of Christmas with us, and even Fred managed to join us for much of our festivities. He and I then took off for St. John's Island to spend two weeks at Cinnamon Bay, a place our friends, Don and Barbara Challman had recommended.

They told us it was beautiful but rustic. "Your plane won't get you there until midnight or later so you will need to have a flashlight handy and the makings of a ready meal," Don said. "The place has a store that sells some basic food items but it'll be closed. There will be someone at the desk who probably doesn't speak English to greet late guests." He must've seen the doubt on my face because he added, "But it will be worth it. Believe me!"

And so it seemed like a good idea at the time, away from a too-long winter, living on the beautiful bay on St. John's Island in the Virgin Islands.

Don was right. We arrived at the dark of night and there were no lights to guide us to the office. A young lady who spoke little English provided us with a carrier for our luggage, handed us some sheets and towels, and told us to pick up our other supplies in the morning.

We ventured out onto a twisting path to find our tent. Fred led the way pulling the luggage cart behind him. I was behind the luggage cart, holding on for dear life and wondering why we hadn't unpacked the flashlight before now. It was so dark I couldn't see my hand in front of my face. "My God, Fred, can you see where we're going?" The luggage started to fall off the rack as it bounced down the path and we stumbled around trying to get it back on.

Fred somehow found the campsite, but we couldn't see into the darkness at all. "Crawl woman! The tent has to be here somewhere!"

On hands and knees, I felt around for anything that resembled a tent. The rocky terrain dug into my palms and knees. "I wanna know, Fred," I whispered in a husky voice. "Are we having fun?" Finally, I made contact with a wooden platform. On top of that platform was our tent.

"Atta girl." Fred whispered back, "*Voila!* We have light! This looks like an empty tent. It must be ours." We somehow managed to get the thin sheets we were provided on two of the army cots. Too tired to do more, we each fell onto a cot and agreed to case the joint in the morning.

By daylight we examined our tent—basic and primitive—set on a wooden platform containing four army cots with aging springs, one on each side and two cots across the back. A wooden picnic table with attached benches on each side completed our furnishings. The attached outdoor light didn't work and the stove had no gas.

Shirley in front of the tent at Cinnamon Bay

Ever-resourceful, Fred found a propane gas tank and a light at a nearby vacant tent and brought them back to our tent.

We were given some basic pans and dishes. That was it. No chairs, no backs to the benches, no other amenities. The washhouse was about a half block away, which provided us with two outdoor showers. Cold water only.

But the spectacular beach was a few steps away. We found ourselves surrounded by sugary sand and very tropical-looking bushes. I could tell it would take some time for me to adjust to our Y-Camp environment—the massive sun, the heat, and oh yes, the donkeys that freely roamed the island. It seemed they were a protected species.

Fred adapted more quickly, learning how to beg certain items from departing neighbors like a three-legged beach chair. "Just lean it up against the table and it'll work perfectly," Fred declared. "Look what else I found." He held up two plastic bottles. "Here's some mustard and still lots of ketchup in this bottle. There's more where this came from." Then he dashed off like a little boy on another hunting expedition.

We saved items like glass salsa jars to use for cocktail glasses. Our supply of packaged pasta (just add water) and tins of tuna and peas became the main course for many a meal.

The lush tropical growth and sandy beaches with the beautiful clean turquoise Caribbean ocean right outside our door made up for the other inconveniences. Eucalyptus trees and berry-laden bushes surrounded our tent. The orchestral sounds of birds could be heard day and night. The beaches were refreshingly clean—no rubbish from cruise ships found on its shores such as we had seen in the Yucatan. No vendors selling junk. Only the occupants of the Cinnamon Bay Camp who were largely Yanks, families, older couples—all much like us. The atmosphere was that of a summer resort—a frugal man's summer resort.

We took a taxi downtown. The taxis, open on the sides, held about twelve people seated on benches on either side. We hopped on, just like we were getting on a bus. As I sat on the bench, looking out at the passing landscapes, I gripped Fred's hand and said, "This is a view not to be missed—what a great way to travel." Although the roads were well-maintained, they were winding and steep and we got our first good look at downtown Cruz Bay.

The colorful little shops were wide open, some on all sides. Throngs of people sipped drinks at countless makeshift outdoor cafes. Men dressed in bright colors wearing funky hats strode about on top of stilts, adding to the carnival atmosphere. Music could be heard everywhere. The tiny little town faced the docks and ocean with unnamed streets that went up and down very steep hills.

It became challenging to walk in the blazing heat, which got to Fred, causing us to cut our downtown visit short. We took enough time to pick up steaks and wine for dinner. Then we caught another taxi home where we hit the beach for a great swim. That afternoon we explored several historic sites at Maho Bay.

Fred continued to have difficulty handling the heat. I found myself feeling older, more passive and slower to adapt to change. This was strange because on former trips, I had thrived on the challenge of adapting to unusual situations. Now I found myself wishing for more amenities and found "the thrill to rough it" – in a dirty, sandy tent in airless heat, while trying to cook in the dark with limited resources – gone. Spending two weeks here would be a test of endurance – not a balmy joyful holiday. With the blazing hot heat and the absence of tall shade trees, I thought *Give me wintry Minnesota any day!*

Hot afternoons were siesta time. Fred would sleep away in our hot tent. He seemed readily adaptable to any situation. If things weren't to his expectation, he would just figure out how to make it work for him – not necessarily us – but him. This did not surprise me. He wasn't used to including others in his decision-making. From stories he shared with me about his life, I was aware that he had become used to traveling alone, keeping his own counsel. It had become second nature to him – in fact part of being an independent person. In making travel plans, for instance, he would have details down before bringing them up for discussion. And with my habit of "letting the universe" make decisions for me, I didn't mind. Several of my girlfriends agreed that one of my endearing traits they most liked was my obedience. This was their teasing way of describing my comfort with letting others make decisions for me on stuff of little interest to me. No one could accuse me of being a backseat driver. He who does the driving makes the decisions on how to get there (unless he asks for help).

About this time, I noticed a slight tremor in Fred's right hand and asked him about it.

"Oh, that. It's just a familial tremor. My Dad had it. No big deal."

"Have you had it long? I've noticed it for a while." He then showed me the palm of his right hand, where he had surgery done to loosen the palm muscles that had stretched so tight they had curled up some of his fingers. He said he'd had it done several times in past summers. His palm looked okay now. But I was thinking that this trip might prove more insightful because, for us, it was not idyllic like our other trips had been. *It will call forth inner strengths and resolves,* I thought.

We began to fall into a rhythm with our days. After siesta, we moved off to the beach with two chairs, the three-legged one and a four-legged one that we had found. There we enjoyed snorkeling and reading for hours. We returned to the beach again after a shower to watch the amazing sunset dominate the sky with its rays spreading out from both sides, deep red in the center, turning differing shades of orange as it spread upwards. It held us spellbound, waiting in hushed voices for the oranges and pinks to slither away and the red ball to begin its drop down to the horizon, gradually slipping further and further down until it was suddenly gone, leaving us in darkness.

This beach life was what made this place famous and kept the campers coming back year after year. We ran into one group who called themselves "The Hartford Contingent," who'd been going there for twenty-five years!

"I must say, Fred, I'm getting into the swing of primitive camping. We now have chairs aplenty. This one with four legs I shall call 'the Rockefeller Chair'—the best one." I named it for the Rockefeller who owned much of the island.

As the days went on, even the cool showers in the open air began to feel refreshing, especially when I could look up at the blue skies above. The shower would stay on as long as the chain was pulled. I could hear Fred on his side saying, "Ideal living conditions!"

We were also learning ways to keep the tent relatively clean and free of sand, and the donkeys were not outwitting us so much now. We had begun packing food in a duffle and keeping the darn tent flaps closed tight. The downside was it kept the tent hotter than Hades.

One day, during a siesta, while Fred slept in the tent, I heard a disconcerting noise. Looking up from my reading, I saw two donkeys at the open tent door, one trying to nose up the latch on the chiller. My yelling scattered them away. A plucky lot—these donkeys.

Fred and I began to feel truly comfortable snorkeling among the coral reefs and underwater sea life. Fred could dive down to get a better look, while I felt safer staying on the surface observing all the brilliantly colored fish swishing about us. The sun from above showcased their vivid hues of yellows, reds, purples. Some fish were translucent. They surrounded us as they swerved in and out of the equally colorful corals. I saw one stingray so large it frightened me away.

One day we took off snorkeling to a little island a ways from shore. In following Fred, I noticed the constant tremor in his right hand as he paddled at a comfortable pace.

Fred preparing to go snorkling

As he turned to begin circling the island, I started to get a bit apprehensive at the different feel of the water, wondering if it was the depth that was making it harder to navigate. It felt like rowing against the tide, making it necessary for me to kick my feet even harder. When we began circling around the back of the island I felt a tidal pull that I feared might whisk me out to sea. When I raised my head up, some water got in my snorkel, making it impossible for me to breathe. My feet started to sink and I started to panic. I flailed about as I tried unsuccessfully to blow water out of the snorkel while preventing myself from being sucked into the tide. *Where is Fred? Am I still near the island?* I wanted to scream but the water in my snorkel prevented me from doing anything.

Suddenly Fred snorkeled up next to me, raised his head, and said, "Just stand up. You're over lots of rocks and coral."

As my feet touched the bottom, I found I could practically walk between the rocks to the other side of the island. I felt completely foolish, until Fred started laughing while assuring me it was allowable.

This wasn't the first time Fred popped up out of nowhere when I suddenly felt anxious or out of breath or feared I was far away from others while snorkeling. I started calling him my Superman, coming to my aide.

One day we sailed the shores of this picturesque island with Captain Wit and his crew of one, Jay, who serenaded us with songs and guitar music. The trip included snorkeling off the boat. My swimming skills improved as I snorkeled because of the deeper water, and I felt secure as long as Fred was my guide.

During our stay, Mike and Sheila Gore, our friends from Chester, England, were scheduled to dock from their cruise boat at Cruz Bay for a brief outing one day. We took them to our Rockefeller Suite, offering them gin and tonics in our salsa jars. They sat in our best stolen chairs, including the Rockefeller chair.

Drinking from salsa glasses with Mike and Sheila

After changing into bathing suits, we raced to the beach where Mike received his first snorkeling lesson from Fred, and Sheila and I gossiped while doing water aerobics. We sauntered to the beach house. Because Sheila was too short to pull the chain that made the cold water flow, I joined her in our shower. We listened to the gents laughing in the other shower while they told tall tales that we felt needed some correction from us.

Acting like a bunch of teenagers, we linked our arms together, singing as we left our luxurious open-air cold-water showers. We took a taxi back to town and reluctantly bid Sheila and Mike a fond farewell as they sailed off into the sunset. They later wrote us that their visit at our Rockefeller Suite was the most fun of their three-week cruise.

One night, in the pitch dark, I awoke to the sound of rustling around inside the tent. I wondered if Fred had gotten up. When my brain woke up enough and my eyes adjusted to the slight movement, I realized that there was a donkey inside the tent searching for bread. I screamed at the beast of burden, but he was stubborn as a mule. I jumped out of bed to slap him on the rear, but he turned around and jumped out before I had the chance.

"What...?" Fred was now awake.

That was our last night in Shangri-la.

Chapter Twelve
Murder and Mayhem at Pearl Mansion
1987

WITH THE ELEGANT QUEEN Anne furniture that now populated my now-beautiful home, I decided it was time to show it off. I decided to host a Murder Dinner set in an English Manor in the dreary month of March. At a special needs organization fundraiser I had bid on and won a Murder Dinner Kit for eight, complete with script, characters, and invitations set in England in the 1880s, as well as help from the organization's staff. My newly furnished home was an ideal setting.

Invitations were sent to seven of my lady friends—half of us playing male roles. All accepted, eager to outdo one another in costumes. I met with the staff and planned to have a very English dinner to be prepared in my Queen Anne kitchen and pantry.

The staff all wore white tops and black skirts or pants. Different wines were served with each course beginning with cocktails in the living room as guests arrived, eager to assume their new identities.

I was the Lord of the Manor who flirted with various ladies such as Tib, the mysterious lady in black. Sandy looked very haughty, dressed in her husband's tuxedo. Clem played the Ms. Marple role. But by the time we were arriving at the solution of the murder in the drawing room by the fire, drinking our brandies, none of us were too clear on just exactly who did murder me. Aunt Edna's fine furniture certainly contributed to the ambiance of the evening.

Not long after that, I received a call from my British friends, Sheila and Mike, saying they were planning another trip across the pond in the summer. My committee of friends were again called into service and we planned gala events for each day they would be staying at my home.

My big event was an English croquet party. My new friend Judith loved to plan parties. She designed the invitations sent to neighbors:

SUMMERTIME –IT IS TIME TO PARTY!

at

THE ALL CROCUS HILL LAWN AND CROQUET PARTY

IN HONOR OF BRITISH VISITORS

ATTIRE: DRESS IN WHITE CLOTHING, PLEASE

HATS FOR LADIES

Sandy, who threw parties at her home practically monthly and Clem, who kept us focused and on task, helped with food, centerpieces, and cucumber sandwiches. Fred "supervised" by frequently saying, "I wouldn't do it that way."

All who were invited came dressed in white, congregating in the backyard among the linen-covered tables placed around the strange little croquet court. One of our English guests supervised the game, playing by the Queen's rules. Gin and tonic and the cucumber sandwiches were provided.

Starting out with sixteen players, those of us among the defeated would cheer on the eventual winners saying, "good shot, that," or "pity" to the losers.

All took their heaped dinner plates to a table of their choice while an abundance of wine was served, honoring distinguished Brits as well as us Yanks. My committee of women again helped plan social events during future summer visits, resulting in us experiencing many cross-Atlantic trips over the years.

Several couples who had stayed with me on summer visits also met my neighbors. Our homes and backyards were so close together that it seemed natural over the years to invite one another over for a drink or barbecue.

Whenever Fred's car was spotted in front of my home, invitations for dinner or drinks would often occur. My circle of close women friends knew when he was expected, resulting in more invitations coming our way. My women friends found Fred witty, charming, and a wee bit naughty. Several thought he looked and acted a bit like Jack Nicholson. Single and married girlfriends alike rather envied my life with "the occasional man" who showed up with great frequency and whisked me off to exciting and romantic places. The neighbor guys liked coming over for gin and cigars on the backyard patio – taking turns telling lies and tall stories.

Fred was a favorite with the young couple on our west side. Todd had lost his father several years earlier and really took to Fred, almost as a replacement. His wife, Laurel, enjoyed jesting with us mornings when she'd spy us eating breakfast on the patio, clad in our white terrycloth robes as she was climbing in her car to go to work. Fred enjoyed teasing their youngest child, Marta, who liked visiting with him.

Ed, the young professor on our other side, also became close friends with Fred, frequently coming over for a beer with him. If I had social plans with friends at night, Fred would invite Ed over for a spaghetti dinner and guy talk. Both were psychology professors and had much in common. Fred was particularly fond of Ed.

Looking back on when our relationship started, I don't recall how many others were aware of Fred's marital status. I had only mentioned it to Sandy and Clem at the time because they were my closest friends who knew how to keep confidences. It was not a problem for my daughter who was equally discrete. Fred was such an outgoing, fun-loving guy, and he was also such a good listener, that people just enjoyed being around him. He had a gift at making others feel comfortable.

I don't think any of my other friends and neighbors knew the nature of our relationship. I certainly didn't mention it and few inquired. But I suspected that Clem and Sandy secretly admired the way Fred could successfully live two lives.

I used to tease him when we were alone, saying, "Fred, you should write a book about how to do it! You seem to have a satisfied life with Sonia and your son, and you certainly have one with me." He just kind of modestly shrugged his shoulders. I continued, "Your wife doesn't know me. I know nothing about her other than she exists. You and I travel all over the world together, yet you leave no paper trails nor have I heard you call her for me to overhear. You have the talents to keep each life separate from the other." He even managed to treat both of us with dignity, respect, and a ribald sense of humor. "How do you do it? Other men want to know!"

Shaking his head no, he'd just laughingly say, "I know nothing! Da nada!" Then he'd cup his hand over his ear and say, "I think I hear my mother calling!"

It was almost the Fourth of July when Fred took the mast off his sunfish sailing boat, attached the boat to his jeep, then picked me up. We were off for an outing on our own Mississippi River. Tossing our camping gear in the boat, we set off to find an island we could make our own for a night or two.

And find an island we did—our very own island. We set up our tiny tent, got out our trusty sleeping bags and, using our fanny packs for pillows, settled down to enjoy some reading. It was a beautiful day, sunny, with the tips of leaves turning yellow or red, letting us know fall was on the way.

Occasionally a motorboat would zoom by. We even took a quick swim before resuming reading. A gentle breeze felt good against my damp body. My book fell from my hand as I fell asleep. It was so peaceful.

By the time I woke up, Fred was already sipping a gin and tonic when I looked over to see him propped up by a tree. Dusk was on the way in. "Thought you'd never wake up," he said. He had gotten out the cooking equipment in preparation for supper. Fred always, without exception, did the cooking whenever we tented. The food wasn't too good, but then, it wasn't too bad either. He handed me a drink as I got up to stretch and looked around the place.

"Our own private island—this is so nice," I said. "Why, you don't have to go to far-away places to have a unique travel adventure. This is truly romantic. Just you and me on our own funky island."

We fashioned a table of sorts, opened up a bottle of wine, and dined by candlelight as Fred stuck a slightly used candle in an empty wine bottle. Absent the sound of music, we listened to the sounds of the woods as insects began croaking and an occasional boat or tugboat chugged by.

As it got pitch dark, Fred got out his lantern for more light and we crawled into our tent, dragging our bedrolls and mattresses with us. We lay down, peeking out the front of our tent at the mighty Miss flowing by when suddenly

Camping on the Mississippi

Fred spied what looked like a huge house all lit up flowing towards us. "Why, it's the Mississippi Queen," I yelled. "Isn't it beautiful at night?"

"It is, indeed," agreed Fred.

The boat's paddlewheel gently churned water behind it and we watched the lights twinkle on the flowing Mississippi. Voices rose up across the water like a soft hum as people enjoyed their night on the beautiful river queen. We quietly watched it wend past us and disappear upstream.

Eventually we fell into a sound, restful sleep.

Sometime in the middle of the night a violent wind pounded against our tent, awakening us both. "What the hell!" Fred cried out. He stuck his head out the flap to see what was happening; he quickly ducked his head back in our tent. "A storm is moving in!"

The rain started quickly, coming down fiercely and demanding, pelting our small tent. It sounded like we were being shot at with machine-gun fire with its rat-a-tat-tat rapidity. We hoped our weight would keep the tent from being blown away by the fierce wind.

"Are we having fun?!?" I teased Fred over the pounding wind and rain.

"You've got to admit," Fred yelled back over the din of the rain. "We have a bird's-eye view of a violent storm!" We hunkered down, preparing ourselves for a long night.

By morning the rain had stopped. We crawled out onto the soggy, muddy terrain. Fred got the coffee going on the cook stove. Shortly, bacon and eggs were sizzling in the frying pan. I got out the paper plates, silverware, and mugs, setting them on a tree stump. The sun actually came out, warming us as we sipped our hot coffee.

"You do good work, Fred." I handed him some bacon on a paper plate, then walked towards our boat. It was filled with water.

It took the two of us to tip the boat.

Eventually, we were on our way back north. Our little boat sped through the water, making good time as we approached an open lock. We sped in. A man high above me threw a rope down for me to grab. When I grabbed it, he let go.

The rope jerked me so hard, it lifted me up, and the back end of the boat began spinning from one side to another. The jerking of the rope caused me to let go before my arm was pulled out of its socket. I was aware of a lot of yelling as Fred and the man above me were yelling at me, and the pilot of another boat beginning to enter the lock shouted, "I'm backing up. She's lost control of the boat!"

Fred maneuvered us again in position for me to grab the rope as the man lowered it down yelling, "Wrap it around the winch, pull it towards you, then cleat it off!"

That made sense. Why couldn't I have figured that out myself?

"Atta girl, now you've got it," Fred cried out as the doors closed and the water began filling up.

Soon we were happily on our way to the next lock, but then Fred pointed to the northwest. "Doesn't the sky look ominous over there?"

Oh no. With the way my arms felt after maneuvering through the locks, I didn't know if I had the energy for another storm!

"Hopefully we can make it through the next lock before it hits, but it does seem to be moving fast."

And within minutes rain was pounding around us. We could see the lock up ahead. Lightning shot across the sky like fireworks. I ducked my head from the pelting rain in an attempt to see better. Suddenly a loud crackling noise accompanied a huge jagged strip of lightning that hit the locks and all the lights went out.

"Fred, what's happening?"

"I think it just knocked out the electrical system! We have to get this boat to shore quick!" He roared the motor and headed straight for shore. Rain was pelting us, practically blinding us, as we both jumped out of the boat and began dragging it on shore, pulling it towards a garage. It was so heavy; we realized it was full of water. We turned it over, lightning flashing around us. It just didn't feel safe. We worked quickly together, eager to get out of the dangerous storm and into a dry place.

"Across the road," Fred yelled. "Looks like a place to stay!"

We ran to the house. It was a B&B. We stood at the door, pounding frantically, hoping the host would be there.

A quiet-looking man, dressed in khaki pants and a tan sweatshirt answered the door. He gasped when he saw these two drenched people. We must have looked like survivors from the *Titanic*.

"Do you have a room?" Fred asked. "Lightning knocked out the power on the lock. We had to get off the river. Our boat is across the road."

A smile crossed the gentleman's face as he beckoned us in. He must have been about our age. He introduced himself as Abe and told us we were in Alma, Wisconsin. "Just wait here until I get the missus to take you to the room." We were dripping on his hardwood floors, so he gave us both towels to dry off.

I was shivering in my wet clothes. "Oh, thank you so much. The sun was shining when we started out this morning," I said.

When we saw our room, it looked like a gift from the Universe. We thanked Abe's wife and then dashed for the warmth of a shower. We hung our clothes to dry, we read a bit, took a brief nap, then went to a nearby café recommended by Abe.

Gratefully, the rain had ended. We strolled down the main street with shops on one side and the Mississippi River on the other. It looked like the lock still wasn't operating

The town was festive, its handful of shops and taverns preparing for the Fourth of July celebration the next day. The excitement of folks, young and old, bustling about its few places of business, was contagious.

After a good night's sleep, we greeted Abe and his wife for

coffee and biscuits for breakfast. We were informed the lock should be ready for business by early afternoon.

Upon returning to St. Paul, we learned that significant numbers of buildings were damaged in Roseville, Minnesota by severe straight-line winds during our last night in Alma. Those winds gave us a night we would not forget.

Chapter Thirteen

Busy Years

1988-1991

I SPENT THE SUMMER of '88 supervising the building of a two-story addition on the back of my house. Linda was spending her "J" month in New Zealand with a class of Hamline students. Fred did something he had "always wanted to do" — hike the Himalayas with a group of experienced Sierra hikers. I desperately wanted to join him, I had even been the one to think of the plans, but Fred said that he would need all his energies to keep himself healthy for such a demanding trip. He had even prepared for the month-long expedition by spending several weeks in Colorado hiking different elevations of mountains while wearing a weighted backpack.

I was feeling sorry for myself that while others were having exotic experiences I was living with no back on my house and the constant noise of bobcats and construction crews loudly at work. Add to that that it was about a thousand degrees in the shade and I began to look like the disheveled Doris Day in *Please Don't Eat the Daisies*.

But one day Fred called me from New Delhi, suggesting I meet him at Steamboat Springs, Colorado at the condo he had leased. *Finally!* I thought. *A break from the constant noise and heat!* I gladly flew to Colorado to see my Fred.

The Denver airport was packed with people. I hadn't realized that the Pope was to speak in Denver. I managed to make my way through the sea of Pilgrims and onto the connecting flight. I felt relief when I finally buckled myself into my seat on the commuter plane.

Turbulence bounced the small plane so much that flight attendants had to cancel the refreshment portion of our flight. Fortunately, the sea of gold of the birches below was so dazzling that I could think of nothing else but Colorado's amazing beauty.

I stood at the door of Fred's condo, groceries at my feet as I tried to fit the key in the lock. I heard someone call my name. I looked down the hall to see Fred running toward me, duffels draped over his shoulders. A huge smile crossed his face.

"What timing!" I joyfully exclaimed as I ran into his arms. He clutched me tightly, lifting me off the floor. My arms wrapped all the way around him and I could feel his ribs through his clothing. I pulled away to look at him. "What happened to you? You're so thin!"

He laughed and explained that he had lost probably twenty pounds or more drinking contaminated water and eating food with dozens of flies lighting on it. In fact, he said the leader got quite sick by the end of the trip, as did several of the other hikers. Now I didn't feel so bad that he wouldn't let me join them. Nonetheless, he loved the trip and had many tales to tell.

Several months after we returned, Fred called to tell me that Sonia had begun a long recovery from two serious heart operations. The surgeries were a continuation of the heart problems she had had for over nine years.

The Graduate

The Pearl Manor, complete with its new addition upstairs and downstairs, filled up with visitors all to help Linda celebrate her graduation from Hamline University. She had graduated summa cum laude and learned the secret handshake of Phi Beta Kappa.

I found the perfect gift to give my tennis-loving graduate. A trip to attend a Grand Slam Match at Wimbledon, England. "Why don't we make a grand tour of it while we're at it, like a couple of swells!" I said to an enthusiastic Linda. "I think we should start on the Costa del Sol to warm our buns. Fred and I had such a grand time there. And then off to probably not-so-sunny England to visit the Gores and the Jenkinses in Cheshire and Mold."

For once, *I* planned a trip! I told Linda we could take a train from Cheshire to London and stay there while we took in Wimbledon. "I'd like to take you to Copenhagen where my college roommate and her husband live. They invited me while I was at the Coe College Class reunion last month. I've never been there and that should be fun."

We had a grand time at various friends' homes where we were treated like celebrities, then saw real celebrities and royalty at Wimbledon. Johnny Carson sat in our row and the Royal Box held both Princesses Diana and Fergie.

Gerda and Jorgen treated us to a weekend at their cabin on the Danish shore as well as a jazz festival on the streets of Copenhagen. They put us on the overland train to Oslo. We found a charming small hotel there with an outdoor garden. Several handsome Norwegian young men in Oslo took a fancy to Linda, wanting to show her the sights, particularly when they found out she was an American and didn't know a word of Norwegian.

Each place had its special charm. Feeling very "worldly," we took the train back to Copenhagen and flew back home from its international airport, bringing back many Danish goodies from its shops.

Fred greeted us at the Twin Cities airport with his arms outstretched, saying, "Welcome home world travelers!" We had a wonderful trip, yet it was good to be back home.

While we had been on our whirlwind tour of Europe, Fred had spent several weeks with Tom in Alaska. They took off from Boulder in Tom's plane. At times they would find themselves forced to land anyplace they could find a suitable spot due to fog. On such occasions they would sleep in their sleeping bags under the plane's wings, sometimes socked in for several days until the fog lifted. Such were their adventures.

Clem and Tib were anxious to hear about our trip, and to see the new addition to the house, so they came over for tea. It was good to see them. They, too, had been doing much traveling together.

Tib was seeing a guy named Paul and the relationship was having its ups and downs. She wanted to know more about how Fred and I managed our lives. "I just can't stand it when I know he is with Ellen.

He used to date her and they continue to have tickets together," Tib said in an upset voice.

"What do you mean 'have tickets together'?" I asked.

"Well, they bought concert tickets together. *And* we all go to the same church. So I'm lucky if I get one night with him. It's driving me crazy."

"I don't know what to tell you, Tib. It just hasn't been much of a problem for me." I refilled my cup with tea and offered Tib and Clem more. As I poured their refills I said, "It took a little getting used to each other our first couple years, but that was mainly because I'd find myself sitting by the phone, waiting for a call, feeling like a damned fool. It kept me from making dates with you all. If I did, and then he'd call for a night I had plans with any of you, I'd have to call and cancel. Some of my friends let me know they didn't like that. Even when I'd give my expensive ticket for a concert or play to them to give to someone else, it was just uncomfortable."

I picked up my tea and blew cool air across the top. Steam rose above the rim and dissipated into the air. "But eventually Fred understood. He sincerely apologized, then said he'd call me twice a week and for me not to hang around waiting. He would just keep calling until he got me. Then I got call waiting for my phone and that helped a lot."

Tib listened closely as I thought back on that time with Fred. I always appreciated how honest he was with me. "Fred finally convinced me that he did not expect me to break any other commitments if he came to see me when I had plans. He'd just enjoy being at my place and could amuse himself until I got home. And you know, that's worked pretty well. It's like I needed him to give me the freedom I had given him." I took a bite of a scone. "He likes that I have a busy life. In fact, he often says, with great pride in his voice, 'you don't need me. You don't need any man.'"

Clem took a scone from the plate and said, "You've got a real winner there, Shirley. That's the kind of relationship I would like."

"I just want a guy of my own," Tib said. "I can't stand feeling jealous or suspicious or upset when he cancels out or doesn't come on our night. It just makes me feel used. And I'm afraid I might run into them when he is with her."

I could certainly understand her situation. "I frankly don't think about Fred when he isn't here because he lives in a different town. I would certainly not like seeing him with his wife. But that isn't about to happen. What does happen is that when he is with me, he is definitely with me." I felt my heart swell for Fred. "My occasional man makes an occasion of each visit. And quite frankly, I don't want 'a man of my own.' It's too much responsibility and I like my freedom."

"Oh, I agree," said Clem. "At my age, I like deciding what I want to do without getting permission from a husband to take a trip or go out with a girlfriend or see a 'chick flick' at the local theatre. But an occasional man would be nice. *That* I would like."

Tib wasn't convinced. I knew that my relationship with Fred wasn't for everyone, but I was very happy to have my occasional man.

Linda was feeling restless. The absence of school and studies in her life had left her with too much time on her hands. She knew what she *didn't* want to do. She was tired of school and didn't want to pursue a Master's Degree. But she didn't know what she *did* want to do.

To work in the field of psychology, she needed a Master's Degree. She tried working at an insurance office for a brief time but that proved heartless — telling clients with serious illnesses that their benefits were being denied.

The idea of being a travel agent appealed to her. She loved traveling and learned that such agents received many travel benefits. In fact, Clem's sister had been a travel agent for years and loved it. So Linda signed up to learn the business at a local school.

She knew I was disappointed that she didn't pursue her Master's. "I'm not Shirley Jr., Mom," Linda asserted. I guess my mom wasn't too happy with many of my decisions. But she did let me go with little discussion. Letting go was harder for me to do with my daughter. How many times had I heard Fred say to me in his own loveable way, "Shut your mouth the fuck up! She's a grown woman who can make her own decisions."

Upon completing her training as a travel agent, she accepted a position at an Edina travel agency, taking to her work like the proverbial duck to water. In time she booked a trip "down under" for the two of us to take in the Australian Grand Slam Tennis Tournament.

We landed in Cannes and spent several days there. We ended up in Melbourne melding into the fun-loving crowd of tennis aficionados watching outstanding tennis. Australia intrigued us with its beauty: lush foliage that surrounded coast cities and exotic animals and flowers abounded. Linda loved the heat, but I preferred the coolness of Wimbledon.

Upon our return, Fred was so intrigued by our tales of adventure in such a colorful and curious country that he decided we should go there the next year when we would be retired. That would give us time to plan a three-month trip to both New Zealand and Australia.

Linda was getting immediate demands for her services. "Isn't it nice to be needed?" Fred said with suspicious sincerity.

Chapter Fourteen

The Beat Goes On

1992

"I THINK I HEAR my mother calling," Fred said as he cupped his ear and walked away from the tirade I was heaping upon the woman at the Reservation Desk.

Here we were, in New Zealand for the trip of a lifetime and I had no travel clothes and no credit card. "What am I to do?" I challenged the Reservation Clerk. As my voice got louder, with a tear or two edging their way out of my eyes, she realized I was on the verge of a major meltdown.

Our plans to visit "down under" came at the beginning of our retirement. Even though I loved my work and felt that I was "at the top of my game," I knew Fred wanted to retire sooner rather than later. I didn't want to receive travel postcards from Fred from all corners of the globe and who knew who might be traveling with him! So my decision was quickly made. Good-bye professional world— hello world traveler.

"If we're going to travel that far," Fred had said, "we might as well spend three months down under. How about six weeks in New Zealand followed by six weeks in Australia?" That sounded good to me. And with Linda, we had our very own travel agent.

But before we left, I had realized that my credit card was about to expire. The new card with a new expiration date would arrive while I was on the flight to New Zealand. I made arrangements with Visa to mail the new card to our hotel at Christchurch by Priority Mail.

When we got to Christchurch I found out the card hadn't arrived yet. Nor had the clothes I inadvertently left in the closet of the Sydney Holiday Inn on our brief layover there. The Holiday Inn was going to ship the clothes to the New Zealand hotel.

That was two days before. I was patient then. Since there were no clothes and no credit card, Fred and I had decided that we may as well pick up our recreational vehicle and take a two-day trip seeing sights around the area instead of sitting at the hotel waiting for everything to arrive. "Not a problem," Fred told the desk clerk as we took off.

It had seemed like a good idea to rent such a vehicle that would be a money-saver while giving us privacy and autonomy. But the recreational vehicle was so small—it could only be described as a tent on wheels. The overhead bin was located over the front seats, providing little space for clothes and gear.

"Simple," Fred said. "We put our suitcases in the back while we're on the road, then put them in the front when we stop for the night."

Checking the cupboards I found two plates, two bowls, two glasses. It was like the Noah's Ark of kitchenware. "Where," I asked, "is the bathroom?"

"Why, that's what this yellow bucket and hose are for. No problem."

The advantage of traveling in our tent on wheels was that we were

The tent on wheels

able to interact with many locals at the trailer camps, getting the local gossip. Fred would frequently invite a couple over to join us for a drink after dinner, cautioning them to bring their own glasses.

The first night in the dark, we had a hell of a time trying to figure out how to convert the table into a bed. Of course, we had consumed a few drinks during the cocktail hour that didn't aid us in figuring out how to do it. Fred was convinced it was broken. I was sure it was not. We finally figured it out. It took longer to figure out the heat and water system. Fortunately, it carried enough water to last about three days. We didn't even know there was a heating system until almost the last day we were in our home on wheels. The yellow bucket was self-explanatory. A small drain was provided at each trailer site. Happily, the table was easy to set up on the patio, giving us more room inside. We purchased two aluminum lawn chairs to set outside with our table. "Perfect," Fred said as he sat down in one of the chairs and opened his book to read.

During our two-day excursion, we stopped near a harbor and saw loads of dolphins leaping in the water.

It was all very relaxing, but now, here I stood, yelling at this poor woman at the front desk of the hotel. She quietly offered me her boss's office to use for doing my calling since he wasn't there on weekends. She helped me write down telephone numbers as I spread my paperwork on her boss's desk, trying to figure out where we would be next, so she could mail credit card and clothing to me there. Then she quickly left, leaving me to make a series of calls before I found out where my clothes were.

Of all things, they were at the airport being fumigated! While on the plane for Christchurch, we discovered all passengers were fumigated while in flight. This was a New Zealand requirement. I guess it was required for the shipment of clothing too!

The credit card people assured me the card had been mailed and should be there. "Give it a few more days," the operator suggested.

Now calmer, I found Fred in the bar where he was on his second beer. I told him the desk clerk would mail the clothes and card to me at the post office at Dunedin, a town we were planning to visit next.

It was with great trepidation that I approached the post office at Dunedin…but…the package was there! Inside it was the priority express envelope addressed to the hotel manager — not me. Evidently it had been in the boss's office when I went into my tirade! It was unfortunate timing that it had arrived on a weekend when the boss was not there.

——————————

Our guests at the various trailer parks invariably were eager to talk with Americans and were just as eager to share their concerns with us, primarily about the Chinese invasion to New Zealand.

When the Brits gave Hong Kong back to the Chinese, many wealthy Chinese feared losing the freedom they were accustomed to, so some began moving to New Zealand where they believed they would be safer. This resulted in increasing the value of real estate, making it difficult for many New Zealanders to own or keep their homes. Their roads were not built for the increased traffic, resulting in increased accidents. We had to admit their roads were quite narrow and poorly surfaced.

Because we planned to hike, or as they say in Australia, "tramp" many of their famed coastal paths, I needed to purchase a heavy-duty red raincoat. It became apparent that rain was to be our frequent fellow traveler. When we arrived at Bluff, a town at the very tip of South Island, we had difficulty standing up because of the intensity of the wind. As the van rocked back and forth with each strong gust, we rapidly agreed we needed to stay in a motel for the night.

It seemed prudent for us to keep a post-it note on the window reminding us which side of the road we should be on. The narrow two-lane roads added to the challenges of staying focused. Items in the local newspapers warned of the increased traffic accidents due to more tourist traffic. That made driving a bit dicey.

One of the scariest roads was the one to Homer Tunnel. The tunnel was dank with the smell of very wet earth, and dark with few lights, leaving us driving in the dark, hoping to be on the correct side of the graveled, potholed road. Above us water dripped from the dirt ceiling onto the dirt below. The tunnel went on for what seemed a lifetime. *Is this a joke? Is it still a work in progress? Will we never come to the end?*

We finally emerged from its grasp into a sunny harbor surrounded by the weeping walls for which the harbor was known. Milford Sound is a world-renowned natural wonder. The mountains stand tall, straight out of the sea. Luxuriant rainforests cling to sheer rock walls. The waterfalls tumble hundreds of meters to the sea below. At the mountainous north end of Fiordland National Park is the classic fiord, famous for its dramatic scenery, especially Mitre Peak.

As dramatic as Milford Sound is in sunny weather, it is even more dramatic in the rain when rock faces stream with waterfalls, mist hangs around the tops of the mountains and rivers and streams rage. We had come to New Zealand to tramp its Milford Track, which Rudolph Kipling called, "the finest walk in the world." Although it rained most days we were there, we tramped many of its trails, encountering other trekkers from many countries. It was excellent exercise and spectacular scenery.

We had planned to spend the night near the harbor but the aggressive sand flies chased us back into our vehicle, leaving us scratching the bites on our ankles. So we once again encountered Homer Tunnel's exit, eager to enjoy a glass of wine while fixing a hot spaghetti dinner. We said in unison, "Good wine—Good food—Ah, life is good!" We laughed as we reminisced on the day's frustrations that resulted in witnessing the remarkable harbor and its weeping walls by boat with other tourists.

That night Fred asked me to check on the car rentals and airline tickets to verify the timing of everything. When I reached for my file folder of trip information, I couldn't find any of our reservation information—or our plane tickets. I was in a panic and said to Fred, "I know I put it in this bag and it isn't here!"

"Are you sure?" he asked slowly, in a measured tone.

I had a really strange feeling. I was looking where all of our travel items were kept. "Fred, everything is here but our airline tickets."

"You mean — *all* our tickets? To Australia, then all over Australia, then back to the USA?" His voice was calm. "They've got to be there."

I couldn't believe it. First my credit card, then my clothing, and now the plane tickets?!? "Fred, do you realize that's *seven* airline tickets for each of us? *Missing?*" Tears began rising in my voice. *Oh, my God*, I thought to myself. *How could I have let this happen?*

"Not to worry," Fred leaned back. "Relax, have some more wine, then we'll look through all the luggage in the morning."

But I couldn't let go. I just kept worrying and worrying about it. "Fred, I have to call Linda right now. See what she can do." So I walked to the phone booth down the road and called Linda to ask her help in replacing my lost tickets.

I forgot about the time difference. I woke her at 3:00 a.m. "You —what?" She said in a half-daze. "Lost *all* your tickets? Mom, do you realize how costly it will be replacing them?"

I was already flustered and she wasn't helping. "Oh I know. Linda, what do you suggest?"

"I'll call the Christchurch Hotel to see what we can do, then call the airlines." Linda's tone suggested she would like a mother replacement.

Fred was in bed when I returned, already asleep. As I lay there on my back, trying desperately to retrace our last day at the Christchurch Hotel, it suddenly dawned on me where the tickets must have been. I imagined myself sitting in the boss's office with my papers and tickets spread out all over his desk when I was on the phone with the Sydney hotel. I must have left them there! When I told Fred about it the next morning, he said, "You're great fun to travel with."

I called the hotel in Christchurch and had them mail our tickets to the airline counter at the Auckland Airport. Everything ended up working out just fine.

One has to hike Fox Glacier while in New Zealand. When we visited it, it was melting more than it should have, but it still looked imposing to us. After hiking straight up the mountain terrain to the base of the glacier, we put on our clamps and followed our leader as he picked steps in the ice for us to climb.

The exhilaration of being there, experiencing it in its wonder, was intoxicating. The mountains were slate grey, suggesting the rocky terrain underfoot when in melted areas. The snow of the glacier was white with a bluish tinge. Tall bushlike grasses popped up among the mounds of snow. In some places it looked like spinach clumps in a sour cream dip. In other places, the glacier was solid white. After following our leader up the glacier in the steps he made with his pick, like a gaggle of geese in a line, we eventually followed his steps down, using our poles to balance us.

When I looked back up at our group, I noticed we were all wearing shorts and jackets, some with hoods and caps. Fred had a wide grin on his face. He was digging it even though he needed some help from our guide going down. Fred needing help surprised me because he was usually such a mountain goat in the manner he tackled hills—up or down.

I scampered like a goat. We felt like veterans of a fierce battle returning tired and worn but alive and victorious back to our barracks in our camper.

Several days later we rented a charming holiday home made of beautiful cedar overlooking a jungle. The cedar came from Washington State. The cabin was beautifully furnished.

One morning while having coffee on the front balcony, we saw a helicopter with uniformed men being lowered to the jungle below on a rope, picking up—we soon learned—illegal marijuana. It seemed to us a strange way of policing for marijuana. At any rate, we enjoyed the show.

A day later we went kayaking on Tasman Bay with a guide and another couple. The laidback guide told us to paddle like hell if the tide started taking us out. With instructions like that, how could we fail? Later he quickly prepared a brunch for the five of us, complete with hot coffee prepared in a French Press pot.

Although it rained much of the time we enjoyed tramping the South Island's famous pathways.

On the North Island, Fred was at the wheel of the R. Tucker Thompson, a sailing schooner like those sailed in the Pacific 100 years ago. It could hold forty-four day passengers and sleep sixteen. Fred stayed at the wheel all the way out to a nearby island while I climbed almost to the top of the tallest mast. I'm not sure why. But it made quite an impression on Fred and he took many pictures of my climb.

After tooling around the island, enjoying its majestic beauty, we headed to Auckland Airport where we dropped off our tent on wheels before taking off for Sydney, Australia, then on to Hobart, Tasmania where we would begin our six weeks in Australia.

Shirley climing the mast

Australia

We started our Aussie journey in a quaint seedy hotel in Hobart. It was reminiscent of a setting where one might expect to find a Humphrey Bogart character eluding gangsters while rescuing Lauren Bacall. I could just see Bogie standing next to a piano, a trail of smoke circling his head.

New Zealand was beyond a doubt one of the most beautiful countries in the world. But when it came to having a riotous out-of-the-box good time with outrageous, fun-loving people, Australia was the place to go. Their language is melodic and actually hard to follow when a bunch of Aussies start talking. They have the strangest animals and creatures on God's earth.

On a golf course near Melbourne we saw our first kangaroos

and were mesmerized by their interaction with the golfers passing through. An elderly lady playing golf ignored the "roos" until one hopped in the probable path of the ball. She then shook her nine-iron at the roo, who hopped a short distance away and resumed grazing.

But the magnificent Coral Trekker at the Great Barrier Reef, with its zany crew headed by a young Robin Williams look-alike, complete with beard and a parrot on his arm screeching "Reef the mainsail," set the stage for a riotous seven days. Its fourteen passengers from about five different countries were expected to help with crewing, and made a pretty sight hanging from the highest masts with their bottoms all in a row as they unfurled the sails. The trekker not only looked like a pirate boat, it *was* a pirate boat with its five huge orange sails unfurled to the wind.

As usual, we were the oldest folks on the boat. But age didn't keep us from being quite popular with all the young folks. We swam in the turquoise ocean many times daily, snorkeled among the coral, and slept on the deck under the stars.

On the last night we gathered together for a party. The crew picked two passengers to compete with two crew members. The challenge was to see which team could be the first to finish eating a creamy dessert with hands behind their backs. The winning team would get champagne for their group. I was one of the two selected to participate — much to my surprise.

The desserts were placed before the two of us. As we knelt down with hands behind us, ready to start eating, a hand roughly shoved my face into the whipped cream dessert. As I looked back in amazement, my tormenter laughed, then ran out on the deck. I followed her. She ran to the side and dove into the ocean. *She's got me there*, I thought. I didn't really want to dive in at night, so I returned to the party room where everyone was getting a glass of champagne.

To conserve water, no showers were allowed until the seventh day of departure. We were each hosed down on deck and were required to sing. If the singing stopped, the water from the hose stopped.

Leaving the boat, we relaxed for several days exploring South Molle Island after taking a much-appreciated hot shower. We then flew to Darwin and Kakadu Country where even more weird sights, animals, insects, and sweltering hot weather awaited us.

Our four-day Kakadu Safari started on the Adelaide River Queen where we watched a twenty-foot-long crocodile jump for huge hunks of steak. We saw even more strange creatures as well as impressive-sized Termite Cathedrals. The hellish heat cut our five-day stay at Darwin down to a quick flight to the cool Blue Mountains and Werriberri Lodge. It was so cool there that we had a fire in the fireplace nightly.

Eventually, we reached Sydney where we had dinner with a couple we met during our stay at Cradle Mountain Lodge. Their lovely home sat on the famed harbour. They were intrigued by us because we came from Minnesota, the home of Garrison Keillor who writes stories about the above-average children who live at Lake Wobegon. They told us they listened faithfully to Keillor's weekly radio show and had a collection of his tapes.

Another day we joined an English fellow traveler from the Coral Trekker for dinner, and several times we kept running into another Trekker passenger, a young gal with a great sense of humor who was a forest ranger. Australians are easy to get to know.

The three months went by too fast. It was incredible how much fun Fred and I had together, and how well we got along. Fred agreed with me but said, "It's not like being married."

"You mean because there's a light at the end of the tunnel— when we stop being together and go our separate ways for a while?"

"Exactly. We're together when we want to be and that's what makes it so good." He patted my derriere. "Now, you *do* have our airline tickets, don't you?"

"Boop-boop-te-do," I replied in my dumb-blond fashion, shaking my head from one side to the other while batting my eyes, "I don't rightly know..."

Grinning in his lascivious way, he pulled me to him, saying, "My poor little boop-boop-to-do-lady."

Enchanted April

Not long after I had arrived home from my long trip away, Clem began discussing a new trip with me and Tib. We were all true fans of English movies such as *Howards End, Room with a View*, and the latest, *Enchanted April.* In *Enchanted April*, three English women, bored with their lives, decide to answer an ad written by a fourth English lady proposing the leasing of a villa in Tuscany for a month in April. They end up having great self-discovery moments mixed with love.

Enterprising Clem found an ad in a local travel magazine offering a Tuscany villa for rent. When Clem showed us the ad for the villa we all said, "Count me in!" We started our journey in April and took off for five weeks.

Our villa in Montenegro had all the beauty that Italy is so famous for and was near lovely cities, large and small.

At times we had clashing agendas; sometimes one or two of us wanted to explore the museums of Florence, while the other one or two wanted to hike the splendid hills of Montenegro, visiting its quaint pubs nestled in among the acres of dazzling red poppies and elegant cypress trees. This required some diplomacy and lots of wine to resolve.

A fourth lady joined us later, which made it possible for us to split up in twos. Maybe one pair wanted to see all the nearby cathedrals, castles, churches, and museums; while the other pair wanted to take the train outside of Montenegro to see some of the sites. For Tib and I, the five beautiful cities of Cinque Terre, nestled in the hills of Italy embracing the Mediterranean Sea, was the highlight of many highlights in beautiful Italy.

Flying home, we each felt we had experienced our own enchanted April.

When I got home, I discovered that Fred's mother had finally died at the age of 102. He planned to stay in Ridgetown, Ontario for some time to handle estate matters and visit some of his dearest childhood friends. For him it was a bittersweet time.

Chapter Fifteen
Into Africa
1993—1995

FRED AND I PLANNED for one of our most potentially exciting trips yet. This time we were beckoned to the worlds of Hemingway and Karen Blixen (*Out of Africa*) and into the wilds of Africa. To go on a safari, we needed to travel with a group for the first time instead of on our own. Shots and vaccinations were required.

Two days before we were to leave, I discovered I had an infected wisdom tooth that required extraction. As the dentist stuffed the now-empty cavity with lots of gauze, he armed me with pills and said, "Let's hope for the best."

On our way to Africa, Fred and I stayed at the Grosvenor/Thistle Hotel on Buckingham Palace Road. So many royals and celebrities had stayed there on their way to such exotic places as Africa.

Rumor had it that the Grosvenor was convenient for illicit relationships due to its attachment to the Victoria Railroad Station, which made it possible to enter and exit the hotel without using the front entrance. This fact made walking through its lobby, cafes, restaurants and bars more interesting. We could almost feel the presence of Hemingway and Prince Edward in its hallways.

Once we got to Nairobi, we stayed at the famous Norfolk Hotel. Any moveable feast must include this hotel. It had hosted Earls and Lords and an occasional Prince in its early days, followed by generals and Theodore Roosevelt on his retirement as twenty-sixth President of the United States. In fact, his big-game safari broke all records for size — 500 porters, each carrying a sixty-pound headload.

For us, the Norfolk was best known as the fashionable rendezvous of the big-game shooter and tourist, Ernest Hemingway, and that famous lady the Baroness Karen Blixen. Now our modest names could be added to the roster of residents.

Much of what I knew about Kenya came from reading Hemingway's novels. But the hunting we planned on doing was with a camera, not a gun.

I was most anxious to see the Karen Blixen Museum, located in the suburb of Nairobi named after her. She began writing in her sixties although she was a storyteller most of her life.

Our guide cautioned us to be wary when leaving the grounds surrounding the Norfolk Hotel. Indeed, the graveled streets were filled with all kinds of transport, including people pushing wagons filled with goods, vehicles of all kinds, three-wheeled bikes, and boys selling newspapers and other items, running in and out between the traffic. The shops were largely one-storied, some with huge umbrellas

serving as roofs, others with tarps or tar.

Big bales filled with grains and goods were stacked everywhere along the streets and under the umbrellas. One merchant told Fred he earned $2 a day and described himself as educated. He was selling dried corn, soy, and kidney beans.

We toured the University of Nairobi across the street from our hotel. Fred engaged several students in conversation, as was his habit wherever we went. We were surprised at how many people spoke English.

On safari

Our group ventured out in vans that had railings inside to hold onto when bouncing over the rocky roads. Our group of about twenty people was divided into small groups of six to fit into each van. Each day we toured a different area and stayed at a different hotel or camp. When there were animals to see, the driver stopped; the top was open so we could stand up to view.

The animals were so amazing! Seeing loads of zebras grazing as we passed by took our breaths away. We learned about their predators such as lions, cheetahs, and hunting dogs — who were careful to avoid the zebras' powerful kicks. We watched a cheetah mother training her young in the art of hunting as they crept amidst tall grasses that concealed them. The rhinos were second in size only to the elephant. It was not unusual to encounter tribes of giraffes, elephants, water buffalo, or gazelles as we toured the countryside. The survival of the fittest was readily observable.

We bounced across a road, which we dubbed the road to hell, and arrived at the Masai Mara National Reserve. Its elegant lodge was flanked by luxurious tents with verandas all facing the Mara River. These tents were furnished with elegant mahogany furniture, a well-equipped bathroom with a toilet, shower, and wash basin. Crocs and hippos were floating down the river, accompanied by exotic songs of unknown birds.

The Masai people were fantastic, dressed in brilliant scarlet red, a color believed to keep lions away. Monkeys and baboons cavorted in the trees. Elephants were everywhere. They were the largest land mammals alive and live to be seventy to eighty-five years. They have neither many friends nor many enemies in the animal kingdom apart from an enterprising lion who may attempt to grab a baby elephant. The elephant's main predator is MAN with his greed for ivory.

Each day was a different treat of sighting exotic animals and learning about their habits. One day we encountered a male lion lying between two lionesses. After being spurned by one female, the lion had better luck with the second and mounted her—giving us a Kodak moment when all one could hear were cameras clicking away.

I later made Christmas cards with my lion photo urging the recipients to "keep the good times rolling during the holidays." The cards were much in demand, even by the president of the university where I had begun serving as a board trustee.

Keep the good times rolling!

Spending time in a Masai Village was like walking back in time 2,000 years. The mud-dung grass huts were in a circle. We were fortunate to tour one and needed to bend over to get into them, crawling through a dark tunnel. That tunnel led into a small room with a hole in the wall for smoke from the small fire on the floor to escape. A big pot of some kind of soup was on the fire. Crawl spaces in three different directions led to bed areas. In the adjoining room was a pen containing a calf, which they were apparently raising. The rooms were very dark, musty, and warm.

The Masai were a handsome people, very tall and slender, dressed in colorful fabrics. They are a powerful tribe that no one wants to mess with. Their nomadic lives require them to walk an average of fifty miles a day.

The wealth of a Masai warrior is measured by the number of wives and goats he has. Our guide, Timbo, told us the man is the boss in the African family. "He can have many wives. Wives get along fine. If a husband comes home, finding a spear stuck in the dirt outside his door, he knows another man is with his wives so he does not enter. This is okay." When I looked doubtful, Timbo added, "That is the African way, my dear. I have no wives because I can't afford any."

I looked at Fred, implying he better not get any ideas. He shrugged his shoulders and said to Timbo, "She is the boss."

I didn't know if Timbo bought it.

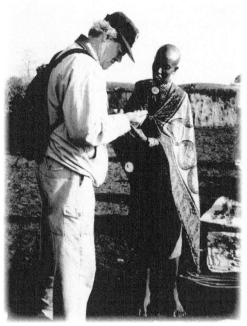

Fred with a Masai Warrior

We stayed in Nairobi long enough to pick up our luggage, then started our drive to the Tanzania border where we would go through passport checks and change to Tanzanian drivers. They would take us past Mount Kilimanjaro to Arusha, and to our lodge at Tsavo National Park and the Serengeti Plains.

While driving through Arusha, we got caught up in the middle of a political rally for the opposition candidate for the president of Tanzania. Four of us somehow got divided from the others in our group. We were suddenly surrounded by 29,000 Africans, all waving blue and white flags, raising their hands with two fingers, making the victory sign. We were the only whites in the crowd. We popped the top of our van and waved the victory sign back as they went marching ten deep on the sidewalks and driving past in trucks and cars. They were excited and joyful, pleased at the presence of these white people with cameras, snapping photos like crazy. We were excited to share their fervor—to see this basic grassroots democracy being born.

Tears of exultation filled my eyes as I witnessed their joy in being able to participate in their first democratic election. We later wondered if they thought we were foreign journalists covering their first political rally. The four of us recognized we had witnessed an unforgettable moment in Arusha's history and it was the high point of our African sojourn.

Later we saw the incumbent president's supporters and their green flags as we drove through a Masai village. In tribal dress, they waved their flags and held up one finger in support of their candidate. Our driver, who was definitely for the opposing candidate, held up his two fingers in its victory symbol and they shook their heads "no" with smiles on their faces while punching their one finger up vigorously. There seemed to be no animosity between the opposing camps — only joy that there were two candidates.

It was a truly incredible experience for us; we felt honored to be witness, and a bit humbled knowing our own country's apathy regarding our political campaigns.

Celebrating their candidate

One of the world's most amazing sights was the endless line of wildebeests and zebras queuing up to get to the river to drink. A solid line of ostriches in formation marched across the horizon flanked by zebras and wildebeests, also in single file, on each side — coming towards us in the Great Migration fashion.

Another amazing sight was visiting the birth of mankind, discovered by the Leakeys. Since 1989, Meave Leakey, a paleontologist, had directed fossil-hunting expeditions and had more recently made headlines with her discovery of a four-million–year-old human ancestor, Australopithecus anamensis, a find that pushed back by half a million years the emergence of upright walking. Fred could hardly contain his excitement at being at that very spot — our homeland — and eagerly bought a t-shirt that acknowledged our very old human ancestor.

This country, full of beauty and poverty, inexperienced in effective governance, gave us much to think about. Bereft of leaders, striving hard to play catch-up with the developed countries, it had not only its own poverty to deal with but increased responsibilities for its flood of immigrants streaming in from neighboring countries (Uganda, Somalia, and Rowanda). Its cities were noisy, dirty, impoverished; its illiteracy and unemployment staggering. Survival was the name of the game for most of its citizens whether urban or outback.

All three cities of Nairobi and Mombasa in Kenya and Arusha in Tanzania were filled with largely open-air, makeshift huts on dirty, dusty gravel roads with the occupants' wares spread about; they were cooking over open charcoal fires. Children were carrying children on their backs, women were carrying water or large bags on their heads, and men were selling wares or hauling goods on carts, pulling or pushing them up and down their byways. Yet they had such colorful clothing, such ready smiles on their faces. As we passed they would yell "Jambo, Mama" and "Mama buys, Boppa pays." A resilient country. It made my heart go out to them.

Fred and I made good travel partners. We suited one another and I believed we would be partners for several decades. We seemed to be seekers of similar goals and were as compatible as lovers as we were as friends. "Fuckin' A" — Life is good!"

South Africa

After leaving our tour group, Fred and I were excited to be among the first American tourists to visit South Africa after the peaceful fall of apartheid. Nelson Mandela had only recently been released from many years in prison and was soon catapulted into its presidency as its first black president.

We landed in Cape Town near midnight. At such a late hour, the very modern airport was practically deserted. "We've got to get some African money," Fred said. We went in search of a cash machine only to find one that wasn't equipped to deal with foreign currency. In his ever-calm tone Fred said, "We'll have to get to a bank first thing tomorrow morning."

"But how do we pay a taxi to get us to our hotel?" I asked.

We spied a taxi driver and one lone taxi. Fred approached him, engaging him in conversation. The driver was willing to take us to the hotel where we could possibly borrow money from the desk clerk.

When we booked the hotel, the agent said it was the closest one to the airport. It turned out to be a very long ride.

As modern as the gleaming city in front of us appeared to be, it apparently was unprepared for many tourists. We could see miles of shanties encircling the edges of a huge, sprawling, very modern city. Our hotel was modern, too, and the hotel clerk agreed to give us money for the taxi.

The next day Fred set off to look for the nearest bank. When he returned he said the bank was heavily guarded. "I had to go through a series of locked doors, one after another. It made me feel like I was being guarded and watched by invisible persons. It was an eerie experience." He said the guards were all whites. "Guess whites are still in charge of the banks and police."

By day, the city of Cape Town looked like a more modern San Francisco, full of shiny skyscrapers encircling the bay. But truckloads of black workers were transported into the city to do labor work. It appeared the city was still run by whites.

President Mandela was trying to improve housing for blacks by building foundations with lots and lots of cement slabs and giving the blacks access to running water. Next he hoped to add simple small houses, then electricity. The bulk of blacks still lived outside of the city limits.

Mandela had only been president for sixteen months, but during this brief presidency, tourist business was booming, catching the locals by surprise. Foreign tourists were mostly from Germany and Japan.

We took a taxi to go pick up our small camper, which was remarkably similar to the tent on wheels we drove in New Zealand. Immediately we headed for Ocean View Drive along the Indian Ocean, flanked by magnificent homes, parks, cultivated gardens, wineries, and affluent shops. It was a two-hour scenic drive of outstanding beauty.

The trailer parks were much like those in the U.S. and New Zealand and were frequented by white families on vacation. We selected a spot, set up shop, complete with our table and chairs placed on our terrace, and then invited neighbors to join us for a drink after dinner. It was during these gatherings that we learned much about their fears, concerns, and predictions concerning the leadership of their country under President Mandela in his first year in office. In the Cape Town area, Afrikaners of original Dutch descent seemed most fearful of the formidable changes sweeping across this remarkable country.

One person felt that the eighteen months under Mandela had been economically disastrous.

Another said, "The country is 'dumbing down' fast and might soon be bankrupt. There's going to be a civil war between the two rival black tribes and that will bring about the final destruction of my beloved homeland."

Another sadly said, "My son, a brilliant computer analyst, plans to accept the first job offered him outside South Africa."

Yet another camper agreed, fearing "One result of the 'dumbing down' will be the return of the abacus since no one knows how to use computers or are willing or smart enough to learn."

"You need to know that the further north you go, the more shanties and poverty you'll see," another couple warned us.

"My wife and I are moving to Canada. She got a good job offer as a doctor. We just know the deterioration of education will affect our children adversely, so we are moving," was the sad report of another.

But an angry view offered by one man was, "I'm not leaving because of the fact that whites can no longer take their money out of the country. I can't afford to flee the country or I would."

Yet others defiantly refused to leave the country stating, "My parents, my grandparents, and I have worked too hard to create this country for me to up and leave with my family."

Only the few South Africans we met of British descent seemed hopeful about the future. In fact, they felt changes were long overdue. Their views might be explained in part by journalist Eddy Harris in his book, *Native Stranger* who says that the Boer cannot easily obtain a passport to Britain, as the British South Africans. "This is his home, his only home. He is an African and he will vehemently tell you so. He has no place else to go. He will live and fight and die here, make his stand here, make it work or lose it all here."

Continuing our ocean drive, we stopped at a quiet spot by the ocean to eat a picnic lunch when we suddenly spied a whale. In fact, we counted seven huge whales cavorting about the craggy shoreline. Leaving our lunch, we rushed to the rocky cliffs overlooking the ocean to watch this magnificent sight. A huge bell started ringing to alert the town's people that the whales were back. Before long, many people arrived, watching quietly, almost reverentially, in awe of these mighty creatures that seemed to be performing for us. It turned out they were mating!

For serious hikers, Tsitsikama National Park was a must. Nature trails meandered into the forest and along the coast. The five-day Otter Trail followed the shoreline for most of its route and it was challenging.

We parked our trailer on the edge of a rocky shore on the Indian Ocean, watching waves twelve to fourteen feet high splash geysers as high as thirty feet. It was like watching continual geysers erupt at Yellowstone or non-stop fireworks on the Fourth of July. We could not take our eyes off the spectacle occurring in our own front yard.

We were like kids—reluctant to go to bed lest we missed something. We slept with the trailer door wide open so we could hear the pounding of the waves and feel the mist on our faces. Definitely the wildest and most beautiful place yet.

We left the affluent white enclave of the Southern Coast— Cape Peninsula and Garden Route—and entered what may have been the real South Africa. We motored through Port Elizabeth onto the East Coast and finally inland north to Kimberly on the way to Johannesburg. The country was much like the Nevada and Arizona deserts, with flat brushland offering few shady spots.

The gravel roads were quite narrow. At one point we got a flat tire. *Now what?* I wondered. It was hot and sticky, with no one around and we seemed to be in the middle of nowhere.

"Do we have any tools or spare tires?" Fred uttered while trying to figure out where they might be. "Boy, there's nothing but cactus and small brush here. We may be in for a long walk somewhere to get help."

Just then I saw a truck coming down the road and excitedly pointed it out to Fred. Fred waved down the man and greeted him as he got out of his truck. We were most grateful for the man's help. "We're kinda used to helping one another in these parts," the man said. "So you're from the USA. Where are you heading? The further inland you go, the rougher it gets. You wanna be careful. These people out here don't know how to take care of things. Best you find a place to stay inside before night." We thanked him profusely, then continued on our way.

When we got to a town, we pulled in for gas and then decided to find a room for the night. Having become accustomed to seeing only whites, we both noted this appeared to be a town of black citizens.

"Fred," I said, "Doesn't this look like an English village? Look at the shops and streets, all clean and orderly." We found a huge white hotel with a balcony across the front. It looked down on the cobbled street below. "Why, it almost looks like a small version of a southern mansion from *Gone with the Wind*," I said and suggested we check it out.

Inside, a white lady was at the counter. As Fred checked us in, I looked into the lobby and restaurant next to it. The high ceilings and velvet drapes framed the mahogany furnishings of the lobby and restaurant.

"Wow," I said quietly to Fred as we followed a person to our room. "This is truly elegant!" As a matter of fact, we had a suite of rooms open to the balcony. We quickly made ourselves comfortable, fixed ourselves a gin and tonic, and strode out to the balcony overlooking the street full of black people milling about. We noted that it was Friday and perhaps they were done working for the day and getting ready for a night of fun.

Some looked up to see who was on the balcony; we waved to them and they waved back. They yelled up and invited us to attend a dance that night. They pointed to the building across the street. It looked like a perfectly ordinary brick business building. "This should be great fun," we both agreed.

We decided to eat at the hotel restaurant. The spacious dining room had only one other occupant who was finishing a meal. We ordered a satisfactory dinner and, once the other diner left, we were the only ones in the huge room. We ate in silence. The heavy drapes at the windows filtered out the heat from the sun, darkening the interior.

Later, we ventured out to find the dance. We entered the building that was pointed out to us earlier. Dance music filled the space. Two adults welcomed us and stamped our hands to show we paid.

The dance appeared to be a high school dance with older people there as chaperones. The room looked like a gym. We were the only whites. We sat down on the bleachers to enjoy watching the young folks dancing. "My, God," I whispered to Fred, "I think they're all dancing the tango." Several adults and students greeted us and were quite friendly, asking polite questions about where we were from.

We stayed several hours, dancing with the young people. It was here that I learned Fred was a pretty good dancer; although we did not attempt the tango. At the end of the night the people we met said good-bye and wished us a safe journey.

We got back to the hotel and had a brief conversation with the white woman at the reception desk. She could not believe what we had done. She told us how dangerous it was to be outside at night.

Fred and I just shook our heads in wonderment.

We left the next day for Kingston. Although the area had had a five-year drought and the farmers were suffering, it was an excellent reproduction of an old mining town. The town told a remarkable story of its early diamond mining history and the Boer War.

At a restaurant in Kingston, we encountered a young South African couple of British descent who seemed comfortable with

Mandela and the future of their country. They invited us to join them at their country club the next morning for a sailing regatta and brunch.

The next day we found ourselves at the lake, which was more like a huge pond, slate grey in color, surrounded by grey slag heaps and dirt. A reminder that we were in diamond country.

Fred was given a small laser sailboat and joined the group while I tried to make myself comfortable sitting on the "beach" of grey slag, in the heat. There was no beach furniture.

The regatta of twelve or more lasers, their brightly colored sails reflecting off the waters of the tiny lake, looked lovely as they moved in a stately fashion around one another. The wives arrived in time to fix the brunch while the men, including Fred, docked their boats. We grabbed a bite to eat but had to be on our way to Johannesburg, where we were to catch our plane to America the next day.

At Johannesburg we hired a guide to take us to the infamous Soweto, Africa's largest black city and a suburb of Johannesburg. The first impression of Soweto was of an enormous grim, undifferentiated sprawl, punctuated by light towers that would seem more appropriate in a concentration camp. Some of the outlying townships looked quite acceptable while others were as bad as any third-world slum.

Life in Soweto

There were the wealthy elite that lived in comfortable bungalows; the privileged who lived in monotonous rows of government-built three-roomed houses with an outside tap and toilet; the lucky who had been provided with a block of land, a prefab toilet and a tap, and who were allowed to build whatever they could; the fortunate who lived in shacks erected in backyards; the squatters who built wherever they could and had virtually no facilities at all; and the men who lived in dormitories in huge dilapidated hostels.

The paved city streets were filled with traffic. Small shanty shops appeared to be selling stuff the owners no longer wanted to one another. All seemed friendly. Busloads of tourists stopped from time to time to wander through the area and take photos. We were encouraged to step inside several one-room homes and a one-room school. We even saw Minnie and Nelson's two homes — hers more luxurious and his more modest.

For the majority of Jo'burg's inhabitants, Soweto was home. Surprisingly, most white South Africans we met seemed completely ignorant of life in the townships and few had ever been to one.

That night we dined at our hotel. We were seated near a black couple and their two adolescent children. I smiled at the family several times throughout our meal. As we were finishing our dinner, the black man came over to our table and invited us to join their family for an after-dinner drink. As we sat down with them, the gentleman said he wanted his children to meet some Americans. When I asked him how he knew we were Americans, he replied: "First, you acknowledged our existence by smiling at us, then while the two of you talked, you engaged in expansive gestures. This is not typical of South African whites who have more controlled body language."

Our informative conversation ended with the exchange of names and addresses.

It seemed to us that the Boer whites we met had a very different view of their country and its problems than we observed during our short time there. Their lack of awareness on how blacks lived made me think of the three blind men, each describing by touch the appearance of an elephant. The first, touching its trunk said it was like a very thick snake; the second, touching its side said "no, it is like a giant wall"; but the third, touching a leg said, "it obviously is like a thick tree trunk." Each man saw only what was nearest, but not the whole. We met even fewer British South Africans, but their views seemed more hopeful of South Africa's future under President Mandela's leadership and more aligned with our views.

Once again we had a warm homecoming with Linda greeting us. Fred decided to spend the night and the next morning, breakfast was interrupted by a phone call. It was Mr. Winslow. "I regret to inform you that Miss Edna died this morning."

I was amazed that what we had been anticipating for so many years was actually happening. I asked, "Should I come down right away?"

"No, it isn't necessary that you be here at all. She made her wishes known to me. She wishes her ashes be sent to Salt Lake to be interred next to her husband's ashes. She wished no memorial services. I will assist you in administering her estate and will send papers for you to sign soon."

"Who was that?" Fred asked while finishing his coffee. "It sounded serious."

"You'll never believe it." I plopped down in my chair; my arms and legs felt limp. "Aunt Edna died this morning. That was her attorney, Mr. Winslow. He said I am the assistant administrator of her estate and he will handle things." I still felt disbelief.

My aunt had used her husband's wealth to set up a scholarship fund named after him to be used for future engineering students. As his niece and co-trustee of the fund, I would now be responsible for directing the proceeds of his estate to appropriate universities. In the event of my death, the responsibilities would be carried out by my daughter. We were each left a modest trust fund.

My head was swirling with what this might mean for the two of us. Yet I felt badly; because Aunt Edna had lived so long, there would be few left to mourn her death.

Fred said jubilantly, "Well, you have the perfect retirement job for you — managing the distribution of engineering scholarships in your aunt's trust. It should be most gratifying." Getting up from the table, he gave me a quick kiss and said, "I gotta go. Be calling you soon."

As usual, I helped him gather his gear and gave him the Penelope wave as he got in his car and waved out the window.

When Linda got home from work that night, I had much information to tell her about Aunt Edna's death. Now all of Grandma and Grandpa's children were dead. We were the end of the line.

Chapter Sixteen
England Mourns
1996—1998

IT WAS HAPPY BIRTHDAY in Shirleyland and once again my gaggle of gal friends had planned an enjoyable evening of food, drink, friends, gifts, and loads of laughter and remembrances of times past—*some* of them truthful. Somehow they conspired among themselves on which one would host this fun event each year. Each year it left me counting my blessings that I had such remarkable friends.

It was Sandy, the beautiful and charismatic one that first stressed to me the importance of girlfriends. She said men may come and go, and kids may do the same, but a cherished girlfriend was just "there" for you. There was no substitute.

Clem taught me how to be a friend, Judith taught me how to make a friend, and all taught me how to keep a friend. I've been blessed with a small circle of dear friends.

Each one brought something different to my life—enriched me in different ways. Some are front burners—others back burners. They may get rotated from front to back and vice versa. These were my front burner friends. There are more, all dear to me.

My friend Judith's decision to remain single intrigued me. That decision required her to be on her own wherever her work took her. She used her interests and hobbies to make new friends and learned the art of being totally self-sufficient.

All three women—Sandy, Clem, and Judith—have had their ups and downs traveling their respective roads. Each one has traits I admire and wish I had. I've learned from each. Sandy was perhaps my major teacher. She, who early on seemed like a *Better Homes and Garden*-type woman, had become caring and compassionate, the most giving, greatest "do gooder" of us all. I held her in awe. She used her boundless energy to help others obtain their dreams. She and her husband together raised lots of money for various local charities but seldom spoke of it. Yet she was fun—I mean stand-up-and-laugh fun. She had been likened to Erma Bombeck by many, but I personally saw her as a lot like Lucille Ball in *I Love Lucy*. I am fortunate to have these women in my life. They have been there for me when I've needed them. I hope I have been for them as well.

It was about this time Sandy became a trustee at Hamline University. It had been her husband's alma mater. He had served on the board in the past and now they both decided it was a perfect fit for me. I found dealing with the issues of higher education stimulating and became engrossed in the new learning required to be a knowledgeable student of national and state trends. Sandy and I became inseparable board members who took our responsibilities seriously, which included providing healthy doses of fun and joy.

Fred was ready for another visit to Europe and England, so in 1997 we planned our usual few days in London followed by quick visits to the Goreses and Jenkinses and then on to France and Norway. Fred and I were watching TV late one night when breaking news about the death of Princess Diana was announced. It gradually occurred to me that we would be arriving in London the day before her funeral. I had booked us in at the Grosvenor Hotel weeks before but with much of the world possibly descending upon London for this event, it occurred to me I should confirm our arrival with them, which I did.

Linda took us to the airport two hours early because she had to get to work. Since we were early Fred suggested we check out where our gate was and then get some coffee. There was a Starbuck's right across from our gate so we each bought a Newsweek magazine to catch up on the Princess Di news while getting a bite to eat. It was great to not feel rushed and just enjoy the beginning of our trip. Maybe we were too casual because Fred suddenly looked at his watch, stood up, and hurriedly began picking up his stuff. "Hurry up! I hope we haven't missed it."

"What's the matter?" I asked. "There's no one over at our gate."

"That's the problem. There should be. Look at the time!" We rushed up to the counter. No one was there. Then we saw the sign behind the counter that said the gate for London had been changed.

We ran through the airport pulling our bags on wheels behind us. We jumped onto moving walkways, said "excuse me" as we passed slow-moving people, jumped off the moving walkway, ran through the crowds, and made it to the gate. We were breathing hard. The gate people were getting ready to leave. "Is this the gate for London?" Fred asked.

"The plane just left. Are you supposed to be on it?"

"Yes. We were sitting across from the wrong gate," I shouted.

"What can we do?" Fred asked.

"Well, I can get you to Detroit and maybe you'll get there in time to catch your plane to London. If not, you can spend the night there and catch their morning flight to London."

"Let's go to Detroit, Fred. I simply can't face my daughter after she brought us here two hours early."

So we found ourselves sitting in the middle seats in the middle section of a very full plane. "Listen, Fred. Maybe the pilot of this plane could contact our pilot to wait for us."

"No, Shirley. I don't think that's a…"

I waved the flight attendant over to me and explained our situation. "Can you ask the pilot of our other plane to wait?" She said she'd try and left.

Before Fred could finish his sentence, she was back. "Our pilot contacted the pilot of your plane."

"Great," I said. "What did he say?"

"No. He said no. But I found out we will be landing at the gate right next to his gate and if we have good tail wind, we just may make it. So we will see that you two are the first passengers off."

"Oh, thank you, thank you so much," I said. I looked at Fred, "You see, my idea wasn't too foolish."

"Ya, ya...." Fred scrunched down in his seat. "I'm gonna get some shut eye."

The flight attendant alerted us as we were landing. True to her word, we were the first off the plane. We ran to the next gate and found that our plane was still there. I held up our tickets, waving them wildly so both the desk attendant and the pilot that I could see through the window could see them. I wanted to make sure they knew we were the missing passengers. The pilot waved as the plane backed out. "What? Where's he going? We're here," I screamed. Fred was busy talking with the desk attendant. She turned to me and said, "Your plane's doors were all closed and he was in the process of backing up when you got here."

"But she has another option for us," Fred said calmly. "She can get us on another plane right now that's going to Amsterdam. From there we can get a plane to London because Amsterdam has frequent flights to London. But we have to hurry!"

"Yes," she agreed. "Just be sure to have the ticket clerk at Amsterdam locate your luggage and have it sent to London." She ran us to the gate and got us on the plane just minutes before it was to take off. The flight attendant took over and hurried us on the plane and up the steps to where we were to sit.

As I breathed a sigh of relief, we sat in a spacious area right next to a window, by a bar. "What is this, Fred?"

"Well, my dear, we must be in first class. I've never been on one of these two-story planes."

I couldn't believe it. We were traveling the seven-hour flight in absolute luxury. At last we both took a deep breath, then relaxed as the attendant said, "Can I get you drinks?"

After we arrived in Amsterdam, we raced to the ticket counter to get on the next plane to London. It took the agent some time to locate both our names in the computer, but at last we got our boarding tickets. I then asked her to trace our luggage. She said our luggage would be sent to Heathrow rather than Gatwick since we were flying from Amsterdam rather than Detroit. "You must go directly to the luggage information center to find out where your luggage is. They will know."

"Not a problem," we both said as we raced to the boarding gate out of breath.

"Just in time," said the man at the gate as he reached for Fred's passport. "We have a full plane. It seems everyone wants to be in London for this historic weekend." Handing Fred's passport back, he asked for mine. After carefully examining it, he then walked back to the gate desk, checking something on the computer. When he returned, I asked, "Everything okay?"

"Madam, I regret to inform you that your passport has expired."

"What?!? How can that be?"

"You see here, your passport expired in July."

"Well," I demanded in my best Queen Elizabeth voice, "Nobody informed me!!!" Glancing at Fred's face, I could see a big smile taking over as he said, from inside the gate, "I'll send you a picture postcard from London, Shirley."

As the gate inspector returned to the back desk to use the phone, I saw Fred standing on the other side of the gate. I said with growing amusement, "Well, what are they to do with me? And how will I get back in America without a current passport? Clearly, I'm here!" Fred shrugged his shoulders, struggling to control his smirking smile.

The gate inspector nodded his head as he completed his conversation, then came back to me and handed me my passport. "I have a note in your passport. Just show it to the passport control man in London." I thanked him profusely.

As we dashed toward the door of the plane I asked Fred, "How do you suppose he worked it with London?"

Fred, guiding me to our seats in the plane, said, "Probably didn't want to be bothered with you."

The flight was filled with many young folks planning to attend Princess Diana's funeral. "One advantage we have is that we have no luggage to drag around when we're getting on the train to Victoria Station," Fred pointed out.

I went through passport check with no problems then joined Fred in seeking out the luggage information center. The lady said, "We have located your luggage. It is in Detroit. They will be putting it on the next plane and it will come here. We will resume responsibility for getting it to you. Where are you staying?" And that was that.

As we left, Fred said, "Not bad for a couple of senior citizens missing a flight: got us on three planes for which we were not ticketed and they are delivering our luggage to our hotel room free."

I replied, "Seems the Universe was taking care of some senior citizens today."

Upon entering the Grosvenor Hotel, only three hours later than we would have had we not missed the first plane, I went up to the desk clerk and gave him our reservation information. "Any luggage?" he asked as our transaction was completed.

"No," I said as I spread my arms wide, displaying my khaki-and-boots travel attire, "We travel light!"

After we got to our little room, Fred said, "Let's go to Buckingham Palace now while we still have some energy." Jet lag had not yet taken hold.

What a shock as we stepped outside our hotel, seeing a city in mourning. All flags up and down the street were at half-mast. The smell of flowers permeated the air as countless people walked by carrying flowers to leave at Buckingham Palace. The city was as quiet as a church full of people. Solemn looks were on all faces that passed us by.

We talked in whispers to one another as we strolled down Buckingham Palace Road. As we reached the gates, covered with bunches of flowers stuck in the grating, we fit ourselves into the crowds of people, families with young children, young and old folks—all looking grief-striken, shocked, subdued. Everywhere mounds and mounds of flowers were heaped up, with notes and letters stuck among them expressing grief and disbelief.

Shirley at Diana's memorial.

Diana was frequently referred to as the "Princess of the People." The only flag not at half-mast was the one on Buckingham Palace. Already we had heard this was an affront to many people. The Queen was still in Scotland but was expected to arrive later that day. It was widely hoped that she would respect the grief of her subjects by lowering the flag.

There must have been thousands of people milling about the grounds — all in quiet reverence. Even small children and babies were subdued.

The word was quietly spreading among the crowd, even among those who had climbed up on the wrought-iron fences, that the Queen was coming.

We could see her, looking solemn, giving a wave of acknowledgment as her car entered onto the grounds. Quickly she was in the castle. The changing of the guards occurred. The surreal silence continued. Then, someone noticed the flag was being lowered to half-mast. An audible sigh could be heard.

After kneeling down to read some of the many letters written by people of all ages, we left to get a bite to eat at a restaurant down the street. We watched out the window as the people continued walking by carrying bunches of flowers. "This is so amazing," Fred said. "It is like the whole city has become one big cathedral. It rather defies the stereotype of the English stiff upper lip."

Upon return to our room, I was taking a shower when I heard a knock on our door. As I peeked my head out the door, I heard the porter say to Fred, "Your luggage, sir." We both agreed, this is what we considered good room service.

After a nap and dinner, we felt revived. We decided to head back to Buckingham Palace at night and see if there was still a crowd there. On the way, we saw a telephone booth and felt we should let the Gores know we were in London. Sheila answered saying, "Good Lord, Shirley, you folks need to come here right now. You don't want to get caught up in all those crowds there."

I replied, "Oh, but we do. We want to witness history being made and believe me, it certainly is here. We'll take a train there late afternoon and meet you at the station. That way we can take in some of tomorrow's funeral ceremony."

It was quite dark when we entered the gates at the palace. Though we couldn't see well initially, we both felt we could sense being surrounded by thousands of people moving about. As our eyes adapted to the darkness, we began noticing lit candles everywhere, scattered all over the grounds, roads, and parks surrounding the palace. The same somberness was embraced by families with infants and small children as well as adults. They seemed content to just be there. Some quietly mentioned they planned to spend the night. We walked among the throng, careful to avoid baby carriages and folks sitting in folding chairs they had brought. It was easier to see as more candles were lit. Eventually, we returned to our hotel.

The next day we caught a bus to see what was happening elsewhere. Everywhere flags at half-mast dominated the city. Rows and rows of people lined the sidewalks around Westminster Abbey, outside of Harrods, along the parade route the royal party would be walking later in the day. It appeared that some people had spent the night holding their spot. The same quietness prevailed. We stayed to see a bit of the procession before getting on the train to Chester.

While on the train, it suddenly stopped and an announcement was made that all of England would be honoring Princess Diana with one minute of silence. All conversations came to an abrupt halt. Faces of passengers near me suddenly seemed absorbed in deep thought, some with lips moving as if in prayer. I couldn't help but think of this lovely woman who had died so tragically and so suddenly. And so young. The world was certainly going to miss her. When the minute was over, the train resumed.

Right away as we got off the train we saw a very happy Mike and Sheila waving. After hugs and expressing condolences, we climbed into their car and all began talking at once. "I shall be missing that beautiful Diana, I must say," said Mike. "I rather fancied having her beauty around for some time."

"Oh, go on with you," said Sheila. "Life will go on." She looked at us, "Now how was your flight?"

"Mike and Sheila! Do you know that you are harboring an illegal immigrant?" I said.

"Now what's this?" they wanted to know. As we told them our crazy story, each of us adding embellishments to our series of misadventures culminating in the expired passport, Mike was having a good laugh. But ever-practical Sheila said, "Well, Shirley, you'll have to get a new passport in London, but it will be far quicker to get your passport photos at our local market tomorrow. We don't need passports now to travel around Europe, but France, for instance, could be difficult for non-Europeans. Best not to take a chance."

We piled into their charming home and the drinking began. The guys wanted to watch sports on the telly so Sheila and I watched the full funeral procession and ceremony on the upstairs TV.

It was a short but happy visit, and with passport photos in hand, we climbed into Mike's new car, wending our way to Sue and Tony's home.

No longer living in two small caravans, Sue and Tony were eager to show us the results of their prodigious efforts. The six of us dined on lamb in their renovated elegant new home surrounded by an enchanting English garden with a peacock or two wandering about. They now had a beautiful little girl named Georgia who was adored and cherished by her parents.

The Gores left for home, but we stayed several more days. During our visit, the petrol crisis hit the U.K. It consumed all conversations. We heard varying views on who was to blame.

The Jenkinses and their lovely daughter Georgia entertained us royally. We were quite sure we had put on five or ten pounds while there. Not only were we impressed with the home that Tony and Sue had spent so many years building, but we were equally impressed with their charming daughter, who was merely a strong desire so many years ago.

We then took a train back to London where I picked up a new passport from the American Embassy.

Later that day we took the Chunnel to Paris. In all his years of travel, Fred had never been to Paris. We took in the usual tourist spots and came upon the site of Princess Diana's death. Flocks of people wandered about, most adding more flowers to the piles already there. It was a kind of hushed moment, then most people quickly left, as we did, to take in more of the sights.

On the subway back to our hotel, we again found ourselves packed in like sardines. I was standing up clasping one hand tightly on the bar, while clutching my day pack tight against my tummy with the other hand. "Here's where we get off," Fred said as we both extricated ourselves from the crowd and pushed our way out the door. Jumping out after me, Fred yelled, "Hold on, I gotta check something." Looking at me, he said in a shocked voice, "I think I just got robbed!"

"Oh no, Fred, how can that happen to you, the experienced world traveler?"

In a sheepish grin, he said, "I might as well have had a sign on my back pocket saying, 'take me.' I sure knew better than to put my wallet in my back pocket. Why, I can't even get out of the subway. My subway ticket was in my wallet."

"I tell you what," I said, "I'll send you a postcard from back home." I imagined myself standing on one side of the turnstyle looking at him trapped in the subway. Oh sweet revenge!

"Guess I had that coming. The bad news is I had everything in that wallet: drivers license, credit card, passport, and about $100 in cash." Fred had bought a special leather wallet on the plane that was big enough to carry a passport as well as money and credit cards. It had seemed such a convenience at the time of purchase, but now it was a major problem.

"Well, you've sure made some Frenchman very happy. Let's get you out of here and then back to our hotel." We were staying at a boutique hotel and I thought the owner would most likely help with phone calls to cancel credit cards.

The owner and his son were most understanding. Even though they didn't speak English, Fred managed to communicate. Motioning to Fred to follow him, the owner raced out the front door with us following him to a nearby store. The owner of the store knew English and made all our phone calls, cancelling cards in a matter of minutes. We couldn't thank him enough. It looked like our last afternoon in gay Paris would be spent at the American Embassy, getting Fred his new passport.

After getting him passport photos, we headed for the Embassy, guarded by a Spanish-speaking soldier who demanded to see Fred's passport. When Fred said, "That's why I'm here. Someone stole mine," the soldier then asked to see some proof of identity. "It's all gone. I have no proof," he said while looking at me.

"Don't look at me," I said as I looked at the guard, shrugging my shoulders. "I've never seen this man before." By this time both Fred and I were laughing and the guard was trying not to smile. "But what can I do?" I asked. "Oh, I guess I could give him this," I said, as I pulled out my copy of all Fred's documents, handing them to the guard. "Is that relief I see on your face?"

"You do good work." He replied with that irresistible smile.

Norway, Here We Come

We had decided to end our trip with a quick trip to Norway. Our late flight was quite bumpy and got us there later than anticipated. A cab took us to a hotel along the dock in Bergen.

Fred said he was very hungry so we stopped in the dining room on the second floor of the hotel.

After eating, we decided to get to our room before we both fell asleep in our food. We ambled over to the elevator.

"You have the key? What floor are we on?" Fred asked.

We made our way to the fifth floor. Our room was a corner room at the end of the hall.

"It's a mighty small room. But you can't miss the bathroom," Fred observed as we turned on the light. "It's right by the door."

"Hey, the bathroom floor is heated," I exclaimed.

"Yah, thanks to discovering oil in their own backyard, so to speak, the Norwegians can now afford heated bathroom floors."

Next thing I knew, Fred had torn off his clothes and was in bed, sound asleep, snoring. I turned out the lights and quickly joined him in deep sleep.

I didn't know how long it had been before I heard someone banging loudly on the door. I reached over to wake up Fred. It was pitch dark. I couldn't find him anywhere in the bed. I groped my way into the bathroom to turn on a light. The banging continued. I looked in the bathroom. Nobody there! Where was he? The banging was louder. I opened up the door across from the bathroom door, cautiously peeking out to see who it was and there was Fred — in the nude — mumbling something about a dream. I quickly dragged him into our room. "What were you doing out there?"

"I've been all over the hotel trying to find our room."

"You — what...? All over?" I looked out in the hallway both ways; thankfully, there was no one around.

"I remember going down the steps, all the way to the second floor, finding myself outside the door to the restaurant."

I shut the door. "Fred, that's all the way on the other side of the building. What were you doing way over there — on the second floor?"

"I was trying to find a restroom. I had to pee. I remembered there was one on the second floor so that's where I headed."

"My God, Fred. Did anyone see you?"

"Just then I saw a couple in the restaurant heading for the door so I quickly ran into the restroom. They may have caught a glimpse of me. I kept thinking, what do I do if someone finds me? I don't know the language. I can't identify myself. What if I end up in the friendly jail?"

We were both laughing by now.

"I'll bet most folks have had a dream like that. Walking around in public naked. I sure have. But for you, it was no dream."

"I kept thinking it had to be a dream. Really! I thought it was a dream!" Fred kept repeating, "I thought it was a dream!"

We must have laughed about it for what seemed like hours as we imagined possible scenarios of what might have happened had he knocked on the wrong door, or bumped into someone in the hallway. And what if that couple did see him. What must have they thought? Would they have reported to the desk clerk that there was a nude man running about the halls? How would I have found him if the police had found him first? We both concluded that he must have opened the wrong door when he thought he was opening the bathroom door, which then shut behind him. Being half asleep, he headed for the bathroom he remembered seeing on the second floor. "I really think I was sleepwalking. The whole thing was like a dream. I don't know how I finally found the right door to bang on," he said, shaking his head as we both continued laughing. This had the makings of being our best travel story ever. We were still chuckling the next morning.

After breakfast, we packed up our gear and got ready to catch the train to Oslo.

The next day we were on the plane, flying home. But now we had two people greeting us at the baggage center. Linda and her new boyfriend Nick were there with big smiles on their faces.

Linda's best girlfriend Kim had given her a great present at her birthday party several months earlier—Nick! Linda had a crush on him since she was in high school but, as Nick said, they were never on the playing field at the same time. This time sparks flew and it looked to Fred and I like a promising relationship. Nick came from a highly respectable family who lived in our neighborhood. In fact, Nick had worked for me once, as an educational assistant at the Behavioral Learning Center. He had been considered eye candy by most the female staff.

"Wait until you hear our misadventures this time," Fred said to Linda.

I interrupted to say, "It wasn't so big a deal, we only flew on three planes for which we were not ticketed resulting in a different airport delivering our luggage free to our hotel—all at no extra cost because we are so special!"

"Well," travel agent Linda corrected, "that is because you both were using frequent flyer miles. Otherwise it would have cost you a bundle."

"Oh, but," Fred added, "your mother was also flying with an expired passport and I had to pull strings to get her into the country."

When Fred left to return to his home, I found myself immersed in the joys Linda and Nick were feeling in the newness of their love. Nick brought her flowers almost daily—even brought me some at times. He was a comfortable guy and fit well into our lives, frequently eating meals with us and taking on small tasks such as shoveling the sidewalks, warming up the cars, fixing a leaky faucet. Eventually, he became Linda's roommate. Both of them stayed in the basement bedroom. Our family was expanding.

Cruising Britain's Canals—1998

"I've always wanted to rent a narrowboat and cruise Britain's canals." This was the way Fred stated many desires that soon became our next travel destination. The internet gave us a wealth of information. We selected the J. M. Pearson & Son Ltd. Company and the Avon Ring route based at Tewkesbury.

A narrowboat is like a skinny trailer with a small living, dining, and kitchen area, a bathroom with a tiny shower, and several bedrooms. The boats were steered using tillers situated at the rear of the boat. Since most boats were longer than the width of the canal, turning could be a challenge.

Quite often a family would rent a narrowboat, giving them several people to crew. But with only two people, Fred was, of course, the captain and I, the crew. We were given some onsite training on steering and going through the locks as well as booklets and navigation maps full of useful information. I understood little of it. *This*, I thought, *is going to be a real challenge for me*. But adventure was what I wanted.

Reading one of the booklets gave me hope that this would be an amazing trip:

> *To tie up at the canal bank at dusk; to wake and find yourself free to choose the pattern of the day ahead — when to start and where to stop; to relax and find yourself stepping back to an age where life moved at a slower pace and there was time enough to enjoy it.*

On the narrowboat

On our first day on our narrowboat, Fred handled the boat and navigation map while I handled the lock with considerable help from the locals. It was tricky and physical for a mechanically impaired person such as me. When it rained, locking was even more challenging. Fortunately, the boat contained yellow slickers for us to use when it rained. The wood would get slippery, making crossing from one side of the lock to the other a bit dicey. All locks were unmanned. We were on our own. The captain's main job was to steer to the right and then yell at me (crew) to jump off, grab a rope, tie us up, then get about pushing the gates open or shut with my rear end and opening or shutting the paddles with my crank. It took about a half hour to get through a lock. Some locks were close together, resulting in no rest for the crew (me). By the end of the week, I was beginning to get the hang of it.

We took to our comfortable digs and the gorgeous English countryside right away. The imperial swans and a gaggle of geese, followed us, waiting for us to tie up. They would perform for us, anticipating food. The swans were huge magnificent birds with banded legs and huge webbed feet. One stretched his long neck to its greatest length, snorting loudly, insisting I deal with him. I had no food. He looked as though he were considering jumping into the boat. I'm sure he could. They followed us, coming up to my kitchen window when I was cooking, big beaks sliding against the window as they threw their bodies against the side of the boat. They could be very intimidating.

Tewksbury's waterfront was as close to heaven as one was likely to find, with its ancient arches of King John's Bridge, the quiet backwaters of the millstream reflecting half-timbered houses and the town's towering abbey.

We took the bus from Evesham to Stratford-on-Avon in order to immerse ourselves in the world of Shakespeare. There we encountered a wonderful guide in the Holy Trinity Church who was a veritable treasure, sharing with us the history of this remarkable church, its patrons, and her views of the historic religious factions from Celts to now.

On the shores we saw tiny docks, more like perches, evenly spaced along the grassy, green shores, used by fishermen, on this rainy day protected by green umbrellas. Each fisherman seemed to have the same equipment — tiny collapsible chair, table for fish poles and hooks, etc., a thermos, a netted bag for holding caught fish — all fitting into canvas commercial bags the size of ski containers.

Once back on our boat, we enjoyed watching the young folks and their coach sculling along the Avon outside our narrowboat.

> *As schuuler, I must face backwards*
> *To move forewards,*
> *So that looking over my shoulder*
> *I seem to be moving into a future*
> *That is already, before its time,*
> *All past."*

(From trip booklet. Author unknown.)

Amazingly fit, the young girls would skim the surface like dragonflies, totally focused. Their coaches jogged along the shore or on bikes and yelled directions to them. The scenery looked unchanged from its earliest history. I had expected it to be touristy and over-developed along its shores, but that was not the case; lily pads, wild roses, hollyhocks, and lilies led the way to villages with manicured English gardens, reaching down to the banks, some stretching out from lovely brick homes, some with thatched roofs, some impressive estates, some hotels on the Avon with tea tables and chairs embracing the shores.

On our last day on the Avon we encountered six locks requiring our expertise. Each lock was guarded by squadrons of geese and swans who would swim out to greet us. I was quite exhausted by the time we exited the sixth lock, but proud that we got our narrowboat safely back to its harbor.

Chapter Seventeen

The Ice Road

1998—1999

W HEN I PICKED UP the phone, Fred's joyful voice beckoned me once again. "How would you like to drive on an ice road and ski for a month on an island."

"Sounds good to me," I replied.

"Get your gear together and I'll be down tomorrow morning," he said.

We'd been many places all over the world, but one of our favorite spots was in our own backyard. Madeline Island, only about a five-hour drive from St. Paul, has two distinctive personalities: summer and winter. It's touristy and full of resorts in the summer but remote with few inhabitants in the winter. Fred secured a cabin to rent for the month of February.

Madeline Island is located off the coast of Bayfield, Wisconsin. It is the largest island in the Apostle Island chain, measuring fourteen miles long and three miles wide.

Its history is fascinating. Madeline was actually the daughter of an Ojibway Chief who traded furs with the French. She married the brother of Jean Baptiste Cadotte, the cheif French trader. After her marriage, she was baptized as Madeline. Descendants of the Cadotte family still live on Madeline Island.

Today the year-round population is approximately 180 people

but swells to 2,500 when summer residents arrive—many of them also descendants of the early settlers.

I had visited this island frequently in the summer over many years—but always wondered what it was like in the winter. Even in the summer it is a quirky place full of fascinating people—young and old. One place of interest to me was the graveyard by the marina where vine-covered tombstones revealed much of its fascinating history. Not only was Madeline buried there, but many women of child-bearing age and babies were also laid to rest amidst its bushes, wild grasses, and vines linking some graves together.

There was a museum on the other side of the island across from the dock. The history of the island was displayed beautifully here. The museum was designed by a friend of mine who made this special island with its rich history even more interesting.

La Pointe, the only town on the tiny island, operates a one-room (K-6) school with sixteen students. High school students make the daily trip by ferry to Bayfield to attend school. Islanders must adjust to the changing crossing modes—ranging from the ferry March through mid-January; then windsled (air propeller driven boat) mid-January during freeze up and break up; to crossing the frozen expanse by foot, snowmobile, or car on the "ice road" from January to early March.

Locals must keep a car (usually a junker) on shore in case students or teacher get stuck on shore when a whiteout or other emergency prevents them from returning to the island. In 1996 the tiny town of Bayfield (population 534 in winter) had one grocery store and limited supplies and newspapers. Madeline Island had one computer with internet access in its small library.

The realtor told us that there were two ways to get to the island. One was via an ice road, which was what we planned to take. However, if the ice was too thin, there was a transport that would take us across the thin ice (I wondered what in the world it could be!) and there would be a junker car waiting for us on the island, with the keys in the glove box.

Since island living had long intrigued me and since living on such a small island in the winter had even more cachet, I was eager for the experience. Remoteness and beauty was what we wanted!

We arrived the first day the ice road was open for driving. The handwritten sign stuck in the snow said: TRAVEL AT YOUR OWN RISK. We eased the jeep onto the ice of frozen Lake Superior.

"I don't know, Fred. I think I'll keep the window down so I can jump out real quick." How did they decide the ice would be thick enough to carry a car *all the way* across?!? I thought maybe the ice would crack and down we'd go. The freezing wind stung my face, but I didn't care, I wanted to be prepared! Then I noticed a row of unevenly scattered recycled Christmas trees that stood about three feet high. Their needles were brown; the trees were dead. I asked Fred what they were all about.

"They're to guide us to the island in case of a white-out or blizzard. Pretty clever, don't you think?"

I was too concentrated on locating the island, wondering what I'd do if I heard the ice start to crack. This was not fun. But then Fred quoted from the material we got about the ice road. "Remember, Shirley. The island is 2.2 miles from the shore. The average ice road lasts 52 days making it to about March 16." He looked over and gave me a wicked smile, "But you can't count on it. We're fortunate –we're almost there."

"What a comfort you are," I teased. When we saw the shore, we couldn't miss the odd-looking contraption that sat halfway on the ice. It looked like an aluminum rowboat with a motor attached to the front. A green tarp covered a homemade wooden enclosure that protected the boat operator and several passengers. There was a big circular wheel covered by some kind of outdoor screen attached to two small wooden wheels hanging over the back end. Attached on the very end over the two wheels was a huge piece of plywood painted forest green with a big white letter "W" painted on it.

I realized this would have been our alternative transport to the island if the ice road had been closed. "Look at that contraption. Why, there's barely enough room in it for two of us plus the operator. How would we have gotten our luggage and supplies for the month over?" I asked.

Fred with the alternative transportation to Madeline Island

We finally arrived at Somtara, the lovely home we had leased for the month. It was on the very tip of the island. While it was nothing special from the outside, Somtara saved its startling beauty for its interior and frontage facing magnificent Lake Superior. A long hallway with bedrooms and baths were located on the backside. A white built-in-china cabinet and buffet flanked a very modern kitchen and elegant dining room with its large shiny black dining room table. A huge sailing ship topped the majestic marble fireplace located at the far end of the long sprawling formal living room. The floors throughout were inlaid parquet covered in part by a subtle pink carpet. Bookcases flanking either side of the fireplace were filled with mostly scientific books on physics, astronomy, and Antarctica, reflecting the intellectual tastes of the owners. Everything looked new.

In spite of the elegance of the cabin's interior, we were truly in the boonies, living on the very tip of this fourteen-mile-long island. Even some of the locals said they seldom ventured out this far from La Pointe on the other end of the island.

La Pointe was a tiny town that consisted of one road running the width of the front of the island with a tavern on each end, both opened for business. A small dock was also on one end and a marina closed for the winter on the other. The shops and business places were all shut. Only one grocery store was open with no groceries and a shelf of magazines from yesteryear. If you took one magazine, you were encouraged to leave one in its place. The grocer did, however, have some frozen milk.

I suspected we were the only tourists on the island. The grocer informed us that they did have frequent snowmobilers who visit once the ice road was opened. Until that occurred, she told us, the local men would get into fist fights outside the local bars, going stir-crazy when they couldn't get off the island.

On the way back to our cabin, we passed the recycling center with a sign on its fenced gate that said, "Recycle or you will have bad karma."

The snow had been falling horizontally all day long. Our decision to stroll downtown was quickly reversed by the chilling force of the lake wind. We did walk inwards among the tall firs and snow-covered evergreens under a full moon screened by falling snow. Laughing and giggling, we pushed one another into the drifts—making snow angels. The next day the ice road was impassable because of whiteout conditions.

During the day we skied a loop of trails that were in ideal condition in beautiful, snowy wooded terrain covered with delicate shanty Irish lace on the trees, bushes, and fallen limbs. Our tracks got covered over daily with new snow.

Skiing for three or four hours each day provided us with a daily change of dramatic scenery. One day we found ourselves overlooking the iced rocky shores of Lake Superior, austere in its fantastic glacial beauty.

On one occasion, we got back in time to fix dinner for Carol and Keith,

Skiing Madeline Island

a couple we met at the pub. Carol was a teacher at the school. Keith operated the septic outfit, was on the town board, and planned to run for its chair in the next election. His platform was for lower taxes and less tourism. He wanted there to be more summer homes instead. They loved it here and skied daily. They had two freezers filled with produce they had grown on their farm, venison from deer they had shot, and chickens they had raised. They owned considerable land on the island but feared increased property taxes as the value of all land increased. Their teen-aged kids went to school in Bayfield, requiring them to have contingency plans when they could not get back to the island at the end of the school day.

We liked the spirit of this independent, self -sufficient couple who seemed delighted to be living their dreams.

How I loved living on that island. Its serenity and simplicity was so appealing.

Dinner efforts were wasted on another guest named Avery. Eat and drink she did not, but a teller of stories she was. She laughingly described herself as living on Madeline Asylum surrounded by water and ice to keep the inmates on the island. "All the crazies live here," she said, "including me." She then told us about the big car race to take place the next day off the shore of Bayfield, Wisconsin.

It sounded fun and exciting, so we ventured off the next day to see the race. The racetrack was easy to find. We could see it from the island as we followed the Christmas trees to the shore. Folks were standing around drinking coffee from mugs, some sitting on aluminum folding chairs, obviously waiting for something. We asked some locals what this race was all about.

Car race

"Have you ever seen anything like this?" Fred exclaimed.

"I wouldn't miss it for all the tea in China," I agreed.

A big racetrack had been formed on the ice near the shore. Around twenty gaily-colored junker cars, each marked with a big number on its sides, were lined up ready to race laps with Indianapolis precision. Flagmen were in place. A small crowd of families, kids, teens, and fans were seated on folding chairs. Thermoses of hot beverages were clutched in heavily gloved hands. Tailgating reigned. Round and round the ice racetrack they went—skidding, sliding, plowing into snow banks on the sides, turning round in circles. Miraculously, several made it to the finish line of each race.

At Big Bay Park, which faced the open waters of Lake Superior, was beauty one can find only by skiing. We kept stopping to absorb its icy beauty—large geometric slabs of ice in varying shades of pale blue, indigo purple, pinks and coral, stacked in careening walls on the island's irregular shores. Our skiing was frequently halted by the sounds of demanding waters, crashing into mountainous slabs of blue-shaded ice piled high, heaped on top of one another, covering the shores, sounding like cannons in the distance. We stood motionless in awed silence listening to the cacophony around us.

How fortunate we felt to be surrounded by such beauty untouched by man and his inventions. The snows continued to fall.

In my opinion, there are no more majestic sights than the seascapes and landscapes of winter. We were happy!

With great reluctance, we drove our jeep off the ice road and wended our way back home.

The Family Has Shrunk

By this time, Fred had become part of the family, staying with me two or three times a week. Linda and Nick had found a cute little apartment near us and moved in soon after our return from Madeline Island. It was a good move. They needed to be away from the interfering eyes of older folks — that would be me. Like most couples, they had many issues to work out if they were eventually to marry — they seemed headed in that direction — and they needed to sort things out on their own.

The house by now had become a home and Fred and I found ourselves playing house by ourselves with only Jasper to care what we did. Life was very comfortable for us, sleeping late, going someplace during the day, getting home to enjoy a quiet evening by the fireplace, Jasper at our feet. We would kick back in the large living room, the glow of the fire warming the room while we relaxed with a glass of wine. Sometimes we watched a movie; sometimes we read or had company over. It was a deliciously lazy time. The seasons rolled by. With spring on the way we biked, going on longer and longer trails.

There was one concern that had come into our lives. Fred was having a great discomfort with painful urination. He later found out it was enlarged prostate problems, or as he called it, "old mens'" problem.

We took a quick trip to Sam and Susie's place and while I was chatting with Susie in the kitchen, I heard the two friends sharing their health concerns. Susie and I joined them in the sunroom. It turned out that Sam's urinary issues were due to prostate cancer. Susie said they had gone online to look up different treatment options and picked the option for them.

Fred was relieved he didn't have cancer, but he found urinating becoming more and more stressful. Sam suggested he try using catheters; Susie suggested he use distracting techniques. It was a good discussion that Fred needed to have. He commented that other than his familial tremor, he had been quite fortunate in enjoying robust health.

Susie asked, "Have you noticed any change in your tremor?"

"Well, it's probably more noticeable. But it doesn't keep me from doing anything I want to do," Fred replied while he held up his hand, which was slightly trembling. "After all, we're all getting up in age — to those golden years." Other than Susie, who was younger than the three of us, we were all marching into or already in our seventies.

On the way home, we talked about winter plans. I suggested we return to the Yucatan and do more kayaking with Gail and her group.

Fred said, "Let's add another week and go on to Anna's for more snorkeling and sun."

"Okay, I'll contact them and set it up." He then dropped me off and returned to St. Cloud.

I was glad he had a chance to share his medical concerns with his best friend. He missed not having more guys in his life to engage in "guy talk." Again, I was thankful for my close circle of girlfriends.

Yucatan

Three different years we connected with a group of kayakers at Playa del Carmen, the starting point for our rugged trip by jeep to the Sian ka'an Biosphere Reserve on the Mexican Yucatan Peninsula, twenty-five miles south of Tulum. The reserve is a UNESCO World Wildlife Area, a major breeding ground for fish and some of the continent's rarest and most beautiful birds. Military soldiers with Uzis guarded the entry to the reserve. Gail, our beautiful and confident guide, would spend time talking with them with her newly acquired Spanish. Finally, after some money was exchanged, we were waved in.

The narrow gravel road was full of potholes, requiring the driver to weave from one side to the other. The road was threatened by the encroaching jungle, eager to reclaim the trail back as we pushed its leaves and vines away from our faces. Up ahead, we saw what I can best describe as "a suggestion" of a bridge. It stood there, daring us to cross the rugged ravine. The rotting wood bridge consisted of two boards with open space in between.

We all jumped out of the jeep, crossing carefully on one of the boards, leaving Gail to drive, following hand signals from one of us on where to guide the wheels. Once she was on the other side—all four wheels on terra firma, we shouted and clapped our hands at her success. I remembered her efforts years ago, the first time I traveled with her across this bridge. If anything, the bridge was in even worse shape then. Living in these parts was primitive and adventuresome.

Our cabanas were spare, providing one huge bed made of several beds pushed together, a table, a rod holding five hangers, and a tiny shower room containing a sink, shower, and medicine chest. The toilet was located in a nearby cabana.

Candles lit the paths at night, giving a shimmering soft glow. Surrounded by palm trees, we ducked as we passed under them. They were pregnant with coconut—some ripe, most green. Dead palm fronds and old coconuts lined the ground beneath the trees. Those trees along the shore were dwarfed by high winds, possibly from past storms.

The days were spent snorkeling, kayaking, and swimming, or exploring Mayan ruins and nearby villages. We didn't do as much kayaking this time because Fred said he had a frozen shoulder that limited his paddling.

We did go off snorkeling on our own quite often. At night we sat on our patio on a bank overlooking the ocean. The skies were heavy with zillions of stars.

Mexico is a land of dubious facts and vague beliefs. It seems no one knows for sure who owns what or who lives where; there were only rumors.

Talking with various people trying to do business in Mexico, we gained some understanding of how difficult it was conducting business in a land with no uniform rule of law, no known authorities in charge who could provide useful information.

It was a very different world culture dominated by a macho mentality. In addition, it was difficult to keep staff at these small seasonal businesses, open only part of the year. Much risk-taking, flexibility, and love of diversity were required attributes to any businessperson.

On our third visit, we made arrangements to spend an extra week at Rancho Punta Pelican located further south, owned by Anna, a woman from Ontario. Located at Ascension Bay, it was known for its fine bonefishing. Anna claimed the first President Bush had come here to bonefish. Bonefish are considered to be among the world's premier fly game fish and are highly sought after by anglers. They are primarily caught for sport.

Anna and Gail had to figure out how to get Fred and me to Anna's place from Punta Allen for our second week. Gail had sent Anna a note via the ice-man on Wednesday, asking how we were to get to Anna's. Gail was set to leave on Saturday and by then she still hadn't received a response from Anna. Obviously there was some breakdown in communication.

Gail thought maybe we could get a ride with the fruit and vegetable truck later in the day when that driver made his weekly rounds of all the nearby ranchos. She thought maybe he would have room. If not, she told us he could deliver another note to Anna.

By 7:00 a.m. Gail and her tour group were gone, leaving us alone with Roberta and Manuela, the couple who cared for the rancho.

Fred looked at me and said, "No problemo."

"I guess." I replied. Together we shrugged our shoulders, started laughing, and looked for something to eat. "I think Gail left us a thermos of coffee. Want some?" Together we fashioned ourselves a breakfast with what was left, then went for a swim, showered, packed, and had the rest of the coffee while waiting for the fruit and vegetable truck.

Sure enough! At 1:00 p. m., we heard the honk of the fruit and vegetable man's truck. I ran out to greet him. He introduced himself as Carlos. He knew about us and said, "no problema." He gave Manuela her groceries, weekly newspaper, and candy for the little one. Carlos and his three helpers loaded our stuff into the upper regions of his small, modest Ford truck. The three helpers climbed into the back and we slid into the front seat with Carlos.

The potholed roads were unbelievable and narrow. He had to make many stops along the way and at each rancho we got out to stretch our legs. We watched Carlos weigh the goods, wrap them in a plastic bag, and give them to the waiting customer. The older boy in the back of the truck knew where everything was. He rapidly lifted up various containers revealing other produce: eggs, chickens (skinny and scrawny with heads still intact) or a bag of chicken feet, garlic bulbs, plump tomatoes, bananas, sweet breads, potatoes, and always the weekly newspaper. It was great fun viewing the process, listening to Carlos's stories and being bumped from side to side as we continued our hot and dusty journey.

Two and a half hours later, we arrived at Anna's. ¡*Vamos a la casa de Anna!* She was much relieved to see us; it turns out she had been wondering how we were getting there since she had not gotten the note from Gail. (She later found it unread on her dresser.)

After enjoying a wonderful dinner prepared by our charming and worldly Anna, we listened to tales of the Mayan religion from our hostess and met the four bonefishermen from Seattle. They fished from 7:00 a. m. to 4:00 p. m. daily, leaving the place to us.

Anna took us on a tour of her new building projects — still in process because of a lack of supplies (cement) and transportation (that pesky broken-down bridge). The four Seattle men had arrived at that infamous bridge in the dark of night at 3:00 a.m. It took them about a half-hour of discussion before deciding to cross it.

Our casa was round, like a huge tepee with twenty-one bamboo poles meeting at the top, supporting the palm-leaf-thatched roof. A tiny patio and four windows faced the ocean — each offering dynamite views of the sea and trees. The floor looked like grey marble squares. In a clean corner room was the bathroom, complete with toilet and shower. There was no hot water, but we found the lukewarm water sufficient. We were urged to conserve on water. Electricity was supplemented with candles.

My days there with Fred consisted of eating, sleeping, lovemaking, snorkeling, swimming, reading, and, of course, the cocktail hour. "Ideal living conditions!"

Anna informed us she would be leaving for Cancun on the 5:00 a.m. bus heading for Tulum. She felt quite sure we could take the same bus when we were to leave, and eventually arrive at the Cancun airport. This was the bus that picked up locals and should have room for us.

On our last day before returning home, there was a strong wind accompanied by a pounding rain. Fred came in from snorkeling, excited because he had just seen a seven-foot-long stingray and followed it for twenty feet. The rain was sneaking into our casa between the palm leaves on the thatched roof. The geckos scurried into dry spots.

We hurried our packing, apprehensive about getting our stuff out on the jungle road in the rain by 5:00 a.m. In the pitch of darkness, Anna's assistant Megan arrived and cautioned us that the bus was often late so we should be patient.

The jungle was not friendly as we stood in the mud, looking up at the black sky while the rain persisted. We took turns running out in the road, looking for signs of the bus. I started singing all the songs I could remember from South Pacific. The sky was getting lighter. Still there was no bus. "Ideal living conditions," Fred insisted. I was running out of songs, beginning over with a robust rendition of "There is Nothing Like a Dame," when the bus finally lumbered down the wet, rutted road.

We frantically waved our arms. It stopped and spots were found to stick us in—me in the front, Fred somewhere in the back. The bus was packed with Mayans headed for Tulum for work or shopping. At Tulum, we caught another bus to Cancun, then back to wintry Minnesota. Just another day in the life of the intrepid travelers.

Chapter Eighteen
Far from Home
2001

Linda and Nick were finally living their own lives elsewhere and I was seeing Fred every other week or so. I was home alone, but I was far from lonely. I had more time to spend serving on boards, socializing with girlfriends, entertaining, and working out at the club. It seemed so easy to make new connections, whether it was with other board members, gals at the club, or new neighbors. How could anyone fear retiring—wondering what they would do with themselves? Learning to say no seemed to be the real challenge of retirement.

Fred and I were spending more time at the cabin when we weren't traveling. Occasionally, Barbara, co-owner of the cabin with husband, Don, would drop in on us in the fall, before she and Don took off for the winter to their place in Arizona. I think they appreciated the extra rent they got for the cabin and we certainly enjoyed its convenience.

But in the spring of 2001, Fred and I were getting restless for another big trip somewhere exotic. Looking through several travel magazines that had come our way, we agreed on going to China with a tour group. We decided that while we were there we would take in the post trip the tour had to Vietnam. We were excited. Soon we were packed and at the airport, waiting to board the plane.

———————

Modern freeways guarded by tall poplar trees lined our way into Beijing. It was a beautiful sunny day and Beijing's busy streets were filled with healthy-looking people; they were nicely dressed in western attire, slim, and seemingly happy. People were everywhere — on bikes, walking, driving. I was amazed by this very congested street, flanked with skyscrapers and neon signs advertising in English a variety of American products. It certainly didn't look like I had imagined. As Communist cities go, I had thought it might look as drab as I remembered Moscow from a trip I took in 1989.

We arrived at the Bamboo Garden Hotel. After dinner, we experienced the real Beijing of people living and playing comfortably in the streets; women dancing in lines, waving red scarves; men squatting on the sidewalks playing Mahjong; cab drivers lounging about the streets waiting for business; people everywhere eating, dining together in family groups, eating from a central foodpot. Open shops were selling goods ranging from groceries to fresh produce or meats to USA CDs to specialty teas.

We hired a cabby to give us a tour in his odd contraption — a motorcycle jitney of rusting metals and an overly loud motor. We hung on for dear life as our driver careened through the frenzied traffic on rough roads, nearly throwing us out the open sides.

Entering a dark alley, we sped towards a place called the Drum Tower, apparently part of the original city walls at one time. Our driver proudly directed us to the buildings barely discernible in the dark evening. Signs describing its importance were in both Chinese and English. The narrow, darkened streets were busy with people enjoying the warm evening. In a large courtyard were groups of middle-aged and older ladies dancing in lines, following the movements of another lady leading the group. Not far away was yet another group dancing with red scarves. Such dancing seemed to be a common activity for ladies of a certain age.

Later we were told that it was common for men and women to gather together in the early morning before work to do tai chi. Because of the small housing accommodations, people tended to live their lives on the streets as often as possible. In this area, homes had running water but no toilets, instead they used common WCs located in buildings scattered about. Prosperity was not too widespread in this area. "You wouldn't want urinary flow problems living here," Fred remarked, thinking of some of his issues as he aged.

As we were walking back from our jitney ride, we saw ladies of varying ages selling exotic teas who waved us over and beckoned to us to be seated. They prepared and served us hot tea in tiny cups. One young lady spoke some English. They watched our reactions to their tea with great interest. We gestured and laughed a lot together and waved to them as we left. The people largely ignored us unless we spoke first. Then they shyly but happily showed an interest in us.

One exception was a family surrounding a foodpot in an open shop who beckoned us to enter and join them. Fred did enter and, with a big grin on his face, rubbing his hand on his tummy, he smelled the soup, nodding his head in appreciation, but then he backed away, again smiling, indicating with his gestures that he was too full but thanks. They nodded enthusiastically as they grinned, giving us good-bye waves. We continued the waves as we strolled away from their shop. We felt safe and appreciated.

The next day we joined our tour group and our guide showed us about the Forbidden City and Tiananmen Square, giving us excellent information on the impressive buildings, parks, shaped sculptures, and their history. Tiananmen Square was huge, paved with horizontal beige-colored pavers. The main building was three stories high with upturned roofs. It was flanked by one-story rust-colored buildings with tan upturned roofs. The whole area was clean and well maintained, full of tourists and school children. All the temples were of similar style, some brightly colored with rose pillars and gold trim. Others might have a huge gold lion-type creature on a pedestal. We entered a primary school through its brilliant, red ornate gates full of delightful children wearing brightly colored shorts, tee shirts, and tennis shoes. Some streets had intricate circular patterns made of soft grey-colored pavers. All shops were of variable colors, mostly two-story tidy buildings with windows or open stalls showcasing their attractive wares. Bike racks filled with bikes were along the curbs. Trees were spaced along every other building.

We were impressed with what we had seen thus far. Our guide said that Beijing's priorities were met first since it was the seat of power and, I assumed, needed to be impressive as the capital of the country. Others, elsewhere in China, must have been envious, perhaps wishing they lived in the big city too.

The next day we toured the Great Wall of China, which is 1,500 miles long, built by over 30,000 men over a period of years completed about 2,000 years ago. Climbing the steps was aerobic exercise.

The Great Wall of China

Dressed in my usual khaki outfit with boots and Tilly hat, I generated some attention. A Chinese woman approached me holding out her camera. I thought she wanted me to take a picture of her, but she shook her head "no." She wanted her picture taken with me! I obliged.

"Guess I am as worthy of a photo to her as the Great Wall of China is to us," I bragged to Fred.

"Point of view," he responded with a shrug of his shoulder.

The day was full of activities leaving us hot and tired, ready for bed.

The side streets of Beijing were often narrow, made of rough stone or dirt, heavily pitted with potholes. They were flanked by two-story shops and shanties in wide open stalls. People were lingering on the graveled or cracked sidewalks, just spending time in the streets. Several chairs were often grouped together with families seated, talking, eating, playing Chinese checkers, with all kinds of bikes parked or scattered about. Some were taxi bikes, others motor bikes, their owners waiting for customers. Much laughter could be heard. The odors of many different foods could be smelled.

Prosperity was evident in certain sections of the city with dazzling colored neon lights and giant red lanterns framing buildings, bridges, and city streets. Huge modern structures with elegant high-rise apartments could be seen stretching out for blocks and blocks.

Quite suddenly the streets would fill with the chaos of hoards of bikes and pedestrians challenging vehicles for the right of way, often creating gridlock, while streets and sidewalks again became more third world. Yet most dressed Western — many looking like Yanks.

Mao would NOT approve of the rise of capitalism and the pursuit of the good life in his country. This was the era of the businessman in China — not the Communist.

Mr Yang, our excellent guide, explained, "In the '70s, people desired watches, sewing machines, and TVs. In the '80s, desires had changed to washers and dryers and computers. In the '90s it is the pursuit of homes, cars, and travel. Even the most modest homes that looked like sheds from the outside may have big-screen TVs, microwaves, washers and dryers, gas heat, and air conditioners."

A Day in Infamy

The first bit of news about the September 11 attacks on New York City and Washington D.C. came from a fellow traveler who had heard it mentioned on the 6:00 a.m. German radio station — the only English-speaking radio news they knew of. They then picked up a Chinese newspaper as they rushed to our dining room to break the news to all of us. One small photo of a plane hitting the first tower was on the front page with a caption in Chinese describing the event. We huddled together, sharing what each of us knew or thought was happening, much to the consternation of our guide, who was ready to get us off on our tour for the day. She finally let us watch the hotel TVs.

What news we could get came from a German, French, and English-language newspaper. It took some time to absorb the horror and vastness of the destruction. We gathered in groups speculating, baffled, in shock. It seemed ironic that we felt safer in China than American citizens probably felt in America. All foreign airlines had cancelled their flights to the U.S., diverting those already in flight to Canada. We were unable to call home. Our hotel lacked the technology. Throughout the day, we continued our tour visiting tombs, museums, temples, city walls, but I had quite lost my concentration.

Sophia, our tour leader, did not recognize how this national disaster was affecting us and she was quite impatient when we would cluster about any newspapers or share fears or hearsay with one another. We were preoccupied with events in the USA, and what might be occurring next. I wished I were there to experience it firsthand.

We joined two couples at their table, who told us they were sure it was a terrorist attack planned by a man named Osama Bin Laden. They were recently retired from the CIA and had worked in many exotic places around the world. One couple, Sue and Bobby, had met in Saigon during the Vietnam War where their romance began. Pat and Ron were not only good friends of Sue and Bobby, but lived near them in Washington D.C. when the four of them were not traveling. Pat considered herself a political junkie as did I, so the two of us shared information and ideas with one another.

However, I was a rookie compared to any of them. Fred was his usual affable, laid-back self who got along with everyone. He especially enjoyed sharing his love of hiking trips with Sue and Bobby, who lived and breathed the world of hiking.

The next day we left by train for Xian, a fourteen-hour trip. We found ourselves ensconced in luxury, each couple in elegant private compartments. Wine glasses were placed on our table, which was covered with a green-and-white-checked tablecloth. A pretty young lady in uniform had already served us our tea. Fred opened the wine bottle — *pop!* Our box lunches were next. The atmosphere was festive.

We bopped in on one another, laughing, feeling astonished, and fortunate to find such joy in such a place while America writhed in agony.

I had purchased travel wine glasses in a cute net bag while still in Minnesota. Now was the time to open and assemble their stems to the glasses. We were eager to show off our elegance to our fellow travelers only to find that the tag in the bag said "Made in China."

Chatting with our neighbors, the Laytons and Taylors, we wondered with them what the possible implications might be of the 9/11 tragedies. We agreed that the Boomer Generation had lost its innocence. Our generation knew that nothing would be the same again.

After checking into our Xian Hotel the next day, we had a full day of museums, opera, and dinner. That day one of our fellow travelers, Sally, had actually talked with her daughter in Minnesota. Sally's daughter was most fearful and afraid of where future targets might be. We were now at a hotel that had international TV and telephone hook-ups so the rest of us were anxious to be able to eventually connect with our loved ones.

Xian

We continued our tour of Xian, a very large city, very polluted by smoke from the many surrounding coal factories, and dust blown in from the clay hills and valleys. We drove through a countryside of cornfields guarded by mountains on the horizon as we headed for our destination of viewing the terra-cotta warriors and horses. They had been buried in the tomb of Emperor Shi of the Qin Dynasty in the feudal era China, but not discovered until 1974 by a farmer digging a well. The emperor wanted protection in the next life so he had these sculptures of 8,000 warriors along with about 400 horses buried with him. All the unearthed terra cottas are great works of art, made about 2,000 years ago. They had all been smashed and burned by a rival tribe who had seized the empire from the deceased emperor's son. Seeing the excavation process was a rare privilege for all of us to view.

The Terra Cotta Warriors

Once back at the hotel, I was able to finally get in touch with Linda. Oh, how I had longed to talk with her—to be with her during this crisis in America.

She echoed my feelings by saying through her tears, "I need you, I need my mama—I want my mama!" Anyone who knew my daughter knew she prided herself on being too cool to utter such sentiments. That she did was testament to me of the severity of what it must have been like back there in America, for those who were there.

She said, "Mom, you have no idea what it is like here. Everyone is frightened about what might happen next. Experts say they could hit any place in America, like the Mall of America." I had no idea that there might be any target in Minneapolis "Everyone's flying

American flags. Fighter planes fly overhead — right here in the Twin Cities! There are no commercial flights." I could hear the fear in her voice. "In the travel business we know travel will never be the same again. 3M is already cutting business travel once commercial flights are back up, for phone and video conferencing instead. You've got to get home as soon as possible before war breaks out somewhere else. Folks think Bush will attack Afghanistan soon and then how will you get home?"

"Darling, there's no way we can get home now with no commercial travel to America. And it is perfectly safe here. We couldn't be in a safer place."

"Mom, you have no idea what it's been like for everyone here. We all saw the whole attack on live TV."

"You're right, I don't know. But I won't be able to contact you for at least another week. We are on our way tomorrow to Wuhan." We had a five-day cruise booked on the Yangtze. "That will totally isolate us from TVs, e-mails, phones, and newspapers." The phone card suddenly disconnected us before Linda could hear me say, "What a time to be isolated." I would much have preferred to be in the U.S. — but that was not to be.

We took a plane to Wuhan, a "small" town of eight million people. There we boarded an unbelievably luxurious cruise boat. Victorian Cruises advertised itself as "The Civilized way to see the Yangtze." Our large and spacious stateroom was much nicer than most hotel rooms. Because there had been no international flights since the Tuesday terrorist attack, only seventy passengers were on this cruise. There were many cancellations. We couldn't have been happier. Our whole crew of fifteen were happy campers. The harbor was lit up like New Orleans, all glitter and glamour. It was as if our whole group decided our fate was "to have a ball doing the expat thing."

We did cluster around the bulletin board in the ship lobby each morning to read the sheet of news fragments revealing little. The TVs in our staterooms showed only foreign movies with subtitles, some in English. We were learning what it felt like to have no access to news. From being frustrated in trying to gain information, we gradually gave up and conversations gradually shifted to our daily activities.

While others took a tour, we wandered off on our own and

became instant celebrities while mingling with the locals. We watched some kids play basketball complete with regulations, referees in uniform, coaches, and a scoreboard propped up on two chairs. A handful of onlookers sitting on some crude benches were cheering them on. When Fred took out his camera, several young boys came over, trying out their English on us, very politely saying, "How are you? I am fine. Welcome to China!"

The tropical climate gave the city streets and shops a Mexican and Caribbean appearance.

The shops were made of corrugated iron with open fronts, selling or repairing a multitude of items. TVs were in some. Many were interested in the two tall Yanks. And others were eager to greet us with the few words of English they knew. They loved having their pictures taken. Fred bought some beer, tried on some thongs (his feet too big), and got some undershorts. Many were involved in assisting him with these purchases.

Later we sat on deck enjoying our fellow expats and viewing the polluted countryside. One could write chapters on the vastness of pollution in all of China. On the train, we had watched it come down from the mountainside to the tops of the trees, covering them with dirt, enveloping the horizon. On the boat, not only horizons but the narrow shores soon disappeared, blanketed by a heavy grayish black fog, even though a blue sky shown on us.

On the Yangatze

Like all Chinese rivers, the Yangtze flows east. Its third gorge is the most spectacular. We continued on to the three-gorge dam project.

There was much talk about it while we were there and many were concerned about the dam's impact on China's people. The one and half million people would be relocated to newly constructed homes elsewhere, which would require an allocation of 40% of the entire budget to meet the expenses. Only in Communist China could such a decision be made in a timely fashion by so few, affecting so many.

We were waited on like royalty by the staff of many to serve so few. The meals and drinks were delicious and the many shipboard activities great fun.

Hanoi, Vietnam

Only seven of our group continued on to Hanoi, but Fred and I fell in love with it and its people almost immediately. Driving to the city, we passed verdant rice paddies and their many workers, flanked by tall willowy trees and French villas, many in need of paint jobs, but nonetheless looking dignified. Our young, handsome guide, Dao Tren Zung—dressed in jeans, tee shirt, and baseball cap worn backwards—was easygoing, highly knowledgeable, and proud of his country's history. He had put together a schedule for us that was both informative and fun.

The food was, quite simply, the greatest. Trip highlights included the Ho Chi Minh home and museum, the Hanoi Hilton where photos of Senator McCain, who appeared highly regarded, remained—the evening water puppet show, the delightful zany Cyclo tour through the Old Quarter, and a day-long private cruise on a traditional wooden sailboat on the Ha Long Bay, swimming in its cooler water, offering us relief from the unremitting heat and humidity.

Street scenes that we found fascinating on our Cyclo tour were dominated by happy people in all settings, young and old alike. School children dressed in cute uniforms with red bows waved enthusiastically at us, as did a wedding party of happy guests. A naked father bathed his son sitting in a plastic blue tub while other sons were on bikes and a mom weaving something. We passed by a series of shops in two-story shanties that were in poor repair but full of hanging clothes and motor bikes. Families here also seemed to spend much of their time out of their apartments and hung out on the streets just as they did in poorer sections of Beijing. And they appeared to be just as happy.

Trying to cross the streets by our hotel found me frozen on the curb with fear. The streets were wide, filled with bikes, motor bikes, cars speeding along, turning left or right with no signs of lights or signs to aid pedestrians. I noticed Fred wasn't trying to cross, either.

There was a family standing by the hotel watching us, probably with some amusement. Suddenly, the teenaged son came by my side, took my hand, and led me into the street, through traffic, walking slowly all the way to the other side. Fred was right behind us. Like magic we arrived safely at the other side with traffic having gone around us, never stopping.

We heard the family clapping as we successfully made our way across. Frankly, I couldn't believe I was still alive, but I was so grateful to the boy and to his family that I waved happily to them from the other side.

We really didn't want to leave. In fact, we even wished we could take a train to South Vietnam and see Ho Chi Minh City, formerly known as Saigon. But we both knew it was unrealistic. Linda needed me and a war was about to start.

Our guide Dao had noticed Fred's tremor of his right hand and asked him about it. Fred said it was familial tremor—that his Dad had it. "Has it seemed to you that it is a bit more now," I carefully asked. "It seems like it affects your right leg now and then."

"It doesn't give me any trouble. Not to worry," Fred replied, brushing off my concern. Dao invited Fred to visit his uncle, an Eastern holistic doctor, who he was convinced could help cure the tremor. Much to my surprise, Fred readily agreed. He was such a cynic about medicine and its touted cures, but the grin on his face suggested he saw it as another experience worth exploring. While he went, I enjoyed our air-conditioned, luxurious hotel suite with CNN where I caught up on the news.

Fred joyfully came back with a paper bag full of what looked like rabbit turds. He was to take so many of these daily. Fred had great fun describing the doctor and his long beard who spoke no English, but frequently took Fred's pulse while murmuring, "Hum," and wanted to know what time of day Fred was born. His small, dark office had walls full of tiny cubby holes filled with different kinds of medicines. This was a story Fred was to tell friends and neighbors numerous times.

He actually took the "medicine" as directed over the weeks, saying it couldn't hurt. He was given the doctor's address to use when refilling the "prescription." Since we would be returning to the USA via Hong Kong the next day, Fred was amused at how airline inspectors might view the paper bag full of rabbit turds. As it turned out, he had no problem with airline security in either Hong Kong or Chicago.

When I called Linda that night, she had only sad and bad news. Fear continued permeating the country and she got laid off from her job as one of 3M's more experienced travel agents. She remained concerned that we might get caught up in retaliatory attacks on tourists since the U.S. had started its attack on Afghanistan. We were aware that Bush was contemplating an attack on Afghanistan, but hadn't known how imminent it was. We assured her we felt very safe but wondered what we would find when we landed first at Chicago's airport, then our own.

The Hong Kong airport was quiet with few passengers there and on our plane home. The Chicago airport was full of passengers and guards and soldiers welcoming us back to the good old USA. Hours later we landed at the Twin Cities airport and my very happy daughter.

It seemed strange driving through all the flag-covered streets, bridges, and homes in our neighborhood. Neighbors and friends welcomed us back, all talking at once about the horrors, the fears, the rumors; some perhaps finding our affects a bit flat. But quite frankly, Fred and I both agreed, that not until several years later, when the *Today* show replayed the whole day's news from 9/11, could we begin to identify fully with the events of that day.

Chapter Nineteen
Last Trip Across the Pond
2002—2006

SINCE SEPTEMBER 11, 2001, we had not traveled across the pond. With all the uncertainty in the world and the increasing frustrations involved with traveling, it just made sense to us to explore more of our own side of the ocean. Too many unsettling events were happening in the Mideast, creating an aura of fear reaching us in our own country. I was beginning to feel like Dorothy in *The Wizard of Oz*: "There's no place like home."

"So how're the rabbit turds coming?" I asked Fred the next time he bopped into town.

"Actually I took them all, but I didn't notice any changes." He held out his shaky hand. "Don't think I'll order anymore. If anything, there's more of a tremor."

"Have you checked it out with a good old USA doctor?" I asked. "You know, Tib found out she has Parkinson's and she doesn't even have tremors. But I've noticed she has more of a stooped walk and a shuffle that she says is typical of some."

Fred allowed that it probably was time to check things out with his friendly sawbones. "I'm spending enough time trying different things for my enlarged prostate and that's a pain in the ass."

In the meantime, we decided to get in a little skiing at our friends' cabin. It wasn't the North Shore, but it was more convenient. The snow was pretty good and each day we'd wander further away, finding even better trails in the many state parks on the Wisconsin side. I could tell, though, that Fred was letting me be the leader more often as we were cutting new trails or going up hills.

As usual, I brought my trusty crockpot and each day we'd come home to those nifty filling meals. "What's it to be tonight?" Fred asked as he lifted the lid of the crockpot. "Um, beef stew," he said approvingly as he lifted the lid. The aroma was great. We got out the bowls, turned on the music and lit the candles, then dipped into the stew.

"What's that clacking sound?" I asked as I looked at Fred. "Are you doing that on purpose?" He looked dumbfounded as he watched his hand banging the spoon against the side of the bowl.

"Now that's more than familial tremor, Fred. Look at your leg." His leg was twitching quite noticeably. "Has this happened to you before?"

"A few times but not this noticeable. Guess I better see a neurologist."

"That sounds like a good idea," I agreed.

The next day when he dropped me off, he came into the house and made an appointment.

Within a few weeks he called to tell me that he had been diagnosed with Parkinson's. I was quickly on the phone with Tib, seeking her advice. She was very forthright and matter-of-fact about her condition, offering to loan me a book on the subject. She said she would even meet with Fred if he wanted. She explained that Parkinson's was very difficult to diagnose because it manifested itself in so many different ways. She had joined a group that met regularly at a Parkinson's Center in Minneapolis. I thought to myself that this was going to be difficult for Fred to add yet another health problem demanding attention, along with his already constant urinary flow issues.

When next I saw him he had a bag of medicines. "Christ," he said, "I'm going to be spending most my time counting pills, trying to figure out which ones to take at what time along with spending so much time trying to pee."

"Ain't growing old fun?" I asked in a cheery voice.

As usual, we both tried to make light of this new information we both knew to be more serious. All of this was in addition to his frozen shoulder problems that had made kayaking history.

Fred's resilience never ceased to amaze me. If he couldn't do one thing, he'd do another. The next thing I knew, he had us booked on a quick trip with a tour group to the Galapagos Islands where we could follow Darwin's explorations of finches that lead to his theory of adaptation.

We sailed among the islands making up the Galapagos in a little boat. Some days we had up-close encounters with colonies of nesting blue-footed boobies and magnificent frigatebirds. Other days we hiked the iguana haven of Punta Espinoza over young lava flows. Although we brought up the rear in walking activities, I was relieved to see that Fred was still able to snorkel and swim; to do so among sea lions was fun and quite gratifying.

However, that summer our three-hour biking outings became a thing of the past. One day while we were out biking, Fred was ready to call it a day after an hour. He now needed me to help him lift our bikes on his bike rack. His endurance and strength was waning.

He had met with Tib several times but seemed uncomfortable engaging in some of the activities with her for people with Parkinson's. I sensed his reticence and wondered if he couldn't see himself *that* impaired, or if he just thought it futile that any such interventions could make a whit of difference. It was evident that he didn't want to discuss it with me and I doubted he was forthcoming with Sonia either. He was seeing his neurologist regularly, trying out different combinations of medications to relieve some of his tremors that now included much of his right side.

Some nights he would frighten me with tossing his arms about, hitting me as he thrashed with imaginary soldiers yelling out to "kill the bastards." I'd sit upright, shaking him until he woke up, telling him what he was doing. Sometimes he'd recreate the dream for me. Other times he couldn't remember. Often he'd be in the bathroom for what seemed like hours before he could urinate and then it was often painful.

And his physical limitations were worsening. Getting in and out of his car was hard work. Falling asleep at the wheel was becoming more frequent. His balance issues were becoming more noticeable.

He insisted on driving, but I watched him like a hawk. His meds were probably making him sleepy and he was good at pulling over to the side of the road to nap a bit, or stop at a station and get some coffee.

He continued visiting me every other week, come rain or come shine. But he was getting weaker, tiring more easily and having some difficulties swallowing.

By 2006, Fred was restless to explore places in Eastern Europe he had not yet seen. It didn't seem like a good idea to me. Yet he found a group trip on a river cruise along the Danube that he thought would be perfect for us. It would start at Budapest and end in Romania. A four-day pre-trip in Prague was included. Quite frankly, these were places both of us had always wanted to see. I finally agreed to the trip while hoping it might be called off at the last minute.

Family, friends, and neighbors alike wondered how wise it was for Fred to undertake our upcoming trip so far away — in Eastern Europe — with all his medical difficulties.

I, too, shared their concerns about him traveling. But I was Fred's lifeline to travel. He needed me to accompany him, assist him in walking, and to understand travel instructions by our guides. That was why the tour group we booked appealed to both of us. We were no longer capable of winging it on our own in a foreign culture.

This trip provided small groups with guides. With the bulk of the trip on a small boat with our own cabin, I knew it might well be a challenge, but my love for the guy, knowing how important this trip was to him, was the deciding factor for me.

Several nights before the trip, Fred woke me up in the middle of the night having what looked like a seizure. He was yelling something, but his words were garbled; he sounded like a stroke victim. His limbs were thrashing about as he was trying to get up. He kept yelling something at me that I couldn't understand. I was terribly frightened, wondering what to do, thinking I needed someone to help me with him. Before I could call the neighbor, he suddenly lurched forward and sat up, still yelling something I couldn't understand.

Then it occurred to me he was hunting for the catheter he needed in order to urinate. I attempted to help him up, but he was very heavy. As he lurched towards the door, I suddenly feared he might fall down the steep steps right outside the bedroom door. I caught up with him and gradually got him to the bathroom at the end of the hall. The whole incident lasted probably no more than twenty minutes. He suddenly came out of it when he was back in the bedroom and asked me what happened.

He said he'd call his neurologist in the morning, but he wondered if it might have something to do with the change of medications she had made for him the day before.

I listened to his conversation with her. She agreed that it probably was due to the too-quick change of meds. I thought it was a Transient Ischemic Attack (TIA) like my friend Clem had some time ago. TIA attacks generally last about twenty minutes and are often precursors for a stroke.

However, the next few days went by with no further problems. The neurologist approved the Eastern European trip so we took off for Prague.

Last Trip Across the Pond
Prague, Budapest, & the Blue Danube

Fred's Parkinson's disease was readily apparent to a couple we met and joined for drinks and a sandwich at our hotel in Prague. This couple had experience with the disease and shared what they knew about procedures and meds that had seemed helpful. We liked this couple and saw more of them during the trip.

The next morning there was a big group discussion by our two leaders, Raz from Hungary and Petr from the Czech Republic. They gave us an outline of what we would be doing during our four days in Prague, before going on to Budapest for three days, then embarking on the boat for our seven-day cruise of the Danube.

I could tell that Fred was having difficulty focusing on the discussion. Later that morning, he also struggled during the lecture on the politics of the transition and transformation of the Czech Republic from 1791 to the present time. Instead of joining the group on a walking tour of that area of the city, Fred opted for sitting at one of the charming outdoor cafes for coffee. His walking was painfully slow.

Back in our hotel room, he had difficulty changing clothes, remembering what we were to do next, or where his things were. At the hotel restaurant, he stumbled and spilled food while trying to get to our table. I could tell I was going to have to seat him, then get food for both of us. Frankly, he was a menace when on his own.

I had not seen him this bad before. His body was so ravaged by disease that he seemed no longer able to function at his previous level. He was tiring quickly, was easily confused, and was unable to focus efficiently or to process information effectively.

The next few days I found myself unable to take my eyes off him because he would wander off, seemingly in a daze, frequently going the wrong direction. He complained of his legs being very achy, causing him to wobble, veering from side to side when tired. The poor guy was a shell of what he was two years before. It pained me to see the effects of the disease on this dynamic, strong, wise, and fun guy of yesteryear. Yet he would show flashes of his old self in some social settings, such as the cocktail lounge with fellow passengers.

I had been using my reluctant brain far more, figuring out simple problems myself; this gave me an unexpected sense of accomplishment. I had typically let Fred figure things out. But on this trip, I had to do the listening to directions for both of us since Fred had trouble following such directed conversations. I also needed to keep track of his possessions, pack for him, even read the Prague city and subway maps and figure out how to use them to get places in Prague—a big first for me. It had taken Fred's illnesses to get me to assume responsibility for doing my own listening to details, thinking and problem solving, instead of delegating such cognitive tasks to others. This trip found me learning many new skills.

We were unable to join the group for a visit to the Prague Castle because Fred was still feeling nauseated and had diarrhea, so we later took a stroll to the neighboring Jewish Cemetery. We peeked through the iron gates and admired its rows and rows of tall graceful trees; it was a beautifully maintained cemetery. The heat was stifling and Fred was having extreme difficulty walking and sometimes even standing. What had seemed like a short walk back to the hotel left us both exhausted.

We took a nap and didn't wake up until dinnertime. After several false stops on the metro, we made it to Old Town for dinner in an outdoor café. Unfortunately, Fred was unable to eat much of his pasta; he had no appetite and hiccups. We were both very discouraged by his deteriorating health and didn't know what to do other than hope that with more sleep he would get better.

We were scheduled to visit the town of Terezin, site of the WWII concentration camp of Theresienstadt, which Fred had been looking forward to viewing. The town was turned into a model ghetto, but in reality had served as a transit point; from here 335,000 people were transported to the Nazi death camps. Only 5% of those survived.

Fred was determined to go, even though the guides tried to discourage him. They said it would involve much walking and they would have to leave us behind so that the others could view Theresienstadt in its entirety. Consequently, we explored it on our own, commenting on the many gravestones, talking with some of the workers, and doing much resting. I was impressed with the quality of the questions Fred asked the workers, who seemed pleased to be asked.

Amazingly, Fred had no memory of being at Theresienstad when we discussed it later that day.

Fred had difficulty getting out of bed, standing up, and walking without support. In fact, he fell in the bathroom, bringing the shower rod and curtain down with him. His balance was truly lacking and he had intermittent hiccups for about three days, even though he was taking an antidepressant for it; sometimes the hiccups rippled up and down his chest, shaking his whole body. He dropped his pills frequently on the floor because of the extreme tremors, balance problems, and manual dexterity difficulties.

He wanted desperately to be as independent as possible and to continue the trip. Petr and I agreed that he was too incapacitated. He needed a catheter to urinate and was easily confused, not knowing at times where he was.

Both Petr and Raz said I must make a decision for Fred. When they recommended to Fred that he cancel the trip, he said, "Well, we've come this far. We might as well continue on." The guides informed me that once we got on the boat going further East, medical help would become less available and reliable. "But," I said, "I can't make a decision for Fred. I am not his wife. I have no legal authority to do so."

"But you must. You see how he is. We cannot assume responsibility for him," both insisted.

I said we'd have to see how he was in the morning.

At 9:00 p.m., Fred insisted on walking along the Vltava River, which involved a ride on the subway, going six stops. So we did and had a good time. The river nightlife was active, the skyline spectacular, framing the historic church and Prague Castle. Sculls and pleasure boats zipped over the water under the two imposing arch bridges under a magnificent sky. We sipped piña coladas at a picturesque outdoor café on the banks of the Vltava listening to melodious tunes sung by Louis Armstrong and Bing Crosby.

"Fred," I whispered into his ear, "they're playing our very own Louis Armstrong here." I snuggled next to him, laying my head on his shoulder.

"I believe they are," he murmured as he hugged me close to him.

With no difficulty at all, thanks to Fred's amazing radar system, which began functioning again, we made it home by 10:30. Fred was in bed shortly thereafter and I did last-minute packing, readying all our suitcases for a 6:30 a.m. pick-up.

We needed a wheelchair to get Fred to the bus fifteen minutes late. It was grim. Fred now seemed reluctantly resigned to seeing the doctor and leaving the trip early, although I was not sure he understood what we were talking about. Not only was he easily confused, his skin often felt hot to the touch.

While on the bus ride to Budapest, using a microphone, Petr shared his life story with all of us in a most entertaining way. When I asked him, "How did you learn to speak such excellent American-type English?"

He replied, "I lived with a family in Waterloo, Iowa for my senior year in high school so I could learn hockey."

"Amazing," I said. "I lived in Waterloo and my kids went to high school there." We became instant friends. But he continued the pressure on me to decide about Fred. I finally said, after a lot of worrying and thinking, "Have a doctor at the hotel waiting for us and we'll do whatever he recommends." With that, Petr whipped out his cell phone and quickly made the necessary arrangements.

In the meantime, I wondered how I'd manage to get Fred on a plane and then to his home. I'd have to call his son, Tom; fortunately, I had his cell phone number with me. I was never without it when with Fred. But I had met Tom only once and that was twenty-five years ago. He didn't even know who I was. And trying to reach him would not be easy. Nor would it be easy to reach my daughter. She only had a cell phone and it was on only when she was home from work. The more I thought about it, the more worried I became.

Two doctors awaited us in our hotel room. Petr did the translating. They said Fred had a temperature of 104, was probably suffering from an infection, and needed to be hospitalized immediately. The ambulance awaited us as we made our way to the hotel front entry, making Fred and I the center of attention among our fellow passengers. The ambulance quickly whisked Fred, Petr, and me away.

Petr and I remained in the waiting room while the doctor examined Fred. Petr handed me a candy bar he got from a machine. I said, "This is about the time I'd ask you to tell me your life story, but you've already done it so I'll tell you mine." I opened the candy wrapper and prepared for a long wait. "I was born on a farm in Iowa…" Before I could tell Petr more, the doctor joined us with good news.

He said that Fred was dehydrated and suffering from a urinary infection. He would need to be in the hospital three days. Then he should be just fine.

Oh, was I relieved! What I thought was a rapid progression of his Parkinson's was unrelated. He was merely dehydrated because of his refusal to drink water during our flight, choosing to drink wine instead. We had had many discussions on the water issue in the past with his repeatedly telling me, "You're not my mother; I think I hear her calling." And a urinary infection was due to his reuse of catheters.

He didn't like discussing his medical issues and so I chose to refrain from asking him questions I sensed he didn't want raised. I did ask him if he had discussed his health issues with Sonia and he mumbled a response suggesting he had. When I asked what she thought he should do, he said, "She pretty much says the same thing you say." That told me nothing. I could only guess how long he'd had Parkinson's without a diagnosis.

I had dinner with the group that night back at the hotel. We set a place in Fred's honor with wine flowing in abundance. Those at our table made frequent toasts to Fred.

When Petr and I visited him at the hospital the next day, we found a more healthy, vital-looking man, reading a book in his hot single room with a sweet plump nurse dressed in white busily fussing over him. She spoke no English. He spoke no Hungarian. They got along fine.

Fred had the only single room with its own shower and toilet because he was "The American!" Petr said the hospital had few single or double rooms and they were reserved for VIPs. The large dormitory-sized rooms contained many beds and were for most of their patients. Since the hospital provided no patient clothing or meals, it was necessary for their relatives to bring them from home.

The building was badly in need of repairs inside and out. The huge block buildings, with cracked paint, roofs in need of shingles, and windows with cracked glass, reminded me of the glum, neglected-looking buildings I saw when visiting Russia in 1989. Office equipment appeared equally dated, long obsolete in the USA.

Fred was as pleased to see us as we were to see him. He was witty, charming, with his old sense of humor, lying in a bed too short for him with a catheter hooked up to a bag. The doctor said he must remain two more days. He would get out just in time to board the river cruiser. Already Fred was asking Petr if he could rent bikes at ports along the way. We looked at one another, both thinking he might be overly optimistic—getting ahead of himself as it were.

Petr and I were so relieved to find Fred displaying his great spirits and ability to converse with vigor and clarity. He didn't seem like the same person who was admitted the day before.

When we went the next day to visit Fred, he was dressed and said he was ready to go. Somehow he had talked the doctor into releasing him a day early. It took considerable time to get the discharge papers ready to be signed by the doctor, largely due to the inefficient old office equipment. We took the city bus home, stopping at a pharmacy to fill Fred's prescription for antibiotics.

There was excitement among our group when we strolled into the hotel with a reincarnated Fred! He still had some balance, swallowing, and tremor issues due to the Parkinson's, but not the disorientation and severe balance problems, which were due to the urinary infection and dehydration.

The river cruiser was delightful. Our private room had its own outdoor balcony complete with deck chairs and made us feel like a couple of "swells." Because of the narrowness of the Danube, we could practically touch the shores as we lounged in our deck chairs.

In spite of the doctor's advice to wait several days before having an alcoholic drink, Fred had a gin and tonic delivered to our room pronto. I couldn't believe it! I angrily and sternly reminded him we missed out on four days in Prague and three days in Budapest— that's SEVEN DAYS— because of his refusal to drink water on the plane and, by the way, to not reuse catheters. I added that this would be my last trip across the pond with him if he continued such careless behaviors. He seemed dismissive but I knew this was it and that travels across the pond were done for me. I was over it!

The days flowed by comfortably with an easygoing schedule. We dined with favorite guests in the beautiful dining room surrounded by scenic windows, and we spent much time on the open deck. Each day we stopped at such interesting places as Vukovar and Osijek, which were heavily damaged during the Croatian-Serbian war of 1991-95. Much of the heavy damage remained.

In the 1960s, Yugoslavia and Romania cooperated on a joint venture that raised the level of the Danube with a series of hydroelectric dams called the Iron Gates. The Danube was now placid through the Iron Gates, its spectacular two-mile-long gorge now underwater. We passed through customs at Ruse, Bulgaria's fourth largest city, and docked during the early morning hours in Belgrade, the capital of Serbia, one of Europe's oldest cities and the center of political and cultural life in the country. Belgrade and the rest of Serbia-Montenegro were just emerging from many years of repressive rule. We finally entered the Black Sea Canal and continued cruising toward Constanta, Romania's chief port. From there we flew home with no difficulties.

The cruise was full of delightful people, the entertainment provided by our plucky staff and crew full of laughs, the food plentiful and delicious, and the sense of history almost too much to absorb.

Even while I was experiencing this whole wonderful trip, it had become very clear to me that this would be our last trip across the pond.

Chapter Twenty
Separate Ways
2004—07

FAMILY AND FRIENDS WERE relieved the Danube trip ended up alright and that I had declared it to be my last trip across the pond with Fred. I could sense they were concerned about my future with Fred in his deteriorating condition. Yet he continued to visit me several days a week, every other week.

The neighbors probably shook their heads a few times at seeing the effort it took him just to get out of his jeep, sometimes asking for help from a nearby teenager to cross the street. A neighbor would often ask, "Should Fred be driving a car?" I'd just shake my head sympathetically and reply with a shrug, "Unfortunately, it is not my decision to make."

One day during a phone call Fred shared astonishing news with me. "Sonia and I have legally separated. I have moved out and will be staying at the cabin."

"What caused this?" His news shocked me. I had no idea they were having such discussions. "Is this as much of a surprise to you as it is to me?" I asked.

"I just decided I couldn't live in that environment any longer. Her words have become too harsh. We have agreed to sell the house and property and split our assets."

Fred was not one to make rash decisions. He was a private

person who kept his own counsel, unlike me who invited my closest friends to help me with many decisions. He had made it clear to me from the beginning that what he did when he was not with me was his business and he would share what he chose to share. The only questions I typically asked him were about Sonia's health or news from his son. And he had not been too forthcoming even to those questions.

Trying to read Fred's mind was like trying to guess what cards a professional gambler was holding by looking at his face or listening to the evasiveness of his words. I often thought that Fred protected himself from wading into possible dangerous verbal water by using his set of favorite high-frequency words or phrases like "I think I hear my mother calling," or "I think it's time for Vespers." This was his way of saying he was done with the discussion. He often said you couldn't get in trouble for words you hadn't spoken.

My friends wondered what the implications of his decision to separate from Sonia would mean to me. My friend Sandy might have been hoping for a marriage between us. She believed marriage was for everyone. Most others, and certainly Linda, probably suspected little change to occur in our relationship.

I wondered about the wisdom of Fred and Sonia separating at this stage of their marriage when they both had such serious health concerns. Linda agreed.

But both Fred and Sonia moved fast to sell their large house outside of town and put their lots up for sale. Sonia soon bought a small house in town that was more convenient for her. It had one floor with one bedroom and a small office. Fred made it clear he'd continue to have his own place. Yet there was no talk of divorce.

Eventually, he rented a one-bedroom apartment in Sauk Rapids that faced a city park overlooking the mighty Mississippi River. The river was magnificently viewed from his living room window. He seemed very pleased. His place was surrounded by tall trees and many bike paths that he was looking forward to exploring. The small town was only twenty minutes away from St. Cloud and had a small shopping area near him. He and Sonia would have lunch together from time to time.

As my friends aged, some deciding to move into condos or apartments, they asked if I had thought about moving. "You don't want to leave that big house of yours for Linda to deal with when you're gone," suggested my dear friend, Geralda, whose husband had recently died from Parkinson's.

I jokingly replied, "It'll give Linda another career, deciding what to do with this house. She could become an expert selling stuff on eBay."

"Now seriously, Shirley, you need to start thinking about living in a smaller place that isn't so much work," she continued.

"That might suit you, but it isn't what I want. I love living in all this space. I have plenty of room for all my toys, all the things I hold dear, and extra bedrooms for the occasional guest. Also, I must have a yard for summer entertaining." I looked out across my sunroom into my small but beautiful backyard. "I love living alone and I thoroughly enjoy my own company." I was a career woman all my adult life, and home then was just a place to keep my stuff. I looked around at my beautiful home and thought of all the work that went into it. I had as much enjoyment creating my home as I did creating my career. "My house is finally a place that reflects me and is truly my castle." I reminded her that I often housed people for the Penumbra Theatre when they needed a place for an out-of-town playwright, dancer, or actor.

"But isn't that a lot of work?" she asked.

"I have more help now than when I was married to men who thought they had handyman skills but did not." I thought of all the projects that sat for years and years. "Now that I am in charge of my income, I am CEO of Pearl Manor and I have five adjunct employees." With hand in front of my face, I raised a finger for each person I counted off, "Brian who maintains the house, Steve who manages my finances, John who takes care of my car, Greg the personal trainer who keeps me in good shape, and Terri who cleans the house." I lowered my hand and looked off again into the backyard. "And Fred who is my playmate. His services are free! It's a heck of a deal. No one is required to work outside of his or her skill level. I couldn't be happier."

That ended the conversation.

———————————

Fred called me from the cabin soon after arriving there for the winter. He was distraught. "What's the matter, Fred? You sound upset."

"Shirley, I can't ski! I tried today and I couldn't stay up! It's all over." He sounded absolutely traumatized.

My heart was pounding in my chest. An ache rose in my throat. I swallowed hard to choke back the tears. "Oh, Fred, I am so sorry. I know how important skiing is to you. I am truly sorry."

"Well, it's been a good run. But now it's done," he said in an absolutely fatalistic way.

This was the most despondent I had ever heard Fred sound. It was more than a statement of loss of balance; it was a loss of what he most identified as his reason for living — leading the active life of travel and adventure. For him, he saw no other reason for snow to exist than to ski on. What would he do with his winters, all cooped up.

Soon he was back at my home. "Darling, this is where you need to be right now. Let me help you with your stuff." I greeted him with all the warmth I could muster. "I've invited some friends to join us for dinner."

Fred walked into the dining room and was pleased to see my neighbor Ed. He came with his new lady friend Lisa, who, interestingly enough, lived just four houses down the street from me. She and Ed had been neighbors all these years but only encountered one another recently when each was out for a walk. Gradually, they started meeting for walks. And the old story of how one thing leads to another became their story and now it seemed possible that they might become an item.

The four of us felt an instant rapport — all living on the same street. They were a quiet couple who projected an aura of acceptance and serenity to others — quite a contrast to the more bombastict style of Fred and me. On the other hand, Ed, being Norwegian to the core, could tell great "Lena and Ole" stories, but his favorite story was Fred's tale of being lost nude in the halls of a Norwegian hotel. We never ceased to get a good laugh from that one.

I served one of my specialty dinners of Chicken Parisienne and noodles with a Caesar salad. Lisa provided a fruit tart dessert. The wine flowed freely.

After they left, Fred thanked me for having them there when he arrived. "You know how much I like Ed. And his lady friend has that same quiet acceptance of the world that he has. They go well together. Strange how people meet and connect."

That summer while Fred was exploring the bike paths of Sauk Rapids, I joined Sandy and Clem for a trip to Chicago to visit museums, see a play, and explore. We took the train there and back, had perfect weather, explored Chicago's famous Michigan Drive, and laughed and giggled all the way home. It wasn't until a day or so later that Clem told us she had Level-4 cancer. "Why did you wait so long to tell us," Sandy wanted to know.

"I wanted to keep Chicago fun for all of us and it was," she replied. "As for the cancer, it is what it is." We marveled at her calmness.

As winter approached, Fred wanted to take one last trip to Mexico. He reasoned that it was "not across the pond" and was only an hour's flight from Houston, Texas if we stayed on the Gulf side again. We secured a small intimate casa for a month near Chuburnna in the Yucatan near where our friends Rob and Joan lived. We met them on our first trip to this part of Mexico. They were from Ontario and had started a business selling and renting property to foreigners. We kept in contact with them and later used their services to rent a casa near Chuburnna.

"Mom, I'm sure you know what I'm thinking about this trip," Linda said. "I know it's only an hour flight from Merida to Houston, but you first have to get to Merida from Progreso and you don't like to drive."

It's true that I would get stressed out driving six-lane metro freeways, but I told Linda that the two-lane cement highway from Merida to Progreso was well lit and had considerably slower-moving traffic than the Twin Cities. "I have driven it before," I told Linda, "and the cinder and dirt roads from Progreso to Chuburnna have some fast-driving families on old bikes and some old trucks chugging along spewing diesel fuel, but I think I can outrun them in a rental."

"Okay, Mom. I rest my case. May your 'universe' be with you."

A Long Night's Journey into Day

After a beautiful first day of sun, blue skies, and sand, of cocktails on the terrace, of a fine meal in our modest dining area, we were aroused from deep sleep shortly before midnight when all hell broke loose. A roaring sound like jets taking off, or trains roaring through, accompanied by sounds of shutters banging—our casa shaking and trembling from the impact—caused us to jump out of bed, stumbling in the pitch dark to find lights. Winds roared through our abode.

Quickly we began closing all the shutters, wondering if a hurricane or huge storm was attacking us. This was weather we had not experienced before. With the last shutter closed, we jumped back into bed, burrowing under all the blankets, hoping our casa would remain intact under the assault. It was a fitful sleep—waking up frequently only to find it still pitch dark. *Will day never come?* We could see nothing in our shuttered dwelling and dared not open one—even a crack—to see what was happening outside. We knew our patio furniture, bath towels, and beach shoes had been whisked away somewhere by the wind that never stopped.

During the cocktail hour our second day, the wind still had not stopped. Our shutters remained closed. There were no screens. We wore the warmest clothes we could find to stay warm. It was necessary to yell at one another in order to be heard over the wind. It took several days to get used to the inconvenience of doing simple daily tasks—with no hot water, a coffeepot that leaked, a heavy jug of bottled water that took forever to pour a half glass of water, and sand leaving its film over everything as the terrific loud careening wind blew it through the shutters that never closed tightly.

In our many trips to Mexico, we had not experienced such poorly operating shutters with no screens, or such unremitting cold, windy weather, which locals referred to as *el Norte*! Weather conditions apparently had to be just right—a climate change or weather occurrence like a La Nina or El Nino affecting water availability or an extreme event like a Hurricane Mitch—in order to wreak such havoc upon the Yucatan's typical warm, sunny weather. Needless to say, it certainly caught us by surprise.

I could hear Linda saying, "Welcome to my world, Mom," since she was convinced that everything that could go wrong goes wrong only on her vacations.

During this one-month vacation, the winds dominated about two weeks of invasion into our tiny abode, covering furniture, floors, and dishes with sand, requiring us to race about slamming the shutters closed, hunting for the squeeze mop to clean up the water, grabbing the broom to sweep up broken glass.

Fred finally figured out how to light the hot water heater. The toilet stopped flushing efficiently. We had already been instructed not to flush any toilet paper but to dispose of it in the provided containers and to include it with our dump runs to a nearby vacant lot used for garbage. On these windy days, we would retreat outside to the back of our villa where we were protected from the wind, making it possible to read the many books we brought with us.

Fred with a good book

Our housekeeping chores were divided between us. Fred did most of the cooking and I handled dishwashing and housecleaning. Yet I seemed to spend much time cleaning up after Fred. He spilled continually, leaving messes wherever they occurred, using whatever was near, whether or not it was his. He left food out for flies to explore; he put nothing away. I would go behind him putting away, sweeping, or mopping up, closing drawers and doors, picking up clothes, making beds. He seemed oblivious to the disorder he created and was annoyed with me should I make mention of it.

Indeed, he seemed increasingly to live in his own world, listening only to his own inner musings. This behavior was not typical of him. I was quite sure it was due to his Parkinson's disease. He said he turned my words off because they were so continuous. Maybe. Maybe not. He probably lacked the patience to deal with minor annoyances that he easily managed before Parkinson's took its toll on him and everything he did.

Whenever weather allowed, we walked the beach and enjoyed quick dips. I've got a thing about sand. I like it in its place. But it seldom stays—in its place—it becomes invasive. It sticks to your feet or the soles of your sandals, making an entry into your home, climbing into bed with you, between the bedsheets. It casts a film over your dishes, your silverware, your furniture, as the wind blows it into your casa, through the screens, between the wooden slates.

Sweeping was a constant here.

With El Norte gone, we fell into a comfortable routine of beach walking, eating simple meals laced with cold beers or iced tea, and taking quick swims while enjoying our solitude.

The beach stretched out endlessly in either direction. On weekends the beach was filled with families, but it was deserted during the week. We quite took to our deserted beach, to its isolation, to its erratic row of hurricane-ravaged beach homes, that resembled a mouthful of teeth, some shiny white, some yellowed with age, some decayed, some missing teeth, leaving an ungainly gap. Few occupants appeared to be living in any of the casas.

Abandoned hurricane-damaged homes

As I grew more accustomed to handling details of the daily ritual, I felt more at home. Already I'd read two books and completed some writing assignments from a book I brought from home. I was determined to begin writing daily and this vacation seemed like an ideal setting.

With Fred sleeping much of the day, this would give me something useful to do. I found it sharpening my observation skills even as I attempted to write what I saw about me on this beach. Initially, it seemed bleak and boring until I began describing it with a pen.

Journaling was something I seldom did when happy with life. Now, sixteen years into retirement, I felt restless, indecisive, in need of new goals or pursuits. Perhaps my putting pen to paper would reveal other options I hadn't considered. Time would tell.

When the tide was out, smooth blond sand would edge its surface, then a layer of sea shells appeared, which crackled like egg shells beneath one's feet. But shells were not the only gifts from the sea. Litter abounded, offering us remnants of other peoples' lives, such as twisted flip-flops, jars, plastic containers, beer and pop cans, pieces of clothing and lots of seaweed and jetsam.

It was amazing how much we were still doing, even with Fred's advancing Parkinson's disease. Perhaps I was too filled with despair too soon when he told me his skiing days were over—that he had too much difficulty walking. But hope and the ability to adapt to changing situations played such a role. Now here, Fred did most of the driving, the cooking, and remained a people magnet. He was also the chief troubleshooter when things didn't work right. So this trip had been an affirmation of hope and joy for both of us—an affirmation we both needed.

We enjoyed reading and sharing with one another what we read. When no other agenda demanded our attention, we read extensively. We'd become more interested in Mexican history and its current events.

The people we encountered daily were unbelievably friendly. They lived so casually with their poverty. We'd walk through the unpaved streets of their village, peeking into their shanty homes, open wide to the street revealing hammocks swinging in a corner, bits of food scattered about the dirt floors, and in one, an aluminum table with some matching chairs with empty bottles of beer and pop left on the table. A feral dog or two might be sniffing through food remains by a cooler. Catching my eye, an occupant would wave while wearing a wide smile.

In the exploration of our little village, Fred noticed a tiny hole that functioned as a door in the cement block wall, that he was sure housed a beauty shop and might offer pedicures. His toenails had become lethal weapons. The giggling ladies and their small children seemed quite amused when this tall *gringo* came in, using his universal language of gestures and such, and provided him with the much-needed pedicure.

Fred with the locals

Further down the street were cast-off plastic bags littering trees and bushes and everywhere bands of feral dogs wandering about. The dogs looked unhealthy, too thin, with scabs on their bodies. It didn't seem to occur to the people of the village to collect garbage or round up feral dogs.

In talking with a group of expats from Canada who spent winters here, we were told that the folks in the local church were beginning to gather up some of these dogs and neuter them to slow down the procreation process. They found it costly and perhaps a strange project but one the church could manage.

The expats were looking around for better digs for the next winter. We thought their impressive casa was quite lovely, giving the three couples ample room in attractive furnishings. Several complained about leaky pipes, things that didn't work, poor response of owners to make repairs. We ran into them days later and learned they had found the perfect casa for the next winter on the other side of Progreso.

It was truly interesting living in a foreign country. That was what I felt we were doing—actually living there as expats. We had not really done this for this length of time in one place. It required one to puzzle things out for oneself, making one more attentive to the surroundings.

So I became more attentive to Fred's newest health issue—an itchy red rash over his legs and chest that was tiring him so much, he even napped through the cocktail hour. In calling Rob to find out where I might take him, Rob said he was going to the Health Clinic at Progreso and would meet us there. Consequently, Fred became the grand recipient of a shot in the ass, pills, and a salve prescribed by a doctor who spoke no English.

What a difference a day or two makes. Most days, other than a fishing boat or two, there was nothing happening on our beach. But on Sunday, the gang was all here—a group of about sixty churchgoers assembled on the gravel path by our casa. Their leader was dressed in white carrying a microphone. They chanted, sang religious songs, marched down the road, gathering right outside our patio by a storm-damaged home that appeared to once have been a very nice casa. Now it had no roof and the exposed remains of what was once a kitchen. The remains became their church as many crowded in, the rest sitting on the gravel road in the heat of the day.

Five men were all dressed in white robes, three with red sashes and two with green. One woman was dressed in black nun's clothing. The attendees were dressed casually—shorts, shifts, flip-flops. The heat was brutal. The service lasted about two hours, then some left, but most headed for our beach, wading into the gulf fully clothed. They stayed for some time—cooling off, laughing, and having fun. The beach was full of families and fun-lovers on outings.

The days passed by in a lazy fashion, starting with early morning beach walks, then running errands in Progreso where we would lunch on the Malecón, watching the tourists and regulars walk by.

Stopping by Rob and Joan's office, we made arrangements to stay at the Hacienda Uxmal in Uxmal, known for its magnificent ancient ruins. We arrived there the next day. The hotel was complete with marbled halls, all open to a courtyard full of greenery, tall trees, many with ropes resembling those Tarzan might use to swing on. Elegant wood-carved rockers, flanking round coffee tables at intervals along the hall, beckoned us to sit for a while and enjoy the beauty. But a gorgeous swimming pool accompanied by a bar and tables full of laughing bathers made us eager to jump in and cool off.

There we met Nancy and Dan, a young couple from Portland, Oregon, who became our companions for the remainder of our time there. We dined at a nearby resort with our new friends. The next morning we met them and our guide George to go through the most impressive ruins I'd yet seen in the cool of what was to become another impressively hot day. The ruins were a different kind of beauty from Peru's Machu Picchu; they were located in Yucatan's only hilly area, full of greenery and tall trees projecting a calm beauty, serene with very tall buildings and pyramids. Many iguanas of all sizes seemed to enjoy posing for the camera.

Dan noticed that Fred was having difficulty walking so he told Nancy and me to go on ahead—they wanted to take their time. I had noticed Fred was running out of energy and felt gratitude for Dan's kindness. Nancy, George, and I sat at a table near our car chatting while waiting for the guys. When we all returned to the hacienda, the four of us jumped in the pool that felt so coolly delicious.

Fred and I headed out for Celestún and the tantalizing Eco Paraiso. The resort was at the end of a very dusty, winding, narrow road, in competition with Costa Rica for title of the "World's Most Bumpy and Spine-Jarring Road." We were greeted by thousands of tiny stinging black sand gnats. But once we sprayed ourselves with great stuff, and got our belongings into our charming bungalow with its palapa roof and numerous geckos, we knew we were on the doorstop of the ultimate Mexican Escape.

Too far from Celestún to make it a practical destination for running quick errands, we knew we were dependent on the establishment to meet all our food and booze needs, which it did. Our bungalow offered privacy and luxury with its two comfortable queen-sized beds, a sitting area with ceiling fans, and a private porch with hammocks facing a remarkable long and wide beach stretching out for miles. The resort housed only thirty people.

We joined a young English couple for drinks after dinner and talked until midnight. They were touring the Yucatan on their Harley-Davidson bike, and had been here two weeks, planning to return to England soon after leaving the next day.

During a political discussion, they shared their views about Tony Blair. "We think he has done well for the U.K. except, of course, getting involved with Bush and his war."

Fred asked how they felt about Iraq. They responded, "We both feel that Blair's Iraq involvement had so enraged Brits that they could not see all the positive things Blair had done for the U.K. economy."

We took an hour walking along a wondrously white sandy beach stretching out for miles with nothing on it — no buildings of any kind, only occasional schools of birds, mostly sandpipers and gulls being lectured by stately pelicans. Afterwards we had several dips in the pool overlooking the Gulf, followed by siestas in the deck chairs and hammocks, interspersed with reading and, at last, the cocktail hour. Gin invariably awaited us.

We heard rumors, but didn't want to believe them, that El Norte was returning soon. Fortunately, we had a great walk on the Yucatan's most beautiful beaches before leaving at noon to return to Churburna and the land of sand, wind, and El Norte!

Sadly, the rumors were true. We returned to loud, beating, forceful wind hammering at every shutter and door in our casa, spewing sand throughout every room — on all the furniture, books, floors, blowing out the hot-water gas pilot light, leaving us with no hot water, and again finding us unable to carry on a conversation without yelling. Rob returned to fix our pilot light. In these beach casas, nothing worked quite right for long. Corrosion, too much salt, water, wind, and poor workmanship contributed to slowing down the pace of daily living. Whatta life!

One reason we had so looked forward to a month in Mexico was to be free of Bush and American politics. But while running errands in Progreso, we heard more rumors that Bush was to be in Merida on Monday, the same day we would be there. We had seen U.S. Navy helicopters flying over our deserted beach several days in a row. They said it was probably advance security for the President's visit.

So we spent our last day at our casa on an outing to the mangroves near San Crisanto where we encountered some folks from Winnipeg we had met our first day in Progreso. The dip in the Cenote was refreshing. We senior citizens laughed and giggled together like a bunch of college undergrads. It was a perfect way to end our stay at Chuburna.

We left the coolness of the breezy beach for the heat of Merida, capital of the Yucatan, which was busy anticipating the arrival of President Bush. We saw groups of protestors demonstrating in front of the Cathedral de Merida. The newspapers also had photos of demonstrations in Bogota and Guatemala, but because we knew no Spanish, we could not determine the reason for various demonstrations.

Merida is a beautiful city of about 800,000 people. Its neighborhoods displayed elegant architectural styles of Spanish colonial, French, Mexican, Moorish, and Mayan cultures—a city of enchantment.

It was hot, hot, hot in the city streets. Fred made a futile attempt to return our rental car before we headed for our hotel. Hundreds of soldiers and police were rerouting the traffic, preparing for Bush's arrival. Fred had been driving the wrong way on a one-way street, saved by several American women who rescued him. So he still had the car and fortunately no traffic ticket.

La Maison Lafitte was a lovely four-star hotel in the heart of the action—on Calles 60 and 55. We took a dip in the lovely pool in the inviting courtyard. We toured the city on a cute bus, shopped in the square, took in a museum and enjoyed the sights, people, and music surrounding us as we sipped drinks in a sidewalk café.

The next day we started our city explorations in the cool of the morning, returning to our hotel when it was wiltingly hot. Stumbling back into the coolness of our hotel, our bathing suits, and the inviting pool, we enjoyed its refreshingly chilly water. Eating poolside, we spent the heat of the afternoon with other couples.

Packing and retiring early, we arrived at the airport earlier than scheduled so that our plane could be out of the way for Air Force One, which was next to our plane. The presence of President Bush had dictated a change of plans for many. Yet it was thrilling to view the famed plane of the leader of the "Free World."

And so we returned to our Minnesota homeland from what was our last trip abroad.

Chapter Twenty-one
Transitions
2007—2009

O N A SURPRISINGLY WARM day in March, I suddenly got Spring Fever. Fred called to say he'd be at my house for dinner. That energized me. I cleaned off the patio, dragged the patio furniture out, did some light yard work, replenished the bird feeders and filled the birdbath. *Life is good!*

Fred's visits would generally last about three nights, then he would head out to one of his places—either his apartment in Sauk Rapids or his cabin in Wisconsin. He did join me for Easter, so we had an intimate dinner for two, complete with champagne followed by a short walk in our favorite nearby woods. These things he could still do, though more slowly for shorter time periods.

Linda and Nick bought the house of their dreams. They were ecstatically happy! It was a house they both loved and planned to live in the rest of their lives. The home was just right for them—like a cabin in the North Woods but much nicer, with a wood fireplace and more than an acre of land full of oak and pine trees populated with loads of deer and wild turkeys. The previous owner had an eye for interior decorating and ambience. Every window had a remarkable view—yet they were only twenty minutes from downtown.

Linda showed me her diamond ring. *Yes!* They were engaged. We were both delighted.

Fred, on the other hand, didn't know what he was going to do. He seemed to know that he needed to alter his lifestyle to accommodate his deteriorating condition, yet he still seemed determined to maintain his independence as long as he could. By this time, he was living in several different places in three different towns, requiring much driving. In addition, he had difficulty remembering where he had what. For a man in the advanced stages of Parkinson's disease, this was no easy task.

When I suggested he simplify his life by staying in one place, he would cup his ear and say, "I think it's time for Vespers." Then he'd leave the room.

Did I hear someone say stubborn?

I remember years ago when I tried to show him skiing tips I had learned from an instructor in Winter Park, Colorado that made gliding easier. Fred was a plodder, but when he was younger, he had the energy to plod faster than I glided. His superior balance served him well in going up and down steep hills. But then he needed a new way. I could tell he was not interested in my tips.

Later, when skiing at Sam's place in Wisconsin, Fred showed the same lack of interest in hearing Sam's suggestions on improving his gliding skills. I, however, was open to trying out Sam's suggestions.

Another time in Mexico, when Fred was using resistance bands ineffectively to improve arm and shoulder muscle strength, I attempted to show him the method my personal trainer Greg preferred for improving strength training. Again, Fred showed no interest.

Greg came to my house twice a week to work with me on strength training. On one occasion, when Fred was having balance and energy problems, I suggested he use half of my hour with Greg to see if it was useful to him. I left them alone. They met several times, but Fred just couldn't get into it. It may have been that his Parkinson's was affecting his attention span when new learning was involved.

My friend Tib invited us over to her condo to show Fred what she was learning from her DVDs on basic self-help techniques for Parkinson's patients. She gave him a set to take home to watch and a book to read. He never looked at them.

I don't know if he was too discouraged to try or if he just preferred working things out on his own. It appeared to me that he didn't like learning from others. He liked to be in charge, but he resisted anyone trying to be in charge of him.

This may be one reason we got along so well. I had absolutely no need to be in charge of him. Indeed, I was content to let Fred be Fred. He wasn't my husband. I wouldn't have to take care of him when it was needed. So I pretty much had a "live and let live" attitude.

Fred enjoyed listening to me talk about what I'd been doing, where I'd been, what I was reading, what was happening to Linda and Nick or my friends, what the big issues were on the boards I was on. He'd offer me encouragement if I was tackling something new and was proud of my achievements big or small. But he had no great need to share much with me, not even the books he was reading.

We would discuss the news that we always watched together and enjoyed political discussions. When he'd take off on trips with his son or friends or by himself to interesting places, he had no need to share the information with anyone. He was content to live, learn, and experience in the now. I admired that about him. The experience itself was sufficient. He had no need to relive it in any way. It was what I did when with him. At times, I yearned for a similar lifestyle when not with him. However, I'd been a competitive person with a strong need to achieve and receive recognition for the results of my achievements all my life.

In this respect Fred and I differed. He was quite content to be and do. He had no need to discuss what he read. I must. He could come back from a faraway trip and have little need to share his experiences. I, on the other hand, am a storyteller, like my dad. And I don't like being interrupted until I've finished telling the story.

During a political discussion when guests were competing to make their views known, Fred listened but rarely expressed a view unless asked. On the other hand, he enjoyed getting their views, often asking for more information.

It was rare for Fred to share with me what he did when not with me. But one day he was obviously depressed about something. He told me that Sonia was transported by ambulance to the Mayo Clinic the day before by the local doctors who didn't feel they had the skills for dealing with her autoimmune disease—Reynaud's phenomenon, an obstructive disease of the arteries. He said this was a recurrence of an earlier disease he had told me about twenty years ago, that left her lacking the energy to do even simple activities. Smoking was a major contributor to the disease, but she had been unwilling or incapable of stopping the habit, as he couldn't stop his drinking. Now Fred was very concerned that she might lose her leg, which he said was totally swollen and black.

What would 2007 hold for me? For Fred? For Sonia? It felt like a transition year — that the future would not be like the last twenty-six years, which for Fred and me had been more or less idyllic: travel, fun, adventure, playfulness, and friends galore.

In the last few years my very dear friend Clem had died, and that affected everything. She was the one who had organized my women friends and me with her boundless energy and intelligence.

Enjoying time in the backyard

Fred's Parkinson's disease had taken a horrid toll on him so that he could no longer be the adventuresome, physically active, fun-loving, insouciant lover. His wife, from whom he had been separated six years, was now hospitalized with a disease that might cause her the loss of her leg.

Another dear friend, Tib, a far-left Democrat, got married that May at the age of seventy-nine to a childhood classmate, who grew up to become a rich Republican. Suffering also from Parkinson's, Tib felt she had about five more years left and didn't want to be a burden to her kids. So she accepted his proposal and her travels now involved having a joyous life being pampered and cared for by a rich husband who adored her as she did him.

Other friends were suffering various ailments that kept them from seeking active travels. Some lacked money or time for such pastimes.

This left me discovering my ineptness at doing much on my own. It didn't help that my fear of driving metro freeways kept me dependent on others to do the driving.

The big world out there seemed too big for me to navigate. It had been Fred who planned and handled the details of our trips and Clem who did the same for us gals.

It seemed evident to me that I would be seeing less and less of Fred as his life became more entangled with the illnesses of him and Sonia.

The bright spot of 2007 happened when Fred and I took Linda and Nick out for dinner to celebrate Linda's birthday. During the meal, Linda quietly announced that she and Nick were getting married the next Friday at the courthouse. I broke out in happy tears. Fred offered Nick a cigar and said, "Well done." I asked them both if the fifteen years they had known one another was enough time to make such a serious decision. They laughed and Linda proudly said she had held out the longest of all her "spinster" women friends to marry at the age of fifty-one. And so they were launched!

Linda had secured a female judge to preside. Nick's mother and I sat in the jury box. Nick's son was his best man. Linda's hairdresser was her maid of honor. Afterwards we walked to a favorite restaurant around the corner in St. Paul, where we met with those friends and relatives who were available on such short notice. The wedding cake was provided by my dear friend, Sandy, who had helped Linda celebrate many major events.

And so 2007 promised to be a year of change for me and those I held dear.

———————

"Has she no one else to help her?" I asked Fred after he told me the bad news one day. "You can barely help yourself." Sonia had asked Fred to move in with her during her hospitalization and recovery from the amputation of her leg. This was a case of the handicapped helping the confined.

"She has no one else but me. She has no close friends. I can do some cooking and walk the dog. It's the least I can do. I owe it to her."

Looking at him, I wondered. His sad red-rimmed eyes, worn, dirty shirt hanging over his drooping shoulders, made him look more like one needing care, not a caregiver. He now wore clothes easy to put on, frequently wearing them long past laundry time. Even his raspy, soft voice interrupted by frequent coughs was that of an old man.

"I can't believe she couldn't hire someone to help her." Linda and I had found loads of resources on the internet for Fred as his condition seemed to deteriorate; I was sure those same resources could have helped Sonia. "And how can you walk the dog? You need your walker or walking poles just to manage alone."

"She has a little electric scooter I use and it can keep up with the dog. Her dog is very important to her. She's always had one. I still feel bad about the time I took her dog for a walk and the darned dog ran out on the road to chase a car and got run over. I felt responsible for that. I shouldn't have let him off his leash."

"Did Sonia give you a rough time over that?"

"She was very upset. She is a real dog lover."

"Does the dog even know you when you walk in the door?"

"Well, he snarls and growls a bit. Only bit me once," he jested.

"Now why do you owe her?" I wondered.

"Well, I haven't been the world's best husband. She's deserved better."

Still, I wondered why she was estranged from family and had no close women friends. Yet I could believe that he felt some guilt in not having been a better mate for her.

He said he slept on a cot in the parlor of her small home. It didn't sound very comfortable. But he called me weekly, sometimes more often. Despite my temporary annoyance at the situation, I was proud of this honorable man, as were some of my closest friends, especially Sandy.

Since Fred was unsure how long he would be staying with Sonia, he encouraged me to go ahead with my life, making any plans that interested me. My new friend Geralda was hunting for a traveling companion. She, too, had considered Clem a best friend. After two brief meetings, we decided we were suited for one another and planned a trip to India, a place on both of our travel lists. While I felt bad leaving Fred, I knew I couldn't put my life on hold. And I knew Fred wouldn't want me to.

The next time Fred called, I told him of my good luck in finding such a person. He sounded wistful, as if he didn't want to be counted out. He lacked optimism about Sonia's progress as well as his own.

He was, however, pleased that his son Tom was arriving that afternoon to spend the Memorial Day holidays with Sonia and him. Both welcomed the visit. Tom was a day brightener for them.

I hadn't seen Fred in three months. He felt he must take care of Sonia until she could be successfully fitted for a prosthesis and able to walk and drive her car. Fred had arranged to have her car fitted for her handicap. He continued to call me several times a week when he slipped back to his apartment. On these occasions he reported that he was getting weaker with increasing balance issues and had started seeing a physical therapist two times a week. I let him know I thought that was a good decision.

He had missed all holidays—Thanksgiving, birthdays, Christmas, New Year's and did not know when he would be able to see me. So I concluded that I now lived in a world of women. My days of being a part of a couple for even short outings appeared to be over. Fred had been my energizer over the years with his *Come on! Come on!—Let's go!* attitude as he dashed out for his bike or skis or van—leaving me hurrying to catch up. I didn't want to be left behind. But now he had no energy or, indeed, physical ability to play that role. And so far I had done a lousy job of being my own energizer. My New Year's challenge was to figure out how to become my own Energizer Bunny.

Anne, one of my traveling buddies, asked me if I wanted to

spend three weeks with her in Puerto Vallarta. She had reserved a place with two bedrooms. We had spent many vacations together over the years, but I was reluctant to go out of the country in case something happened to Fred. And I hated to go someplace without him. Our winter retreats were always important to us. He made it clear he didn't like being stuck in cold Minnesota when he could no longer enjoy winter sports.

Since he was reluctant to make any winter plans with me, I left with Anne for Puerto Vallarta and had a really fun time. However, when I returned I was astonished to find out that Fred had somehow managed to get himself to Pedro Island in Texas, where his best friends Sam and Susie were vacationing.

Now I really felt awful. I so wanted to be with him. But even more importantly I wondered how in earth he could manage to get there and function while on his own.

Fred was quite a spin artist when he felt the need to be. He acted as if it was no big deal — that his condo was in a building with an elevator and that he spent time with his dear friends. He later confessed that other than having several meals with them at their condo, he really didn't see much of them.

I understood Fred's need to minimize obstacles. I often did too. And often he was right when he said, "No problem — not to worry." He was very aware of his declining health, which necessitated the need for him to minimize even more.

"Fred, how much longer can you drive this car?" I asked. "It is agonizing to watch you pull yourself up into the driver's seat, work hard to get your feet under the steering wheel, and work even harder to stay awake when you are driving back and forth to my house."

He looked directly at me with his tired-looking eyes and, working hard to keep back tears, said, "Shirley, when I am behind the wheel in the car is the only time I feel like a normal man. I have to hold on to it. There is so little I have control of anymore."

I leaned over and gave him a hug. I tried hard to hold back my tears. "I understand," I murmured. "I truly do."

This man was so remarkable to me. It was easy to love him when he was so strong, so virile, so sexy, and resourceful. But at that moment, I loved him even more for being so stoic, so courageous, so uncomplaining in the way he faced what no one should have to deal with. There was a time when I wondered if I would be up to staying with him as his disease further immobilized him. But seeing looks of appreciation on his face when I did special things for him and knowing how arduous it was for him to continue seeing me, I felt my devotion and admiration for him only strengthen.

Somehow, when the snows thawed, Fred began driving the commute to my home to visit for several days most months. We even managed a short outing to our beloved Minnesota North Shore in the summer, staying in a new hotel with its rooms facing Lake Superior. It turned out to be a relaxed and enjoyable outing. Stares from strangers came our way as Fred labored to get in and out of his van, needing much assistance from me to help him out, giving him his hiking poles to use as a kind of walker.

He refused to use a walker or wheelchair and his Parkinson's disease had affected his ability to get his feet moving. He was kind of like the tennis player who must bounce his tennis ball four times before each serve. Fred needed to shuffle his feet so many times in place before one would finally move forward, allowing him to take maybe five or six more steps before the shuffle process would begin again. This was particularly frustrating when going through a door at a store, knowing there were people lined up behind him waiting to go through — or when he was waiting for an elevator door to open, only having it shut before the magic shuffle was completed, allowing him to step forth into the elevator.

Just having him at home with me gave me great comfort. Judy and I had fixed the sunroom so that he could rest on the new, more comfortable sofa while being in the thick of conversations, listening to food preparation in the kitchen, catching his favorite show, *Jeopardy*, on TV, and napping whenever he wished. It became his favorite place.

One day he was sitting in the rocking chair while I sat at his feet. We were listening to a Frank Sinatra record. I was telling him how I had hoped to meet his son. "I kept hoping you would tell him about me. I was proud to share you with my daughter. I had hoped you might feel the same way about me."

"It's hard to explain. I wanted to. But I didn't want to make it uncomfortable for Tom to relate to Sonia. That relationship is important to both of them," he said.

Fred's words filled me with a rush of emotion and pride in him; that he could be faithful to me and still committed to preserving the stepmother/son relationship. His actions and words over the years revealed his desire that no one be hurt.

I just enjoyed being near him while we listened to Frank singing "Young at Heart." We looked tearfully into each other's eyes as we listened to Frank's telling us how dreams can come true if we live long enough and are young at heart. Fred softly said, "The timing is a bit bittersweet." We grasped one another's hands, holding on tight as the music ended.

With winter fast approaching, he once again expressed his frustration at having to stay in his tiny apartment, unable to drive anywhere until spring arrived. He wanted so badly to go with me to Puerto Vallarta but knew he couldn't handle airplane flights anymore. The Old Town section of Puerto Vallarta was not accessible to handicapped people with its cobblestoned streets and houses built on the hills requiring excessive climbing to get anywhere.

So once again I left him feeling dejected but assuring him I would call him several times a week. He knew he could call Linda if he needed to reach me.

This was to be his first winter spent entirely in Minnesota. It was painful for me to leave Fred behind. I thought about him continually. And then I received an e-mail from Linda saying she had received a call from Fred. He was on a train on his way to Boulder, Colorado to visit his son. I couldn't believe it! How could he possibly navigate a train on his own?

I called Linda and she said, "It took him four days to get there. He had to spend a night in Chicago in order to transfer to a train to Denver. His son picked him up there."

"But how could he even get on and off the train and to the hotel? How did he manage it?"

"Mom, he said he just gave out lots of tips and he got all the help he needed. He sounded triumphant."

I wanted to know what was going on! I hesitantly called his son.

Tom answered and I identified myself as a friend of Fred's. "Could you tell me how I might reach him?" I asked.

"Just a second. Dad, it's for you," he called out to Fred with a teasing tone and a lilt in his voice.

Fred was in a jocular mood. His story amazed me. "By being a big tipper, I had loads of help from porters and redcaps getting me in and out of the train and into a cab that took me to a hotel for the night. Hotel people arranged my ride to the airport where redcaps got me back on the right train in the morning. The porters took really good care of me and Tom met me at the station."

I didn't know whether to be angry at him for putting himself in possible jeopardy or to be proud of my stubborn guy for refusing to "go down for the count." Resourcefulness and resilience — these traits had impressed me from the first time I met him. Now he became a kind of folk hero to me.

He assured me it was okay to call him at Tom's. So now I knew where to reach him when I needed contact. The next time Tom answered the phone when I called, I heard him yell to Fred, "It's your girlfriend, Dad." I could hear some laughter in the background.

The impromptu train ride turned out to be a trial run for our final trip to Destin, Florida by train the following February.

In the meantime, my neighbor gave us information about subjects being sought for a study by the Mayo Clinic on brain stimulation on advanced Parkinson's patients. Fred was excited and filled out the application, which was accepted.

He asked me if I would go with him to the Mayo Clinic. I was surprised and pleased to be asked since Fred was so reticent to discuss medical concerns with me. We set out on what we hoped would be good news.

The neurologist started the interview by reviewing Fred's meds with him and the times he took them. Fred seemed vague and uncertain so I suggested that Fred's sleeping pattern often kept him from taking them at the times scheduled.

When asked to walk down the hall, Fred did so with no difficulty. In amazement, I asked the doctor how that could be. He replied, "That's the doctor factor." He asked Fred more questions on his medication habits, then excused us.

Fred asked, "Is that all?"

"Yes, you're free to leave the clinic now."

Fred was quite disappointed. We both concluded that they were seeking candidates who rigidly adhered to the medication schedules since even more requirements would be added. We left a day earlier than planned with our hopes dashed. But we did some sightseeing on the way back as a means of making some lemonade out of the lemon we'd been given.

Chapter Twenty-two
Final Trip
Destin, Florida
2009

O N HIS FEW VISITS to see me, Fred was getting weaker each time. He needed help getting up the stairs. He had arranged handgrips in strategic places and a seat in the bathtub. I'd help him get in bed and cover him up, leaving on a nightlight. He was now in a bedroom right by the bathroom.

Yet, once again Fred was desperate to get out of Minnesota for part of the winter. I wasn't sure how possible it was. I was concerned about his ability to determine if he was well enough to take such a long trip. He had gotten all the information on Amtrak routes and felt sure he knew the drill. I was amazed he was able to handle the many phone calls required to secure our tickets. "Not to worry," he would say. I found the ticketing process most confusing. But Fred, in spite of the fact that he had had several strokes, understood the ticketing process much better than I. His trip to Denver had been an excellent trial run.

We would have to take three different trains to get to Hattiesburg, Mississippi and then would have to stay overnight there before we could pick up a rental car to drive to Destin, Florida. There would be several layovers each way: Chicago for three hours and Washington D.C. for six hours. I felt inadequate to manage both him and our luggage. I would have to get him mobility help at railroad stations in both cities and get us on the train to Hattiesburg where we could not check our luggage because the station offered no checking services. That meant we would have to store our luggage in our tiny roomette, leaving little space for us.

I was also concerned about getting our rental car, helping him walk at Hattiesburg, then getting us to Destin by car. At least we were still in the USA if health issues emerged, and I had Tom's phone number.

I wasn't sure Tom even knew we were attempting this trip. Fred was not too forthcoming about any information concerning his "other" family.

But I had sincerely underestimated my folk-hero guy. He really did understand the system and was lavish with tips. He was so excited to be going anywhere. And then it was he who knew the ropes, explaining to me what would be happening next.

As we left St. Paul, we had breakfast on the train and he was like a kid, looking out the window, pointing out our neighborhood as we zoomed by, then each little town along the Mississippi River as we passed through La Crosse, Wisconsin heading for Chicago.

I was delighted to see his enthusiasm. It made me feel good that I had supported him in making this trip. I had become his only lifeline to the outside world and was pleased I had not let others talk me out of it. Bringing enthusiasm to his face, seeing him excited about our venture, helping him achieve his goals, overwhelmed me with great feelings of love for this remarkable man.

"I am so glad, Fred, you talked me into this trip. You really do know how to 'ride the rails' as it were." I told him how baffling I found the stack of train tickets we were given. We each had six different tickets going each way; one for each stop and one for train and car number at each stop.

"Well, I did spend lots of time pouring over all the tickets, focusing on all the details," he remarked, giving me a professorial look.

"Oh, you mean a person is supposed to read this stuff in advance?" I said in my dumb-blond way.

"I keep forgetting you're from Ioway," he said with a grin on his face.

Riding the tracks takes a different skill set from other forms of transportation. During the day, the bed had been turned into a long davenport and the upper bunk was folded up, out of sight. Across from the davenport by the door was a sink and some narrow shelves containing room for basic necessities. Two washcloths and towels with soap were folded and by the sink. At the end of the davenport by the window was a steel table that folded up to the wall when not in use. A stool folded out of the wall on the other side of the table providing room for two to eat. Across from the stool was the bathroom containing a toilet and shower where two bath towels were provided. It was pretty handy if you liked to shower while peeing.

Two people squeezed into a tiny roomette, particularly when the beds were made up for sleeping, made the simplest movements an act of endurance. I felt like a trapeze performer swinging through the air as I tried descending from my upper bunk to land just right in order to make it to the bathroom door without knocking anything over or banging into Fred, who was trying to crawl into his lower bunk. Such tortuous movements of one's geriatric body required much patience and forethought. It was also a memory challenge to find what one needed without disturbing the other. But when the beds were put away, we had enough space.

We were provided menus from which to select each meal. The porter took our orders, opened up the tiny table from the side of the wall, then brought us our meals, placing each on the table. The food was delicious and our porter most accommodating; he even brought us wine, which greatly enhanced our dining pleasure. During the day we watched the scenery pass by, often commenting on various sites in the small towns as we passed through. "I'm loving this," I said to Fred.

The arrival at Chicago provided us with what turned out to be a well-orchestrated performance by porters and redcaps. Together they got our luggage and us safely on a tram, then Fred in a wheelchair, and me into the station where the redcap took over. Three hours later, that same redcap mysteriously reappeared with luggage and a wheelchair for Fred. He knew exactly which car in which train to transport us, placing us in the hands of the porter waiting for us. The porter quickly checked our luggage somewhere, then assisted Fred up the steps to our compartment after Fred generously tipped the redcap. I followed. If it was near mealtime, our orders were taken as the train sped on its way.

This same seamless performance was enacted the next day when we arrived for our six-hour stay at the Washington D.C. station during a gentle but persistent snowstorm. There we met two charming ladies who explored the station with us. Together we all dined at a quaint café.

I dashed out to enjoy the soft snow as it made a fuzzy cotton carpet of thick snow on the sidewalk. Reluctantly, I returned to my group. Fred sent me on various missions to get wine and other necessities while he enjoyed the amenities of the comfortable and stocked waiting room of snacks, coffee, and soft drinks.

I could understand now why Fred was so knowledgeable about the details of our train trip. When he had said, "Not to worry," he spoke the truth. It was the efficiency and good humor of the redcaps and porters who took such good care of us that made the trip downright enjoyable. And Fred kinda liked handing out big tips of $35 or $50 for their efficient services. It couldn't help but make him feel he was still in charge. That made me feel good and very proud of him.

The snow followed us through the deep south, blanketing its towns and meadows with much unaccustomed snow until we finally reached Hattiesburg, where we were tossed out unceremoniously by our porter, with bags being thrown out on the ground around us as the train hurried on and the porter waved good-bye.

It seemed the well-built station there was closed nights. We suddenly found ourselves on our own in the cold of night, seated on a bench with our luggage at our feet. I called the hotel we had booked on my cell phone, but they did not provide transportation. They gave us a phone number of a taxi service that kept hanging up on me until finally one stayed on the line, but he had only one taxi on duty and it was busy for the next few hours. We would have to wait.

And wait we did. Welcome to Hattiesburg, home of Brett Favre. Fortunately, we still had on our Minnesota warm clothing and gloves. We huddled together on the bench and waited.

"Ideal living conditions," I said through chattering teeth.

Fred just laughed and pulled me closer.

_____

After a good night's sleep, we got our rental car and had an uneventful drive to Destin, Florida. Our condo was in a huge spacious building right on the beach in a well-groomed gated community. Even though our one-month stay was the coldest February in forty years, a good fifteen degrees below normal, we enjoyed even more our spacious, well-designed and decorated condo with its two bedrooms and baths, a wood-burning fireplace, an efficient kitchen, dining area, laundry room, and two balconies, one overlooking views of sagebrush, dunes, the awesome Gulf of Mexico, and a spacious beach that looked and felt like soft sugar on one's bare feet.

"Ideal living conditions!" Fred announced.

So although the weather outside was chilly and overcast and predicted to remain that way for some time, it would have been highly unlikely for us to be outside anyway due to Fred's serious balance issues.

Our first night there, Fred had a bad night trying to sleep in his bedroom, leaving him looking frail and tired with red eyes peering out from his old man's body. His once robust, strong body had become frail, his skin dry and flakey. His once strong arms and legs had become skinny, lacking good muscle tone due to the sedentary lifestyle imposed upon him by his illness. He had lost probably twenty or more pounds partly due to his difficulty swallowing, another side effect of Parkinson's. Even his face was thinner, his skin more blotchy, and his mouth frequently wide open, both when sleeping and awake, as though he were gasping for breath.

Watching him walk was like watching a balancing act as he slowly concentrated on where to place each foot as he walked stooped over. All this required so much concentration that he had little energy left for dealing with much else.

The sky was grey, gentle rain falling, the day cooling as it progressed. It was even too cold to enjoy sitting on our patio. Fred didn't venture out until our last week there. But eventually we fell into a pattern that included some daily exercise.

Fred was able to get by himself to our building's tiny gym on the main floor where he worked out on several machines. I tried out the gym in the Community Center, starting with an aerobics class that consisted of three gals in their twenties, reminding me of how aged and stiff my body had become. As they twisted and turned and jumped and lunged, I struggled to keep up; my body just didn't move that way anymore. It was amazing that I endured the never-ending hour. They praised my efforts, hoping I'd join them daily, but I knew they would not see me again.

I opted instead for the gym and its familiar machines and weights, and the huge expanse of sandy beaches with silvery pools interspersed along the shoreline for my long walks. It was just pure Nature—no planes in the skies or birds in the air or boats on the water—only an occasional sandpiper flitting about seeking dinner.

It was necessary to dress in Minnesota woolies on these walks the first week or so until it gradually warmed enough, resulting in more people frequenting the beach. Some younger folks even wore shorts.

No way could a person using a walker or wheelchair master these sands, but our last week Fred ventured forth with his trusty hiking poles and did manage a short walk. He beamed with pleasure. I cannot tell you how rewarding his smiles were when he had those rare moments of feeling like a can-do independent man. Such fleeting moments made these trips with their occasional frustrations worthwhile to me.

Valentine's Day was the first day in our two weeks that it had been warm enough to sit on our patio. The view was spectacular rain or shine, cloudy or sunny. We had a grand time celebrating Valentine's Day at a nearby elegant restaurant. We enjoyed watching the happy celebrants, listening to the live band, and dining on excellent steak and shrimp. Fred even had a martini.

Fred frequently slept late most days until I would wake him around 11:00 a.m. Even when sitting up, he would nod off while reading. It would take him several tries before he could get up from a chair. He seemed increasingly more self-absorbed and less aware of events around him. Rarely could I engage him in a conversation during the day. When I attempted to, he would pick up something to read or fall asleep, totally ignoring me unless he needed something.

If I confronted him about his solitary ways, he would seem annoyed and say, "Eat your sandwich!" then walk away.

I was feeling like I was just someone to handle the details, get the groceries, dispose of garbage and recyclables. Fred's antisocial behavior was probably a product of his Parkinson's draining him of energy to do much of anything. If I were him, I'd probably be angry as hell that this disease was happening to me. He didn't complain about the disease, but this seemed to be the way he expressed how pissed he was that he couldn't do the simplest damned thing.

He drank about a six-pack of beer a day and had several glasses of wine nightly. At least then he was more likely to engage in conversation.

My friend Geralda called, wondering how we were doing. I shared my frustrations with her, that Fred slept most the time and resisted any of my attempts to involve him in our usual daily rituals. He wouldn't get up for breakfast, he ignored joining me for lunch, he'd spend much of the afternoons sitting on the sofa, asleep with his book having fallen on the floor and his mouth wide open, resisting any of my efforts to wake him up. "This is not the Fred I've known for thirty-one years." I said.

Geralda said, "Shirley, you've got to remember that just getting through a day takes up more energy than he has. He has little energy to spare on social conversation and he never knows what's going to happen to him next. He just knows something will happen and it won't be nice. He's not resisting you. He's resisting this awful disease that is gradually controlling every part of him. Just trying to urinate, or swallow food, or get up out of a chair unencumbered, or get in an elevator when it opens its doors—any of those simple acts—are beyond him. He's at war with something he knows is going to defeat him."

Tears streamed down my face as I listened to her, knowing she was right. What a horrid way to go. Yet he kept desperately fighting, trying to control what he could. I needed to hear her advice.

Talking with Linda and my various friends who called meant much to me. I decided to turn the control back to Fred. Besides, trying to control others only made me uncomfortable. I decided to let Fred be Fred. I let him eat when he wanted and sleep when he wanted. I didn't know why it took me so long to figure it out. It helped him feel more in control of his life and not under the watchful eye of a controlling mother. He then fixed his own lunch and fixed dinner numerous times, with me doing clean up.

Luckily, the Winter Olympics had just started in Whistler, B.C. — a place where we had frequently spent summers — and we were looking forward to excellent viewing on any of our three TVs. Fred and I both enjoyed watching the Olympics nightly, rooting for our favorites to do well. This gave us something safe to discuss.

Occasionally we made a grocery store run or explored the neighborhood. The spaciousness of our condo full of enticing books to read and a choice of TVs to watch made it easy for us to coexist, each doing our own thing when interaction became too uncomfortable for either of us.

One day while he was sleeping, I caught the news about a strange plane accident in Denver, killing two. Apparently a glider plane connected with the accompanying plane when their lines crossed. I awoke Fred, saying, "Doesn't your son fly a glider plane? One just crashed in Denver!"

Fred was immediately on the phone to his son and learned that it was the plane Tom usually flew on weekends, but his friend took his place that weekend. Tom was badly shaken up. He had just returned from a meeting of officials involved with reviewing the accident to determine what went wrong. He and his Dad had a long conversation that was good for both of them. Fred shared Tom's news with me. "I came close to losing my son," he said in a somber voice. That was all he could say.

Tom called him several times after that to keep him informed of how the accident was being investigated and how Tom was doing.

The restful, well-organized condo was exactly what Fred needed. This man loved reading. He finished reading a formidable book entitled *The Maps of Time, An Introduction to Big History* by David Christian. The book had been a Christmas present to me from my first husband, Ron, whose reading interests were similar to Fred's.

The book attempted to unite natural history and human history in a single intelligible narrative. It commanded most of Fred's attention. He loved history — especially the histories of various wars. His own library was rich in Civil War, WWI, and WWII battles, along with studies of the presidents and generals who dominated them. But he also liked natural history, starting with the Big Bang and studies on the universe with its expansions and transformations. These were the subjects that dominated many of our cocktail discussions over the years. Fred was on the road a lot and he always had books on tapes that he devoured while driving.

His tastes were eclectic and included mysteries, spy thrillers, movies on tapes, and all kinds of biographies. When he tired of listening to me talk, he'd simply turn on the tapes. I got the message.

The guy had a wonderful gift of compartmentalizing. If he didn't want to think about something, he could always pick up a book and read. To me, that had been one of his great gifts. He'd read when waiting for me too. That took the pressure off me to hurry faster than was comfortable. I always carried a book or magazine with me to read whenever I had to wait so that was a habit we both shared over our lives.

Our last day in Destin was the warmest — sixty degrees and sunny! We left for Hattiesburg where we would spend the night, then take the Empire Builder back to our eventual destination from our thirty-four day vacation.

On our way back to the Twin Cities, Fred left most details to me, except giving tips. He mostly slept and became increasingly weaker each day on the road. This made the journey even more challenging. We did have good cocktail conversations on the train, reminiscent of the old days, revealing a Fred with many of his fine cognitive skills intact.

Riding the Capitol Limited Train from Washington D.C. to Chicago, we passed many historic sites from the Civil War. Fred's eyes would light up with passion as he shared his knowledge of the history of each sighting. It was like having my own travel guide or Civil War tutor.

The many competent porters and red caps we encountered on each train continually impressed us. Our last porter called Fred by name, saying he remembered him from being the porter on the train to Denver that Fred had taken the year before. We were amazed the porter would remember him. Airports could learn much from Amtrak on how to provide more humane services to travelers, particularly seniors and those with special needs. We chatted with various passengers who echoed these views. Many said it was their preferred way to travel. Riding the rails certainly was a vacation in and of itself with great food, great service, and captivating scenery.

Fred wished our trip wasn't coming to an end. I didn't tell him, but I was ready to return to my more active lifestyle.

Chapter Twenty-three
And Thus the Moveable Feast Ends
2009-2010

ONCE I GOT HOME, I felt anxious about all the unread magazines and mail, and the taxes that needed to be done. Fred called to say he had purchased a treadmill that was to be delivered that day. I was excited and pleased to hear his enthusiasm. It sounded like he was more hopeful about his life—that maybe regular exercise could be helpful.

Fred called again several days later saying he had a bad day. No one turned up to help him at his apartment. "I've been having more urinary infections. The doctor put in some urinary device two days ago and it caused me such pain that I had to see the urologist again the next day." His voice was failing, his speech interrupted by coughing. "They installed another device to fill me up with antibiotics."

I felt bad for him and could only imagine what he had been going through. He seemed confused by what was happening to him. He was surrounded by a sea of dirty laundry and disorder. He didn't know who was in charge of services being delivered to him.

I felt his call was a plea to me to help. "Can't Sonia make phone calls for you?" He didn't respond. "She can get you a housekeeper to come in regularly to keep your place clean and orderly." I reminded him that Linda and I had gone online to find home care support for him. "I gave you the pages of folks in the business. You even picked out some who looked interesting to you. Do you still have them?"

"I don't know what happened to them," Fred said in a weakened, discouraged voice.

I tried to schedule interviews for him, but had been told repeatedly that he needed to be the one to ask because as a friend, I could not. Fred had no computer and had difficulty making such phone calls. He told me Sonia had a computer that she knew how to use, but he seemed reluctant to involve her. That had me in a conundrum. I wanted to help but legally could not. Sonia had the legal authority and computer skills to help him but seemingly did not want to.

Once again I sought advice from Geralda. She cautioned, "There is nothing you can do since Fred has kept you out of the decision loop."

I decided that I would write his son when I had more information on how dire his situation truly was. The last two days may have been an anomaly. Once his infection cleared up and his new urinary tube became comfortable, he might have felt better and the helper aides might have resumed their schedules.

I was very cautious in entering Fred's other world without his permission since I had no desire to encounter his wife.

In the meantime I continued to call him daily. Fred and I both knew he would never be able to visit me again. And because of my discomfort driving that piece of interstate, I would have to ask a friend to accompany me.

For now, he was pleased to be back in his Sauk Rapids apartment where his books, movies, and the mighty Mississippi that flowed outside his door surrounded him. I was relieved he was there. He got help several times weekly to monitor his meds and to give him a shower. He was where he needed to be, but it was apparent to me that he required more services. I felt frustrated that I could not be there to get him the services he needed.

But that was Sonia's role and I had no idea how they interacted. When I asked Fred if she had called or visited him, he typically mumbled some response or changed the subject. The strong tie between them eluded me. From what little Fred had told me about their relationship, it seemed they had little social life and seldom made a celebration of the little joys of life such as birthdays and holidays.

Their behavior baffled me and I was not alone. I had called Tom several times over the last four years with my concerns about his dad. I wanted him to become more involved without my saying so. He'd say, "I'm not too good at this taking care of an aging parent, especially one who lives a long distance away."

I replied, "It wasn't easy for me when my mom, who lived in Florida, began letting me know she needed help. She always seemed so self-sufficient."

"Well, that's it. Dad is so lucid. He seems able to make his own decisions. And I have such a busy schedule. My moon project is about to launch and I really need to be here."

"Your dad does not want to be a burden to you. He's a very proud man, but he does need to be in an assisted living environment. He doesn't take his meds correctly. He falls down a lot and he really shouldn't drive."

Tom replied, "Yah, I, too, have been concerned about his driving and I could see when he was here that he wasn't taking good care of himself. I tried to get him in a gym a block away so he could get some help exercising, but he didn't seem interested. And each time he got in his rental car, I was relieved to see him come back okay."

Tom would call Sonia to find out if she had similar concerns. After all, she lived twenty minutes away from Fred and should have had a good grasp on his condition. She was also the one with power of attorney.

She apparently didn't share my concerns. When I'd ask Fred if Sonia was visiting and calling him regularly, his responses were vague. He'd say something like, "Uh, she calls sometimes. It's hard for her to get around." Occasionally they might have had lunch somewhere, but again, Fred was vague about the details.

Tom wanted to believe his dad's and Sonia's take on the situation.

October 2010

Fred had another of several small strokes and was again in the hospital. He sounded quite defeated. Linda and I were to have visited him that day until he called to say he was again in the ER. I was on the verge of tears. He said Sonia visited him the day before and his son Tom had called. Fred expressed appreciation for my phone calls and many visits to wherever he was.

After he had returned home, Fred had seemed content in his apartment. He was looking forward to showing Linda and me around his beloved village with its many parks and trails. My friends took turns visiting Fred with me over the months. He was in and out of the St. Cloud hospital and at the VA hospital. Sometimes he was at his own apartment. I tried to visit him every other week and took special care to clear all my visits with Fred to avoid encounters with Sonia.

I sought his permission each time before I contacted his son, and showed him a copy of a letter I was going to send Tom. But Fred waved it away, saying he didn't need to see it.

Again I called Tom and again he expressed his reluctance to make decisions for his dad; yet he could see that his dad needed daily help now in showering and in taking his meds. Although he did not wish to be intrusive in his dad's life, he knew it was time for him to get more involved and make another visit in hopes of helping his dad see the need for looking at assisted living options. Fred called while Tom was visiting him and said, "I think son Tom wants to get me in one of those units, but I have plans of my own."

After visiting several apartments in different facilities, Fred told me he saw several that weren't so bad. In fact, one in particular was much like his apartment. He would remain at the VA Hospital until that apartment became available.

Chapter Twenty-four
Fred's Two Worlds Meet
March 2010-July 2011

T HE TIME HAD FINALLY come. Tom was moving Fred into his apartment at the Good Shepherd Home. With Fred's okay, I had e-mailed Tom asking him to pick up Fred's possessions at my home. There wasn't that much and it would all fit in Tom's rental car.

I called Linda. "Can you help me pack up Fred's things, then stay and meet Tom when he comes?"

"I'll be right over. I really want to meet him," she replied. She sounded excited about the prospect, as was I. "We need to talk about what we'll say." We talked about showing Tom some photos of Fred's other life.

I wondered how prepared Tom might be to meet Fred's other family. I simply wasn't sure how much Fred had told Tom about us. Or how much Tom might have figured out on his own from my infrequent phone calls when concerned about Fred's whereabouts or health.

Linda arrived, dressed casually in jeans and sweatshirt, as was I. We quickly found plastic clothes bags to pack up Fred's better clothing, then retrieved some of Fred's large plastic packing containers to use for his books, boots, and other bulky items. Fred's possessions were scattered in at least three places and a storage center in two different states. This was just one of his ports of call.

With our work done, Linda and I settled in the sunroom to anticipate how our quick visit with Tom would go. I poured us some coffee, then settled in my rocking chair. Linda crossed one leg over the other, then leaned over in her "let's get busy" mode.

"How do you think Tom is going to react to finding out about us? And how do you think this might change how he sees his dad?" Linda asked. Then she reasoned, "He is a big boy, after all, a rocket scientist, who was old enough to know about this from the get-go and after all, he and I are the same age. I've known about it from day one."

"It's hard for me to believe he hasn't had suspicions." It was years ago when I called him to find out where his dad was. In fact, I had called Tom a few times trying to find Fred. I reminded Linda of the train trip Fred took to Denver to see Tom. "Remember how worried I was?"

"Do I." Linda reminded me of another time when Fred told me he was visiting Tom in Denver. Then the weeks rolled by and Fred never called. I was worried sick and called Tom that time, too, only to find out that Fred was not in Denver. Tom didn't know where he was. Linda said, "Nick and I were going to drive up to the Wisconsin cabin to see if he was there. We honestly feared he'd had a fall or had fallen asleep driving again and was in a ditch somewhere in the snow."

"That was the first lie I'd ever caught Fred telling me. I didn't know whether to be angry as hell or worried," I took a deep breath just remembering my concern. "When I called Tom, he said his dad had mentioned something about London. The thought raced through my mind: Does he have yet *another* family?" I didn't know the answer then and I still don't know it now, all these years later.

Linda wondered if Tom might become angry at his dad. "He might feel his dad didn't trust him enough to tell him. Or that he couldn't handle it. Or that Tom would think poorly of him."

"Well, Linda, I've had many conversation with Fred on how left out I felt that he wouldn't share our friendship with his son, that I was too insignificant in his life or that he was ashamed of our relationship. Fred usually just mumbled something incomprehensible in reply. But I do remember something he said just the other day when we were having a serious discussion about his illness and its effect on us. He said he had feared that if Tom knew about me in his life, it might interfere with Tom's relationship with Sonia — it might make it awkward for him — that relationship was important to both of them."

"I think you should let Tom know that. That could well be his reasoning."

The doorbell rang. I took a deep breath and Linda and I greeted Tom at the door. He was smiling and reached out to shake hands with each of us. He seemed genuinely happy to meet us and said he had no trouble finding our house.

We ushered him into the sunroom where he sat down, declining any beverages. Like us, he was wearing jeans and a sweatshirt. He was a tall, slender, and attractive man, and like his dad, seemed immediately comfortable with our home and us.

The first thing he said was, "I didn't know you existed until you contacted me. This has just come out of the blue."

We took that as our opening to tell him about his dad's relationship with us. We told Tom about when Linda met Fred thirty-one years ago. Linda said, "He was like a dad to me. My own dad has not been a part of my life for years and years. And Fred played a similar role in my husband Nick's life. Nick lost his dad several years ago. They had been very close. So we did lots of things together." Linda then shared with Tom pictures she had brought of several vacations the four of us had taken together to places like their cabin up north, Mexico, and Costa Rica. She showed him photos of Fred and Nick fishing from his boat at Nick's cabin up north.

Tom was looking at the pictures with great interest. "Nick shares the family cabin with his six brothers and one sister. They each sign up for specific weeks. Mom and Fred and our four cockatiels joined us for several days there. And these photos were taken when Nick and I joined Mom and Fred in Costa Rico for a week. The guys did all kinds of fishing, including night fishing — and we all rode on the zip-lines over the treetops. Your dad volunteered to go first."

Tom was in awe. "Wow, I can't imagine how dad could have managed that."

Linda continued, "We had a great time. These photos were taken on the west coast of the Yucatan where we spent a week with Mom and Fred in a huge, gorgeous casa with about five bedrooms and baths — and a cook and housekeeper. We brought home lots of fish in refrigerated containers. And our cook did amazing work with the fish the guys caught."

Tom was really shaking his head in amazement by this time, shuffling pictures and repeating, "Wow, Dad had another family. I sure never knew. I think you both know my dad better than I do!" In a more thoughtful tone, he slowly added, "I don't think Sonia knows anything about you and I don't plan to tell her a thing."

I asked, "Who did you think your Dad was traveling with the many months he was gone?"

Tom shifted in his chair and crossed his long legs. "You know, the many times I've visited Sonia and Dad over the holidays, I've never remembered anyone visiting them or the phone ever ringing."

We commented on how we had wished Fred might have shared him with us but suspected it just might have been too awkward for Fred. I added, "He also feared that if you knew, it might complicate your relationship with Sonia and he didn't want to do that. Your dad is very proud of you. He told us much about the wild childhood you and your sister shared and how you managed to pretty much grow up on your own once you joined the Navy and got out on your own."

Tom just shook his head in wonderment.

I added, "You know I got his permission to contact you about picking up his belongings here. I wouldn't have done so without his permission." I told Tom that Fred might even have been a bit relieved about this meeting.

Eventually, Tom got up and said, "I better be going if I'm to get to St. Cloud on time." As he was putting on his jacket, he again said, "I'm just blown away by all this." He had a smile on his handsome face and seemed quite sincere in making his farewells as he left.

"Do you think we'll see him again?" Linda asked.

"I just don't know, but he did seem pleased to meet us, didn't you think?" We each agreed that Tom was very easy to get to know— very comfortable with himself. We hadn't quite known what a rocket scientist would be like, but he seemed like he'd fit in most anywhere. He was a lot like his father in that respect. We both hoped we'd see more of him.

Several months later, I went to Fort Meyers, Florida to spend some time with my friends Anne and Jim. Years ago, the three of us had worked together in the St. Paul public schools. He was now separated from his wife and spending more time in their Fort Meyers condo.

One day while Jim and Anne were out golfing, I decided to do some journaling. I got lost in so many thoughts that when Jim and Anne returned from their fun in the sun, they caught me in tears. I shared my fears that I might never see Fred again. With nothing of his belongings left in my home, it dawned on me that our thirty-one year relationship had ended with Tom's departure. Fred was too impaired to drive. And I risked encountering Sonia should I try visiting him at the Home. God, I didn't know what I'd do if I ran into her.

Fred had been reticent in discussing his end-of-year plans and whether or not he would let Sonia know of my existence. She obviously had known of some woman's existence when Linda's boyfriend called and told her years ago that Fred was seeing a nameless woman in St. Paul. Perhaps as the years passed, Sonia assumed the relationship was over. Fred didn't mention it again.

Tom was convinced she didn't know.

One of the last times Fred was at my house, I had asked how I would know if he died. Fred said that someone would call his best friend in Wisconsin who would, in turn, call me.

Is that it? I thought. *Does our history of thirty-one years have no more meaning for him than that? Will my life from this day forth consist of me living without him?*

I had been sharing with Jim and Anne the many joys I had experienced those thirty-one years, but now the reality of its end was making me feel miserable. I couldn't contain my tears. I knew from the beginning this day would come. But now it was hitting me like a ton of bricks.

Anne abruptly excused herself, saying she had to make a phone call.

Jim said, "Your stories about you and Fred and your travels and times together are nothing less than wonderful. You had a full life of play."

"But, Jim, I knew the day of reckoning would come one day, but I made the decision to think about that later, much later, and now it has come."

Jim continued, "Listening to you describe your relationship makes me think of some of the textbook descriptions of the various phases of relationships. What you did not do was take on the encumbrances of marriage with Fred — the details of children, the details of cars, jobs, insurance, money, house ownership, cleaning, and so on. You did not do these things with Fred. You then also did not receive the benefits of sharing these things with a mate.

"Sharing these details of life creates stress and often removes a lot of the play, or all of the play for that matter. You got to do it your way and have your space and you had a life of your own. Not many have done it your way."

"You're right. I had all the encumbrances in my marriages. But none of that with Fred."

"There is a progression to now, when Fred is losing his health. To me, the fact that he now wants to go on is not what I would think is consistent with the way he lived his life. You are the consistent one with your acceptance of it all. It is a wonderful story. Whatever you might write about it should probably be mostly for you."

I was deeply touched by his thoughtful, insightful words. Indeed, I had lived the "day by dayness" of marriage in three different marriages and apparently wasn't too good at it. I couldn't help but wonder if I was cut out for it. What I did know when I met Fred was that I no longer needed a mate to help me get an education, build a nest, have a family, and deal with the ups and downs of family life. What I did want was what I chose with Fred — to live a life of adventure and romance. It was Fred's choice to end his life with the wife with whom he had shared the encumbrances of marriage. It was a choice I would honor.

Tom helped his Dad make a home out of his Assisted Living Apartment at Good Shepherd Home, his new permanent residence. Once there, Fred began calling me regularly, letting me know he would welcome my visits. In fact, his phone calls were more frequent. My friends were urging me to go see him, assuring me they'd take turns going with me, knowing I feared encountering Sonia. I managed to okay my visits with Fred in advance. In no way did I wish to embarrass either of them.

Judith was the first to join me in these trips. The first ones were at the hospital. We learned he could only tolerate two-hour visits, then fatigue would set in. We left behind a potted plant Judy brought for him. "Don't worry," she said. "I left no card."

My neighbor Ed and his girlfriend also joined me when Fred was still at the hospital. They also joined me at Christmas time when he was at the VA. Lisa had brought sweets and a winter scene in a bottle that snowed when tipped upside down. Fred beamed with pleasure at these dear friends. He still had several more falls and bladder infections that resulted in more trips to the St. Cloud Hospital, then the Acute Care Ward, and finally back to his Good Shepherd Assisted Living Apartment. His trips were now taken by ambulance from one facility to another.

Our visits continued no matter where he was. Judy, Ed, and Lisa were perhaps the most frequent visitors, but many others wanted to be included. One was one of my newer friends, Phyllis. I had met her when on the Hamline University board. Later I joined her on the Penumbra Theatre board and we became the best of friends even though she was probably fifteen years younger than I. Phyllis often joined Judy and me.

Jim had returned to St. Paul to get a divorce and stayed with me until his divorce was finalized. He, too, offered to take me to see Fred. Fred liked Jim. They took to each other immediately. Jim and I would take a picnic lunch, pick up Fred, and take him to a local park to picnic. Jim was strong enough to assist Fred's walk to the picnic table and help him get seated.

Fred wanted to know more about Jim's cabin on an island several hundred miles from Sauk Rapids. Fred wondered if he could visit the cabin, but Jim said getting in and out of the pontoon would be too difficult. Bless Fred's heart, he was still up for adventures as unrealistic as he knew it was.

The gals and I were able to take him for several lunches at a nearby city park. Linda and Nick joined me several times. The picnic lunches occurred with Fred often saying on the phone, "Don't forget the deviled eggs, or the summer sausage, or the ice cream."

Fred enjoyed exchanging zingers with Linda and talking football and guy talk with Nick. As an Ohio graduate, Fred seldom missed watching Ohio State's games. Other friends sent him funny cards or sports magazines featuring his beloved football team. He was not forgotten.

He was getting thinner and thinner, finally down to about 110 pounds; he needed a feeding tube because of the deterioration of his esophagus. Still, we kept visiting him, bringing picnic lunches at his request. "Aren't you supposed to only drink fluids?" I'd ask.

With a wink of the eye, he'd reply, "Well, they don't have to know everything."

This was a stubborn streak I had seen in Fred more than once over the years. He was well aware that he was to avoid solid foods because of the risk that it could end up in his lung instead of his stomach and that could lead to pneumonia. But such prudent behaviors did not fit his image of who he was.

Chapter Twenty-five
What Next?
July 2011

PHYLLIS, JUDY, AND I became hardcore regulars at the Good Shepherd Home. Of all my girlfriends, Judith probably saw Fred the most in every setting over the years. She seemed to intuitively know when he needed assistance going up stairs at her apartment or needed a hand at his elbow when waiting for me to pick them up at the theatre. She also knew how to shake him a mean martini when dining on her porch.

Whenever we banged on the door of his assisted living apartment, he was so glad to see us. It took much energy for him to stand, holding his hiking pole for balance, as we entered, laughing and giggling. He gave his endearing smile as we each stood in line for a kiss.

On one particular visit it was rainy and very windy out, so we decided to relocate the picnic to one of the cheerful hospitality rooms at the Good Shepherd Home.

We ladies busily worked to get him seated and to get the food, plates, and beverages out. An elderly man walked by, stuck his head in the doorway, greeted Fred, and probably hoped for an invitation. Fred acknowledged him with a slight turn of his head and a wave. He later commented on the man as someone he was getting to know.

When an elderly lady called out his name while passing by, Fred told us quite a bit about her in admiration. He said she had taken it upon herself to tend the flowers and gardens each day. "Look, look out the window. She is over there kneeling down to weed the garden. I see her do that every day. And she is over ninety years old," he said with pride. We were all amazed. She had the posture of a soldier and a quick gait. He added he was learning that many of the people he was getting to know had interesting stories to tell.

As we ate, we each took turns telling funny stories about friends and relatives, or relived such incidents from movies we had seen like the Chevy Chase movie *Vacation*, where the family was driving to Wally World with a dead Aunt Edna strapped on the roof. Our laughter echoed from the walls of the room. Fred was in good spirits as we wheeled him back to his apartment.

Our friends left for a walk while Fred and I talked. I asked him if he had read the last chapter I had mailed him about our last trip to Mexico when we had dealt with El Norte and our battle with the wind and sand. I had been sending him chapters of our various trips as I finished writing them. He smiled as he said, "As a matter of fact, I did. I really enjoyed it. It felt like I was there. I could feel the sand between my toes."

It pleased me to see him so animated. I'd been used to his frozen face, typical of many folks with Parkinson's. Even his voice seemed more forceful. When I asked him if he had told his son about the memoir I was writing about our trips, he said he had and that his son knew about it. He thanked me as I kissed him.

I was eager to send him completed chapters, eager to get his reactions, hoping it would help him remember our adventurous, romantic, and often crazy times together. I sought his reactions, taking his suggestions seriously, making revisions he requested. He seemed to be getting more involved as chapters increased. He was pleased with the project, but I noticed that he managed to lose each chapter I gave him after reading it. I wondered if he was continuing to keep his two lives separate.

I felt I was getting closer to the finish line with perhaps another week or two of writing, anticipating his joy when I would present him with the finished product—especially since he seemed to be showing progress in his involvement with those around him. He had even gained ten pounds, making him look a bit less like a skeleton.

The boisterous ladies returned. I told him I would be spending the Fourth of July at Jim's island cabin with Anne—we were driving up the next day but would be back to visit him on the fifth. "Anne is going to be my co-pilot and will be the navigator. She says she knows a good way to get me here. So wish us luck, Freddie dear." We each said our good-byes and left, collecting a kiss on the way out.

As we headed for home, Judy later told us that while I was in the bathroom, Fred had kissed her, telling her he loved her and "to take care of Shirley." I was moved by those words.

I returned home from my Fouth of July trip to find the message light blinking on my answering machine. Tom's name was on the display. My heart sank. I immediately feared the worse. I called Tom's number immediately. Tom's girlfriend Alex answered the phone. She softly said, "Fred is dead."

I gasped for air. "Oh, no, no—he was so good when I saw him two days ago. He seemed more engaged in his surroundings, so animated. He'd even gained weight," I cried out. I couldn't control my sobbing.

Alex was most soothing, giving me more details. She added, "Fred has had such a sad life—so much death of loved ones and a rather grim marriage."

"Au contraire," I said, trying hard to control my weeping. "He has had a long happy life of travels and fun."

Alex added, "You know, Fred doesn't share much of what he does, but one day when just he and I were talking, somehow the subject of his first wife came up. He felt badly about how that marriage ended and implied he had gotten involved with another woman. I don't think Tom had known anything about that."

"Yes," I added, "He mentioned her to me. He was quite taken by her and said that, like you, she was Greek. Her parents were born in Greece. I met him long after that. But his last three or four years were trials of endurance for him, which he handled so stoically. I just don't remember him complaining. He seemed determined to make the most of it," I said while still trying to stifle my crying.

"Well, do call Tom right away in St. Cloud," Alex requested.

"Oh, I can't call him now, not until I can control my emotions. This just isn't like me, to be so emotional."

Alex replied, "No, Shirley. You need to call him now. He needs to know how his father's death has affected you."

What also affected me was how Fred handled his steadily deteriorating condition with quiet dignity, sometimes accompanied by a quiet sense of humor, continuing to live his life on his terms, imposing his views on no one. He accepted what he could not change, making the best of a debilitating situation, continuing to enjoy his daily diet of documentaries, political events, favorite mysteries, and his favorite TV show *Jeopardy*. He knew most of the answers.

Fred uttered no complaints and exited this world in the only way open to him. His ability to be comfortable with his own company, to need much time alone, must have been important to him those last months when his actions were so restricted.

When I called Tom, he was matter-of-fact in giving me details of his activities at his Dad's apartment and the storage containers. He said his Dad had wanted no funeral or memorial services because he was an atheist. I didn't see what being an atheist had to do with it. Memorial services are for the living as well as the dead. I told Tom I would have to honor Fred by some sort of ceremony.

I asked if Linda and I could join him in disposing of his dad's things. He said that quite frankly, we would be in his way. It was scorching hot outside and moving all Fred's stuff from his apartment was going to be hard work. I couldn't imagine that Tom would find any help from the Good Shepherd's Home. Tom chuckled at the likelihood of finding strong-bodied people at an old peoples' home.

Sonia was helping Tom find good places to donate much of Fred's furniture and equipment, like the Epilepsy Foundation.

When I asked Tom if he had found any of my manuscripts, he replied, "No, I saw nothing like that and believe me, I would have noticed." He also said his dad had not mentioned that I was writing a memoir about our trips.

I thought, *Once again he's left no paper trail for Sonia to find. He's protected her to the very end. This was his way of honoring their bond until death do them part.* I was impressed.

I then asked Tom if he would stop by and see Linda, Nick, and me on his way to the airport. He assured me he would arrange it. With some timidity, I asked him if I could have some of his dad's ashes. He laughingly said I could have all I wanted. He only needed enough to throw on a park in Boulder where his Dad said he had happy boyhood memories.

Perhaps this was the way Fred left something for me that would mean the most to me. In previous conversations, I had laughingly suggested memorials to him I might create, like benches alongside some of our favorite spots on the river with our names on it, or places where I might scatter his ashes, or in the event of my death, Linda might scatter both our ashes together, so we could spend an eternity together. He made some ribald responses to these suggestions as we laughed together.

I rushed out to purchase an elegant urn before Tom arrived later that day.

Nick arranged to join Linda and me, as did Jim, who turned out to be a gift to me. Jim had endured some tragic losses in his life recently that sensitized him to grief and methods for dealing with it. Having him here, ready to step in with ideas or assistance as more people became aware of Fred's death, was extremely helpful. Linda and I arranged pictures of Fred on various trips over the many years around the perimeter of the extended dining room table—some of him alone, others with me and various family members and friends. Tom was to learn even more about his father's other life.

Tom appeared quite jovial as he burst into our home, hugging first me, then Linda, then shaking hands with both Nick and Jim as each was introduced. Again Tom expressed how blown away he was by all he was learning. He seemed eager to know more details and shared much about his life with us. We were equally amazed at his many ventures into the world of drugs, sex, and rock and roll while growing up, often totally on his own—and how comfortable he was in sharing those adventures with us.

He also shared information about his father's will. The only donation Fred made was to Planned Parenthood, which did not surprise me. He had often expressed with great emotion how insane it was that women were denied equal status in most countries and that 50% of the world's population was denied a voice or the opportunity to earn a living and make significant contributions to their countries. He firmly believed that the great threat to the future was global over-population. No, his donation did not surprise me.

What did surprise me was that he left Tom only his ashes,

asking him to toss some on the park in Boulder. He left the rest of his money to his wife, Sonia. When she offered to share some with Tom, he emphatically said, "No, it's yours. Dad wanted you to have it." He confided to us that she truly needed it because she had serious health concerns and she had to handle all the paperwork from his dad's estate. Somehow I had thought Tom would be in charge of Fred's end-of-life decisions and will since Fred and Sonia had been legally separated for many years.

I asked Tom if he could share with us the last moments of his father's life.

"Well, apparently the nurses had checked in on him at about seven in the morning and he was up and dressed and seated in his wheelchair. He seemed in good spirits. The staff spoke highly of Dad, said he was an easygoing guy to be with. When they returned about 10:00 a.m., they found him dead, lying on the floor. The doctor thought he died at about 9:00 a.m."

"Did they think it was a heart attack or did they say?"

"Well, the strange thing is they found a hundred dollar bill in his pocket. Why would he have money in his pocket?" Tom wondered. "Maybe he had an appointment and he needed money for a taxi."

"But would he have an appointment on the Fourth of July?" Linda asked. We all thought that unlikely. Yet another mystery that Fred left us with.

Tom went to get Fred's ashes from his car, and thus, the "great exchange" began. Jim and I hurried out to the kitchen, preparing the center workbench with covering and proper tools for the exchange. As I got the impressive urn, Linda, Nick, and Tom came into the kitchen.

"Don't anyone turn on a fan," Tom joked. There was joyousness in the room as we all huddled about the workbench while I spooned out the ashes from one receptacle into the other. When I said we just might have a backyard memorial party for his dad, Tom suggested, "Just toss a few of Dad's ashes on the grass and he'll be there. I think he'd like that!" We all agreed.

I couldn't help smiling inwardly at how successfully Fred had kept his wife from knowing about his other life. By insisting there be no funeral or memorial service, he saw to it that these two worlds would not meet, that his wife would remain untouched by his other life. I had to marvel at the irony of Fred's handling of his double life. He was the kind of man who honored his wife and his lover, showing respect for both, while being true to who he was and what he wanted to do with his life.

Sonia's illness marginalized her from his active lifestyle and my being "the other woman" marginalized me from being part of his final moments. *Now that*, I thought, *was something to write about.*

That's when I decided to enlarge the scope of my memoir when writing about this man who repeatedly told me, "What you see is what you get. Nothing complicated about me." When Fred died, many secrets died with him. He turned out to be one of the more complicated men I've met.

Tom said he would never tell Sonia about me, which was a gift Fred would have appreciated and probably anticipated. He knew from my past behaviors I would honor the way he chose to live his life. Now I hoped I could do justice writing a memoir about the most fascinating man I've yet met.

Fred taught me how to live his lifestyle, then I assisted him in maintaining that lifestyle, and when that was no longer possible, he stubbornly did it his way with no counsel but his own, leaving me to the care of my friend, and his wife to the care of what was left of his money and worldly goods.

ODE TO FRED

A true romantic with Hemingway's sense of adventure
A man with charisma who could entrance
An audience of students,
Or fellow travelers in faraway places,
A lover of boisterous exchanges
Flavored with a touch of "zingers,"
Yet hermit-like in his
Enjoyment of his own company,
Who could spend days alone tenting
Or sitting by a campfire,
Absorbing the sounds of the woods and its inhabitants,
Thinking his own thoughts with no need to share them.
His love of history influenced
How he saw the world and its players
And enriched his perceptions
Of what he saw and did in our travels.
He conjured up the most amazing trips
Filled with serendipity that added spice,
Turning each trip into "a moveable feast."
This man was truly one of a kind,
True to his vision of how he wanted to live.

GREETINGS FROM MINNESOTA

September 22, 2011

Dear Tom,

I thought you might like to know that we celebrated the life of your dad at my home on Sunday, September 18. About forty of my friends arrived, including my daughter, Linda, and her husband, Nick, to enjoy Fred's last party. Tag boards displaying pictures of Fred, some from the early years and others from the later years, stood on each side of the fireplace. On the mantle was the urn of Fred's ashes flanked by two framed photos of him along with a bottle of Tanqueray gin, a martini glass, and a container of Fred's cigars. At the appropriate time, we all raised our glasses in a toast to your dad.

I shared with the group some of the adventures we had together on various trips to faraway places, and other times we spent closer to home skiing on our own North Shore trails or Yellowstone Park, hiking in Steamboat Springs, Colorado or Whistler, B.C. Over the years we made new friends in other countries who in turn visited us. I summarized for the group some of your dad's traits that so endeared him to me. Some remarks evoked laughter, others respect for how Fred lived his life. Linda and Nick and others shared why Fred was so important to them. Frequently mentioned was the way Fred mentored and reinforced others to live their dreams. Others were impressed with how his love of history influenced his travels, what he read, and how he interpreted world and current events. His simple lifestyle, how he could live out of a duffle bag or live in a tent impressed others. Those who had been frequent visitors to Good Shepherd Home were visibly impressed with his quiet dignity.

Your dad greatly admired the courage your sister displayed in facing her death. He hoped he would be as brave. His quiet dignity in the way he maintained his independence made him my folk hero. I only hope I can be as courageous as your dad in the way I live out my life.

It was a wonderful event for people grateful to be there to share memories. His best friend from Wisconsin couldn't make it, but his daughter, who knows and cared for Fred, did make it. The food and drink was plentiful and folks seemed reluctant to leave. In fact, a hardcore of immediate neighbors stayed longer for these were the ones who knew him best. I was amazed at the number of cards and flowers I received. We knew you and Alex would be unable to attend. Nonetheless, you were missed.

Best ever,

Shirley

[Tom called to say that he received my letter and the program from Fred's memorial service. He said he enjoyed reading the letter, thought I was a good writer, and wondered how I was handling my grief. We had a great conversation. He was easy to talk with, very forthcoming, unlike his father. Not the least guarded in what he said. He again reiterated how stunned both he and Alex were at the life they never knew Fred had with me, my family, and friends.]

Epilogue
Havana, Cuba
December 2011

ONE OF THE LAST times I saw Fred, he had urged me to join my friend Anne on a December trip to Cuba. It was a place he had always wanted to visit, partly because Hemingway had lived thirty years there.

One day, as I was wading in the waters off the sandy, sugary beaches of Cayo Largo, I spied a seagull flying in the sky, followed by another gull. As it dipped towards me, it swerved away with the other gull following. I suddenly felt alone, terribly alone, without Fred to share this moment. Then I recalled words Hemingway used in his novel, *For Whom the Bells Toll* – which I paraphrase:

Where you go, I have gone.
Now where I go, you go, too.

FRED WILL REMAIN THE LOVE OF MY LIFE.
I HAVE BEEN BLESSED!
THANK YOU, UNIVERSE.

Shirley White Pearl

January, 2012

This memoir is more for Tom than anyone else. My daughter has lived it with me. But my closest friends and neighbors had felt this was a love story that should be shared with many. And so the memoir is also for them. The writing of it has been a journey into the past, seeing Fred through my eyes over the thirty-one years, remaining the fun-loving free spirit throughout those years, only partially dimmed by the acceleration of his disease. If anything, he had seemed more remarkable in his determination to remain true to the way he had chosen to live and end his life.

I was rereading Anne Morrow Lindbergh's book, *Gift from the Sea*, and found much of Fred's basic belief systems discussed, on ways of being true to oneself during one's middle-aged years. She, like Fred, questioned if part of being middle-age should be a period of shedding earlier responsibilities such as ambition, acquiring material possessions, and pride in order to become truly oneself. She also stated that relationships need to change over time because as our bodies age and change, so do our ways of being and spending time change.

This also reminded me of some of Gibran's teaching that stress the importance of non-controlling and non-possessive behaviors so necessary in relationships that grow and evolve as one ages. All three: Fred, Gibran, and Lindbergh, seem to define security in a relationship as neither looking back to what was nor forward to what it might be but instead living in the present.

For Fred, my occasional man, living in the present was making each day an occasion and a moveable feast.

Acknowledgements

This is my first book and my first memoir, largely based on journals I kept during my thirty-one years traveling with Fred. Some were typed, others scribbled on varying-sized spiral notebooks. When old age began catching up with us, and Fred learned he had Parkinson's disease, I decided to write a travelogue including some of our more adventurous travels as a gift for Fred.

A good friend leased me her time-share on the North Shore of Lake Superior for a week in April so I could begin writing. I packed my car with laptop, files and files of journals I had written, lots of quick meals from Trader Joe's, classical and jazz CDs and wine, then took off to become a writer.

There was a wealth of data to plumb. Starting with travel journals, I quickly typed thirty or more single-spaced pages from some of our more unusual trips. My purpose was to depict how our travels would become a moveable feast, as we made each trip a celebration of life similar to Ernest Hemingway's as described in his memoir, *A Moveable Feast*, but on a more frugal scale.

A good friend of mine, Pat Pelto, was an editor for a non-profit organization. She gave the first read of my growing manuscript.

Knowing nothing about professional writing, I had lunch with Mary Rockcastle, a professional writer who was also head of the graduate program in writing at Hamline University. I had met her while serving on the Hamline Board of Trustees. She gave me the names of three writers, all with Hamline connections, who were professional editors. I started with Patricia Francisco who stressed the need for creating a strong narrative providing the reader with background information on Fred and myself, describing how our relationship began.

Scott Edelstein, writer and instructor at the Loft in Minneapolis, taught me how to show rather than tell in a journalistic style, by creating scenes and dialogues throughout the manuscript, creating more interest in the material. This rewrite easily added another hundred pages for my fourth and final editor and publishing consultant, Patti Frazee, who did the final edit and preparation for publishing. She tightened an expanding manuscript, improving its pacing and descriptiveness.

When I asked Fred if he was comfortable with including much about our personal lives, he replied that it should be my story.

My daughter helped with some dialogue and balance issues between travel and narrative sections. My friend Sandy Klas, who lived through my years with Fred, felt I had the makings of a memoir. She felt its major theme should be a frugal version of Ernest Hemingway's *The Moveable Feast*, a favorite book of Fred's that was his inspiration for turning one's life into a daily celebration. She was the first friend to read the finished manuscript. She said it took her on many trips to places she had never been, illustrating how our pursuit of adventure enhanced our great love and enjoyment of each other. This was the kind of encouragement I needed in order to persevere through the writing of the story. Other friends gave me the constant support I needed to keep Fred involved in what he could still do as his disease progressed after he could no longer visit me. I am especially indebted to Judith Pfankuch and Phyllis Goff who were my frequent companions when visiting Fred. Other visitors were Tom Skovholt and Lisa Yost, Linda and Nick Brill, my son-in-law, and Jim Bohn, Geralda Stanton, Rosemarie Park, and Frances Winsor.

Fred was touched by these friends who did not forget him.

CPSIA information can be obtained at www.ICGtesting.com
Printed in the USA
LVOW03s2319220914

405270LV00020B/204/P